Shoptalk for College Writers

Shoptalk for College Writers

Sheryl I. Fontaine
California State University, Fullerton

Cherryl Smith
California State University, Sacramento

Harcourt Brace College Publishers

Fort Worth   Philadelphia   San Diego   New York   Orlando   Austin   San Antonio
Toronto   Montreal   London   Sydney   Tokyo

Publisher	Earl McPeek
Acquisitions Editor	Julie McBurney
Market Strategist	John Meyers
Developmental Editor	Diane Drexler
Project Editor	Andrea Joy Wright
Art Director	Sue Hart
Production Manager	Kathleen Ferguson

ISBN: 0-15-503808-7

Library of Congress Catalog Card Number: 98-71200

Address for Orders
Harcourt Brace College Publishers, 6277 Sea Harbor Drive, Orlando, FL 32887-6777 1-800-782-4479

Address for Editorial Correspondence
Harcourt Brace College Publishers, 301 Commerce Street, Suite 3700, Fort Worth, TX 76102

Web Site Address
http://www.hbcollege.com

Harcourt Brace College Publishers will provide complimentary supplements or supplement packages to those adopters qualified under our adoption policy. Please contact your sales representative to learn how you qualify. If as an adopter or potential user you receive supplements you do not need, please return them to your sales representative or send them to: Attn: Returns Department, Troy Warehouse, 465 South Lincoln Drive, Troy, MO 63379.

Printed in the United States of America

8 9 0 1 2 3 4 5 6 7   0 3 9   9 8 7 6 5 4 3 2 1

Harcourt Brace College Publishers

We dedicate this book to our sons
David Matthew Fontaine-Boyd
and
Jeremy Joel Smith-Danford
and to the memory of Frances Smith

PREFACE

Teachers who write textbooks often do so because they can't find one that fits the way they teach or what they believe about their subject. In our own case, before we began writing *Shoptalk for College Writers*, we had stopped using traditional rhetorics in our classrooms. The modes of writing around which most rhetorics are organized didn't reflect our own experiences as writers or teachers, nor did these texts reflect the discipline of composition as it has evolved over the past fifteen years. With these needs in mind, we wrote *Shoptalk for College Writers* to be the first rhetoric that teaches writing by introducing students to the field of composition and that allows students to write for their own purposes and from a variety of sources of information rather than from pre-selected modes or strategies.

❧ *Organization*

In *Shoptalk for College Writers*, we have set out a framework in which to compose, develop, and complete college essays. We've organized *Shoptalk* so that students begin composing college writing from the very first pages of the book and do so in the course of reading about and reflecting on the nature of written language and of college writing itself.

Shoptalk has two layers of content that are intertwined throughout the text. The first layer forms the three main sections in the book. This layer includes "shoptalk" about the history of college writing and the student's place in this history, about the way we all speak and write within various language communities, and about how one learns the conventions of particular language communities, especially of academic disciplines.

The second layer is a series of writing activities (writing log entries, freewriting and focusing) and essay assignments that appear throughout the text. The assignment sequence is structured around the three sources that inform all non-fiction writing: information that emerges from recollection and memory, information from observation or conversation, or information from written texts. The particular rhetorical mode used in each essay is selected by the student according to the purpose for which he/she is writing. This sequence focuses students' attention on the most important features of college writing—the kind of information you use, how you use it, when, for whom, and for what explicit purpose. This writing sequence will prepare students much more effectively for college writing than do modally-based sequences in which students write to fill certain structures—structures that seem to precede and be disconnected from content or purpose.

The text is arranged in three sections each of which follows the same basic structure. In each section, the first three chapters discuss a language/writing issue and are followed by chapters on **Creating and Discovering Your Essay, Response and Collaboration,** and **Editing and Proofreading.** Sections One and Two include an extra chapter, Writing to Learn, that repeats and reinforces the arrangement of each section. This repetition helps with the planning of class time and provides a clear structure for the student.

Shoptalk is a complete rhetoric that includes readings, writing prompts and guides, response activities, and editing or handbook materials. The text can easily be adapted to terms of varying lengths or supplemented by reading materials of the instructor's choosing.

❧ *Distinctive Features of* Shoptalk for College Writers

Writing Logs

The text in the book is punctuated by **Writing Log** entries that engage students in a writing to learn process in which they are given prompts that help them to reflect on and extend what they have been reading. Beyond helping students with the readings, the **Writing Log** entries become an initial source from which students discover and create their essays. That is, by the time they have reached the point in each section of the book where they are to begin creating and discovering an essay, they have already generated pages of **Writing Logs** to which they return to find ideas, questions, and so forth that can be used for more sustained, essay writing. The **Writing Logs** help students engage more fully with the reading and provide instructors with a rich source for class discussion or activity. Students also get to experience, like real writers, the process of beginning to write long before they actually have an assignment.

Writing Activities

There are two types of writing activities found in *Shoptalk*. Either of these activities can be used independently by the student or in a collaborative classroom situation.

The **Perspective** activities promote analysis and reflection on the material that students have gathered in their Writing Logs. The close analysis of this material allows the student to look for connections, contradictions, similarities, and congruencies among the items in their Logs. They can be used in the order in which they appear in the book, or at any point in creating the essay.

The **Focusing Your Direction** activities provide a series of writing prompts that help the student find direction in the thoughts they have recorded in their reflective writing. These activities are interspersed with freewriting exercises that allow the student to further refine their thoughts.

Student Writing Demonstrations

Interspersed throughout the writing activities are demonstrations of student writing that show how different students have responded to them. These demonstrations will focus students' attention on the creation and discovery activities of writing.

Professional Writing Demonstrations

The professional demonstrations that are included provide students with illustrations of how particular writers have used the same sources of information that the students are being asked to use in their own essays. The texts were selected because they are close to the kind of college/essay writing that students will be asked to do and because they primarily use one particular source of information. Rather than use these essays as models for how their own essay should look, students are provided with questions that help them to look at these demonstration essays in terms of the information they contain, the way it is presented, and how it supports or develops the writer's point.

Computers & Technology

Three chapters of *Shoptalk*—11, 17, and 20—include discussions about the use of computers, e-mail, the Internet, and the World Wide Web. The discussions place these topics in the overall context of evaluating and citing information, allowing instructors to use them to extend and illustrate issues already being raised. Reading about computers in this manner, students will come to understand technology as part of a process in which they already engage rather than as a separate or ancillary feature.

✷ *The Instructor's Manual*

The Instructor's Manual includes suggestions on ways to use the writing assignments in the classroom, strategies for classroom activities, and suggestions on different ways to pace the assignments. Each section of the book is reviewed, and its various features explained. Expectations, suggestions, ways of anticipating and guiding students reactions are also included.

✷ *Acknowledgments*

We wish to thank the following people whose encouragement helped us write this book:

Richard Boyd, Olivia Castellano, Angus Dunstan, Ted Feldman, and Sylvia Vivrette; our editors at Harcourt Brace, Diane Drexler, Mark Gallaher, Julie McBurney, John Meyers, and Andrea Joy Wright; from California State University, Fullerton and California State University, Sacramento, Debi Esquivel, Cherry Honeycutt, and Karen McClendon, and our composition students.

We would also like to acknowledge the assistance of the following reviewers who provided their insights and advice in the creation of this textbook:

Rise Axelrod, California State University-San Bernadino; Wendy Bishop, Florida State University; Susan Booker, Iowa State University; Marvin Diogenes, University of Arizona; Deborah Holdstein, Governors State University; Judy Pierce, Montgomery College; Elizabeth Rankin, University of South Dakota; Paula Ross, Gadsden State Community College; Gail Stygall, University of Washington; Victor Villanueva, Washington State University.

Finally, we acknowledge the important ways in which our educations in composition at University of California-San Diego and University of California-Santa Barbara as well as our connection to BARD Institute for Thinking and Learning and the South Coast Writing Project have shaped *Shoptalk for College Writers*.

ABOUT THE AUTHORS

Sheryl I. Fontaine is Associate Professor of English at California State University, Fullerton where she directs the Writing Center and teaches undergraduate writing courses and graduate courses on the composing process, responding to writing, and the relationship between reading and writing. She has also taught at Claremont McKenna College and State University of New York at Stony Brook. She has written and edited books and articles about teaching writing, writing centers, and professional issues in composition. She has served on the Executive Committee of Writing Program Administrators.

Cherryl Smith is Associate Professor of English at California State University, Sacramento where she directs the Writing Center and teaches undergraduate courses in composition, literature, poetry writing, and teacher education and graduate courses in composition theory and pedagogy. She has also taught at California State University, Northridge and Harvard University. In addition to essays about basic writing, assessment, and teaching writing, she also publishes poetry.

CONTENTS IN BRIEF

CONTENTS

CHAPTER 6
Editing, Proofreading, and Final Reflections

CHAPTER 7
Writing to Learn: Writing a Second Essay from Recollection and Memory

PART ONE

LOCATING COLLEGE WRITING

Sources for Essays 1 and 2: Recollection and Memory

CHAPTER

1

STARTING POINTS
An Introduction

❧ *What Are Your Expectations about College Writing?*

You bring to this book your own expectations about what college writing will or should be. Your expectations may be based on other writing texts you have been asked to read; they may grow from experiences with writing in general or from having heard stories about college writing from friends, siblings, or teachers, and, these expectations are likely to affect the way you initially read and react to *Shoptalk.*

Expectations for college writing may also be influenced by beliefs you hold about what it means to write, particularly, what it means to write in college. Writing is often mistaken for being primarily a skill that could have been or should have been mastered in high school. But all writing occurs in a specific context: high school courses that included writing assignments similar to those found at the university are, nevertheless, high school courses. Yours may have succeeded in accomplishing the goals of helping build your confidence as a writer and increasing your range of experience with writing, and therefore, your high school courses may have provided good preparation for the writing you are about to do. Keep in mind that college writing occurs only in the context of college; the constraints on a college writer–the expectations of the audience, the length of assignments, the writer's relationship to his or her subject matter–are different from those that occur in the context of high school. College writing is the form of written communication found in the academic world of universities and colleges–and nowhere else.

Another belief about college writing courses is that they are "warm-up" courses lacking subject matter, prerequisites for the "real" writing students do in all their other college classes. This book argues, however, that there is nothing preliminary about a college writing course; not only is there subject matter related to the study of college writing, but any time you write you must choose some subject to learn about or reflect on with enough sustained attention that you find thoughts of your own to express. You might think of it this way: Rather than preparing you for writing at college, this book and the writing course you are currently taking will help get you started writing at college and will provide you with the experience of being a college writer.

A final belief about college writing is that it is something you can take in a semester or two and "get over with quickly." The writing placement exams and discretely defined writing requirements at many colleges falsely suggest that writing can be mastered once and for all–before you enter college or in a specific course or two. You may have the impression that one need only learn a particular format or some new vocabulary in order for the difficulties of college writing to be resolved.

While this textbook will consider vocabulary and sentence structure and how one distinguishes certain physical conventions of college writing, all writing is creative by nature, a process of using language to create new meanings in new contexts. From moment to moment and from occasion to occasion, meanings and contexts change, so all writing is unique. Presented with this endless variety of contexts in which to write, no writer–college or professional–can ever really finish learning. Writing does involve familiarizing oneself with skills and conventions, but the most substantive challenges of writing are those associated with any endeavor that relies on one's own creativity. Whether you are enrolled in basic or advanced writing, freshman composition or a senior seminar, or you are writing on your own, except for using set phrases like "once upon a time" or "after serious consideration," every phrase, every sentence you write, has never been said just that way before.

Writing Log Entry 1

Expectations, Fears, and Hopes about Writing

Spend ten minutes or so writing a quick, off-the-top-of-your-head response to the following questions: What beliefs about college writing have you brought with you? What do you expect will happen to you as a writer by the time you finish this course? What fears do you have about college writing? What do you imagine might get in the way of your development as a writer? What do you hope to learn?

❉ *Using* Shoptalk *as a Travel Book for College Writing*

Because writers find themselves in a variety of situations, they must become accustomed to distinguishing the qualities of the particular places, the context, in which they will write. You might think of this text as a resource for familiarizing yourself with the place of college writing, something like a tour book that is helpful when you are traveling or have moved to a new city. It is a book to help you find your way, to help you understand the unusual signs and odd markings on the map. This book can also help you see yourself in relation to the new territory in which you are traveling. There are certain customs to college writing that may seem unusual in relation to your own, places of particular interest to be visited, blind alleys that might be avoided or, at least, identified, and names that may require translation.

Although writing at college certainly resembles writing outside of college, the academic environment where college writing takes place, is, in a sense, a culture with its own set of expectations and values. The positions of authority that academics are expected to hold and the kind of value that academics place on conveying knowledge result in language and essay structures that may be, to the outsider, mysterious or imposing. This book provides an insider's view. You will find information about kinds of writing courses and assignments, about how teachers and programs evaluate writing, and about the demands of college writing and ways to meet those demands.

❈ *Valuing Your Own Language Experience and Interacting with Others'*

Shoptalk is designed to help you become familiar with the idiosyncrasies of college writing, to feel comfortable navigating its geography, yet the book has other aims as well. It will help you use the language experience you already have to make sense of college writing and to make it more personally meaningful. The voices in which you write and the languages you use to shape ideas grow from your personal knowledge of your individual experience, cultural background and history, and your sense of yourself both as a writer and as an individual; so, it is useful to consider the significance of individual and cultural knowledge on the process of writing. While introducing you to the academic environment as it relates to writing, *Shoptalk* will also help you identify cultural and creative resources of your own that can assist you in navigating this territory. Such resources bring you power as a writer; for while you may be new to college writing, you have a long history of using language outside of school that can be your foundation for writing in college.

As a student, you have lots of opportunities to take in the voices of experts. Sometimes you may choose to sit quietly at the back of a classroom, listening to and recording material from a lecture. Other times you may sit silently at your desk, reading and recording information from a written text. In both cases, you have the option to be still, to remain detached as you hear or read someone else's words. But when you write, a different option is presented to you, one that the activity of writing itself seems to encourage. When you write, it is unlikely that you will remain detached or distant from your subject, for your own words create a connection between yourself and the material you're thinking about, and, at the same time, your words create a connection between yourself and your reader.

One final aim of *Shoptalk* is to remind you that as an individual student with personal experience and cultural knowledge entering this new territory of college writing, you are not traveling alone–even if for some reason you would prefer to be. Writers usually compose by themselves, yet writing is very much a social activity; to some degree, all writing is part of a collaboration with individuals who, themselves, bring to the writing situation their own set of experiences and cultural histories. College writing puts you into an interaction with instructors, other students, professional writers, and scholars, with people who may be sitting right next to you and with others whom you will never–could never–meet.

✵ *What Kinds of Reading and Writing Does This Book Include and Why?*

The word "shoptalk" refers to the specialized, insider conversations shared by people who work in the same place or who study the same subject. As a composition text, *Shoptalk* will engage you in such specialized conversation by means of two complementary learning tools: reading and writing. First, *Shoptalk* asks you to read extensively about college writing as it is perceived by people who study the subject closely, and secondly, it asks you to write reflections about what you have read and to create your own college writing. The text shares with you "shoptalk" about the history of college writing and your place in this history; about the way you speak and write within various language communities; and how one learns the conventions of particular language communities, especially of academic disciplines.

The book presents you with assignments for five essays. Each essay will draw primarily on one of three sources that inform all nonfiction writing: information that emerges from recollection and memory, from conversation and observation, or from written texts.

Some of the essay assignments ask you to focus on your own questions, concerns, or issues that interest you about language and writing, topics emerging from the reading you are doing in *Shoptalk*. Other assignments ask you to write about your own questions and concerns, issues that interest you about any topic you choose. Each assignment includes writing activities designed to help you discover ideas and create the purpose and shape of your essay.

Each of the sections of the book is titled and subtitled to describe what the shoptalk will be, and what will be the primary source of information you will draw on to write your essays in that part of the book. So, in addition to introducing *Shoptalk* itself, Part One, "Locating College Writing," talks about the history of college writing, how college writing is located at the intersection of one's own history as a student and writer and the histories of all other students who take college writing, instructors who teach it, and administrators who determine its requirements. After offering an explanation of how college writing came to be and why you now find yourself in the midst of it, this section (subtitled, "Sources of Information for Essays 1 and 2: Recollection and Memory") asks you to use your memories and recollections as a place for finding your own questions or concerns about writing, which will provide you with a purpose and subject for your first essay.

One assumption dominates *Shoptalk*. The single best way to improve your writing is to immerse yourself in written language: to write, and, at the same time, to read—as much and as carefully and reflectively as you can. For this reason, in addition to writing essays, you will be reading this textbook and writing entries in a **Writing Log.** The **Writing Log** entries, like the one earlier in this chapter, ask you to pause in your reading, to use writing as a way of thinking about what you have read. These entries are personal, representing your first thoughts or impressions about what you have read, so they will vary in length and depth. Some **Writing Log** questions and some sections of the text will rouse more reaction and response from you than others. As a general guideline for **Writing Logs,** write for at least ten minutes per entry—sometimes this will be all the time an entry seems to require; other times you will want to go on longer. You can think of **Writing Log** entries as ideas-in-the-making, first impressions, thoughts, and reactions. From time to time you will be asked to share **Writing Log** entries with your classmates, since hearing what others have written can expand your own thinking. And, having a nonjudgmental audience with whom to share your own reflections can be beneficial to you as well, as you will see.

Chapter 4 will say much more about how writing can help you find and focus your ideas. For now, use the **Writing Logs** to write freely about what you read. Do not stop to change words or make corrections; write down your thoughts just as they come to you.

Writing Log Entry 2

Writers' Conversation on Expectations, Fears, and Hopes

Get together with one other person in the class and either exchange *Writing Log Entry 1* (your expectations, fears, and hopes about writing) or read that entry aloud to each other. Your job as a listener/reader is to take in what the writer has to say and to listen or read attentively and nonjudgmentally. Give yourself a chance to reread the writing or to hear it again one or more times before you do the following.

Write *Writing Log Entry 2,* a response to what the other person has written. You can respond to what he or she has written as you might in a conversation. You might give your reactions to the writer's concerns, tell how his or her experience differs from and/or

(continued)

Writing Log Entry 2

(Continued)

is similar to your own, and offer your own insights into what he or she has said. You might raise questions, if you have some, and tell about what the writer's reflection triggers in your own thinking. When you have completed *Writing Log Entry 2,* exchange *Logs* one more time so that you can read the responses you have written to each other's original entry.

❋ *A Summary of the Writing Assignments in* Shoptalk

- Essay 1:
- Write an essay in which your analysis and interpretation of information from recollections and memories you have about writing or college writing provide a purpose for writing and support for the points you wish to make.

- Essay 2:
- Write an essay in which your analysis and interpretation of information from recollections and memories you have about an issue or concern of your own choice provide a purpose for writing and support for the points you wish to make.

- Essay 3:
- Write an essay in which your analysis and interpretation of information you gather by observing other people or by having conversations with them about language, language situations, and language behaviors provides you with a purpose for writing and support for the points you wish to make.

- Essay 4:
- Write an essay in which your analysis and interpretation of information you gather by observing other people or by having conversations with them about an issue or concern of your own choice provides you with a purpose for writing and support for the points you wish to make.

■ Essay 5:

■ Write an essay in which your analysis and interpretation of information from professionally written texts in the discipline of Composition provide you with a purpose and support for the points you wish to make.

2

YOU ARE HERE
Looking at Your Own History as a Writer

❋ Taking a Stance: The Sound of Your Voice in Your Writing

In the first chapter of *Shoptalk*, we, the authors of this book, often wrote in a tone of voice much like the one we use on the first day of class—a bit formal as we outlined the purposes of the book and gave some idea about what you can expect. Similarly, on the first day of class, we try to outline what we'll focus on during the semester, what the assignments are, what books to buy. Usually, we have our students write a little during the initial meeting—to get started. On the first day, we keep at bay the fact that all of us—students and teachers—are unique individuals with complex lives. We disregard the fact that talking about something is a pale and often distorted shadow of doing it. We talk, instead, in that generic way teachers do, a way that seems to assume that all the students in their classes are alike and need to hear the same thing.

Since the purpose of the first chapter was to introduce the book and convince you of its value and authority, we let the book do the talking. Recall some of the phrasing you read in Chapter 1 (we've added italics to highlight our point): "*This book* helps you see yourself . . ." "*This book* argues . . ." "*This book* provides . . . ." As in these examples, some writing appears to achieve more authority by keeping the writer's individuality obscured and, as a result, creates some peculiar language. It leads the writer or speaker into "passive" rather than "active" constructions: "This book is intended for. . ." rather than "We are writing this book for . . . ."

In order to accomplish our purposes in Chapter 1, we chose to use the "first day of school" stance and the voice it creates. We selected this stance because it seemed appropriate for the introduction to a writing text, and because we thought it would establish our authority.

To select a stance, finding the words and organization to create a corresponding voice, writers rely on their personal histories and past experiences. As writers of this text, for example, we are teachers who, after many years of experience, have become comfortable with both the college writing we assign and with the formal, professional version of college writing that is called "academic discourse." We are also generally approachable, friendly teachers who tend to present to students both a personal side as well as the professional. In writing the first chapter, we chose a stance that would combine the two sides, leaning slightly more towards the formal and professional. That is, we wrote in our most teacherly, professional voice, one that is neutral and somewhat distant and in a way that we hoped would sound authoritative but not intimidating. Had we opted for a stance that was more personal and not quite so formal, the writing would have been different.

Look again at one section from the first chapter in its existing, formal version and in an alternate way that we might have written it had we taken a different stance:

EXISTING VERSION WRITTEN IN A FORMAL, DISTANT VOICE

A final belief about college writing is that it is something you can take in a semester or two and "get over with quickly." The writing placement exams and discretely defined writing requirements at many colleges falsely suggest that writing can be mastered once and for all before you enter college or in a specific course or two. You may have the impression that one need only learn a particular format or some new vocabulary in order for the difficulties of college writing to be resolved.

ALTERNATE VERSION WRITTEN IN A PERSONALLY ENGAGED VOICE

Finally, many of you may believe that college writing is something you can take in a semester or two and "get over with quickly." We're concerned that by using writing placement exams and discretely defined writing requirements, administrators of college writing programs give you the false idea that writing can be mastered once and for all before you enter college or in a specific course or two. By creating such requirements, we teachers and administrators may be giving you the impression that if you learn a particular format or some new vocabulary, you will solve all your difficulties of writing at college.

Notice that in the original version "you" exist, but "we" don't seem to be there. We have constructed the sentences so that the placement exams and writing requirements–not human beings–appear to be responsible for any beliefs you may have. In the alternate version, "we" not only exist, but "we" have feelings ("we're concerned"), and "we" become identified among the group of teachers and administrators who institute the exams and requirements that may be giving the wrong impression of college writing.

The differences between the two versions are subtle. Certainly there is nothing wrong with either one. And though you may have personal preferences, one is not inherently better than the other. The audience for whom a piece of writing is intended, the purpose for which the writing is created, and the way the writer wishes to present him or herself affect the writer's choice of what stance seems most appropriate for a given writing situation.

Writers have a lifetime of experiences on which to draw when placing themselves in what they write and taking a stance in writing. Unless writers take the opportunity to identify and reflect on these experiences, to use them in their writing, they are likely to shortchange themselves, their writing, and their readers. When we selected a teacherly, professional stance and its corresponding tone of voice, we drew on those related parts of our lives, and we did so because of the audience for whom we are writing (students in college writing classes), and our purpose (to introduce our textbook). In the present chapter we draw on another part of our history as teachers and writers, shifting our stance slightly to one that, we expect, is less distant than the one you heard in the previous chapter.

Writing Log Entry 3

Writing with a Different Stance for a Different Audience

Reread your *Writing Log Entry 1,* in which you described–for yourself–some of your expectations, fears, and hopes about writing and writing courses.

(continued)

Writing Log Entry 3

(Continued)

Imagine that the person who coordinates the writing courses at your college or university wants to get a better understanding of students' perceptions of writing and has asked students to write a letter to him or her about their fears and expectations as they begin the term. This writing situation, its audience and purpose, requires a different stance and voice from those that you used in *Entry 1.* Rewrite that piece in a way that would be desirable and appropriate for responding to this request.

❧ *Taking a Stance: Finding a Perspective from Which to Begin*

Taking a stance in your writing means more than selecting the most appropriate or effective voice. Along with selecting and finding this voice, you must find your own personal perspective on a particular subject area. For it is only by starting from this perspective that you will ultimately identify the purpose for which you will write: the question to answer, the point to argue, the position to explain, and so forth.

On a location map in a park or mall, there is often an arrow with the words, "you are here." Given the importance of finding and understanding your own perspective when you write, we believe it is useful to pause longer at the word "you" in relation to the history and evolution of college writing. Where are you in these surroundings of college writing? What do you see from where you are standing? What writing situations have you found yourself in previously? To locate your perspective about the subject of college writing, you must recall and record your own personal knowledge of past experiences.

You have already written on your hopes, fears, and expectations about college writing and college textbooks. Now let's consider your history as a writer. Though you may never before have thought of yourself as a writer, you have been one for some time, from the moment you began to use written language to hold and shape your ideas. You have been a writer outside of school—at home, at work, in the community—and a writer in school—in classes, at meetings, and where you live. Writers' previous experiences, the ones they remember most vividly, influence what they now believe to be true about writing and about themselves as writers. Our experiences shape our assumptions and attitudes toward writing and our sense of our own writing abilities. Losing the poetry award in third grade to your best friend, suffering through an impossibly demanding eighth grade teacher, learning the responsibility of being editor of the school paper–as experiences like these accumulate over time, they affect us in ways we may not immediately be aware of. Predominantly positive experiences will have one kind of effect, which may be obscured or even wiped out by one or two especially painful experiences.

Similarly, before writing about any particular subject, writers need to be clear about how they experience or understand that subject–identifying what is described in the chapter or the piece of literature they are to discuss, recalling the events of the historical period they are to study, and so on.

Identifying and recalling such experience is a first step toward one of the most important parts of college writing: reflection and analysis, making sense out of complex ideas and concepts. If you have a clear picture of the material that provides the basis for the essay, you can then more effectively work toward the final goal of a college essay: to analyze material as a means of reaching and supporting a particular purpose. As writers clarify their perspective on the subject to be examined, they can then step back and reflect on it, looking closely and systematically at its parts, analyzing these for points of similarity or difference from which to draw generalizations, and, ultimately, determine a purpose for writing, a focus and direction for the essay. Based on this process of reflection and analysis, the writer may chose to evaluate the material, to argue for or against it, to interpret an aspect of its significance, to explain its occurrence, and so on.

❋ *One Author Explains How She Recalled a Story*

To illustrate what the beginning of this process of recalling, reflecting, and analyzing might look like, I have searched my memories and written from my own history as a writer.

The story you will read is made up of experiences remembered or half-remembered from the time I began writing until now. Some occurrences in my writing history may turn out to have had a long-term effect on me, while others may be only curious stories to tell. I don't think it matters where one begins in telling stories from one's writing history or which incidents get recorded. I chose two events that stood out when I worked on this writing, though it might have been just as valuable for me to have chosen two others.

To begin recalling this story, I first had to think about my own writing history. To help me do this, I jotted down a word or phrase to stand for any events I could think of in my life as a writer. I listed anything that came to me in about a five minute period. Here's my list:

```
sixth grade graduation

the complainers' club

plays/performances

first poems

poems at night

publishing not writing

poem book

stories for J.

dissertation

first cccc talk

Mrs. Donaldson

Yaddo

Cummington

running poem

freshman comp.

storytellers
```

A list like this is written in a kind of code, not intended to be meaningful to anyone but me, the writer. But it is important to recognize that this list *is* writing, the first writing I did to recollect something from my personal writing experiences.

Next, I looked over my list to find topics I felt like thinking about. I did this by process of elimination, rejecting one event because I felt too close to it, another because I remembered it only vaguely, still another because it made me feel too angry. On a different day, these grounds for rejection might be the reasons I would choose a subject for writing.

I then found on the list one event that seemed to stand out for me that day. What I wrote eventually became the section you will read below about the PE teacher, Mrs. Donaldson.

I don't think it is necessary, or even a good idea when you first write them down to try to make sense of these memories, to draw conclusions from them. The conclusions and connections and analysis come later. If you give over your attention to the storytelling, you may find that new perspectives will appear to you, quite naturally, in the process of writing. In fact, I wrote the section about the PE teacher and then a second, separate piece about the running poem, without thinking of the two incidents as related in any way. Only later, when I looked at the two pieces side by side, did I see a connection.

Keep in mind that what I have written and included below is not meant to be an example of a college essay, but, rather, an example of how a writer might start working toward writing an essay by collecting, focusing, and refocusing some personal recollections. It is not first draft writing. However, the revisions I made were not prompted by the purposes of a college essay, but by my initial purpose of recalling my writing experiences, of telling my stories. These recollections, as we will explain later, provide a perspective from which I might make some reflections, begin an analysis and, finally, identify a purpose for which I would then write a college essay.

In seventh grade I learned that I could not "just be" a writer. I don't remember how it happened that I wanted to be a writer, or why. It's likely that I came into Westlake Junior High in Oakland, California, thinking of myself as a writer, already. I know that I had been answering the question, "What do you want to be when you grow up?" with "a writer" for several years before I learned that this was not an acceptable answer.

Mrs. Donaldson, the Physical Education teacher in whose presence I felt even more clumsy and skinny than I felt at all times during junior high, enlightened me. "You can't just be a writer," she responded when I took my turn to tell the career I'd chosen on seventh grade career day. "You have to have talent."

Years later it occurred to me that Mrs. Donaldson not only believed that writing abilities are impossible to develop, but that it was possible to tell, perhaps from the way I stumbled at gymnastics, that I had no talent as a writer.

I learned her lesson well enough to never again say I wanted to be a writer, not even after I was publishing and, in at least some people's eyes, becoming one.

I also learned from Mrs. Donaldson's Physical Education instruction that I had no athletic ability. All through junior high and high school, I avoided sports whenever I could. It wasn't until I was in college that I started swimming, and not until I left college that I discovered I could run. On my 27th birthday, I ran 27 miles. Just before my 28th birthday, I broke my leg skiing so I didn't run 28— or any—miles. In fact, the 27-mile run was, and looks likely to remain, a one time only event.

However, I can't resist saying, I got a lot of milage out of that run. I published a poem about it, "The Center of a 27-mile Run," in a local newspaper. For some reason, the production editor of the newspaper had extra copies of that issue, 200 of them, which he gave to me. I cut the poem out of about twenty copies and sent it to friends.

Eventually I used the newspapers as packing material, boxes of dishes, glasses, photographs, packed with layers of newspaper containing my poem. And, sad to say, a lot of newspapers were thrown out. I thought of packing up boxes of the newspapers to move them too, but I didn't do it. I wish, though, I had sent a copy to Mrs. Donaldson.

Writing Log Entry 4

Moving Toward Analysis: Drawing Assumptions from Writing Experiences

Using as your source the story the author tells from her writing history, reflect on her experiences, analyzing them for connections and identifying some of the assumptions and attitudes that you imagine the author to have about writing and about herself as a writer. What events or comments in the narrative lead you to these conclusions?

❧ Using These Recollections to Make a College Essay

Because the story you have just read has been revised from its most early form, and particularly because you are reading it in a book on college writing, it may appear to you as complete. From one perspective it is complete: The story is published, here in this text, and it has achieved the author's purpose of recalling some incidents from her history as a writer. From the perspective of college writing, however, the piece would serve only as an important step in exploration. To develop this material into a college essay, the writer would reflect on the events described in the story, analyze the connections, draw some conclusions, and, most importantly, identify an explicit reason for using these experiences in her writing. Returning to this story now, analyzing the events and her reactions, the writer likely would see connections she had not seen before, find new directions that her thinking could take. This kind of thinking would lead the writer away from narrating and recounting stories, toward a different kind of writing, one in which the stories and events would become a sources of data from which to make some explicit points about writing or learning. For example, the author might eventually write a college essay whose explicit purpose could be to argue what the author believes it means to "be a writer," to propose a high school course in writing, or to draw some conclusions about the relationship between her writing and her running, or other topics suggested by this story and the author's other writing experience.

The original narrative of the story that you have read would not be the sole point of the essay, rather it would have provided the writer with an understanding of her own perspective, one from which she could search for a purpose for writing an essay. The story, as it is written, might appear as an example to illustrate a point she wishes to make, or might appear in a greatly shortened form, or it might even disappear from the essay altogether. Were she to continue this process of recalling, reflecting, and analyzing, the writer would be using the act of writing as a way of uncovering or putting together a purpose for writing.

It may be disappointing to learn that most writers only figure out what they are going to write by writing. It's less magical than many of us suppose. We are used to reading published texts that simply look like they have always existed in precisely that form. But even an accomplished writer has to spend a lot of time writing, exploring, and searching. Indeed, the more accomplished one becomes as a writer, the longer it takes to write. The stakes rise higher; the ideas you wish to express grow more complex. Your ear for language becomes more alert and critical. You take on bigger writing projects and expect more of yourself. The positive side of this phenomenon, however, is that writers make their work better by working on it. No matter what comes out on the page at first, the final result can be a piece of writing that is meaningful to you and important to your audience. So, in this way, when a piece of writing is complete, sometimes even before it is finished, it may seem magical, after all.

Writing Log Entry 5

Writing from Your Own History as a Writer

Begin to discover your own personal perspective about writing from which you could, later, make connections, observations, and draw conclusions. First write out a list of experiences in your life as a writer. As in the example, use fragments or code words so that you can concentrate on searching your memories, not on creating a well-crafted list. Choose two or more of these experiences. Write out what you can remember of each of these stories.

3

A MAP OF COLLEGE WRITING

❧ *Locating Yourself in the History of College Writing*

Having recollected some experiences from your personal writing history, you may now have a clearer sense of how this history has influenced the way you currently think about writing. In this chapter, we would like to move outward from the point marked "you are here" on the map to the larger territory of college writing, asking you to consider ways in which your personal history has intersected with the public history of American college writing and writing at your school. This public history is not, by any means, a chronology of events that occurred and ended years ago. Rather, it is part of a continuing story involving college writing courses, writing exams, standards, and expectations–all of which exert influence on you and every other student enrolled in a college writing course.

Familiarizing yourself with the nature and development of college writing can clarify for you the impact that this larger, public history has had on both the form and content of contemporary college writing courses, as well as on individuals' beliefs about what it means to be a college writer. Much of what may seem mysterious or arbitrary about college writing, and your relationship to it, can be explained.

Because you are taking a college writing class you have probably begun to hear stories about past writing classes from roommates, friends at other schools, or even parents and grandparents. While it may seem from these stories that college writing courses have been around since the time of the cave dwellers, until the late nineteenth century, no writing courses, and certainly no college writing requirements, existed in the United States. The closest a college student might have come to taking a writing course would have been a course in rhetoric and exposition, a class more like a present-day speech class than one in writing.

❧ *The Beginnings of College Writing in America*

The first American colleges and universities, particularly the elite, private universities, were built to provide higher education for young men of the wealthy, upper-class, students whose college careers had, most likely, been selected for them long before they entered grammar and preparatory school. By the mid-nineteenth century, the middle-class population of the United States had become more socially and economically diverse. Immigrants were arriving from Europe and elsewhere, and the country's economy was becoming increasingly industry-based, allowing more Americans to earn middle-class incomes. More colleges were built to accommodate the increasing numbers of young people who could afford higher education. As a result, the population of students on college campuses was gradually becoming more diverse; college students included not only men from wealthy economic and social backgrounds, who, in a sense, had been preparing for college all their lives, but also young men (and some women) from the growing American middle-class, individuals who had not been "trained" in private schools and social clubs.

As the student population changed, so too did the language experiences that students brought to the university. While all the students at American universities spoke English, they did not all speak in the same dialect or register. Some had, throughout their lives, become used to hearing and speaking "standard," formal constructions; others had grown up hearing a mix of formal constructions and slang or street language. The conventional "king's English" of the wealthy class that had been the norm for entering freshmen, was mixing with the more everyday language or vernacular English of the middle-class. Faculty and administrators, themselves part of the social elite, were concerned about this apparent lack of standardized spoken and written English among students. In 1874, partially in response to these changing demographics and the perceived needs of a more diverse student body, the president of Harvard University began the designs for English A, a course that was soon to become the first required writing course at Harvard and the most influential writing course in the country.

```
┌─────────────────────────────────────────────────────────┐
│                  Writing Log Entry 6                      │
├───────────────────────────────────────────────────────────┤
```

Your Place in College Writing History

As we have tried to suggest, any one individual's experience with college writing is influenced by centuries of personal and public history. Think about where these two evolving histories of college writing intersect for you. Locate yourself and your family history in the evolution of college writing within the American college system. In the 1870s, when Harvard instituted English A, what language or languages were your ancestors speaking and where were they living? To what extent and in what ways do you imagine writing was a part of their daily life?

❧ *The Evolution of College Writing*

The diversity of students enrolled at universities in the late nineteenth century is slight compared to the diversity of today. Those faculty who were dismayed by the prevalence of vernacular English among students more than a century ago would surely be surprised were they to walk across a contemporary college campus, hearing not only the many dialects of English, but any number of different languages spoken by students from a broad range of cultural backgrounds. They would be similarly surprised were they to listen in on contemporary college writing classes and hear the way college writing is now described.

The relatively singular vision of college writing that existed in American universities in the 1800s was, in large part, a reflection of the equally singular set of beliefs and values shared by early college faculty. But as student populations became increasingly diverse, faculty gradually diversified as well. White, male instructors were joined by men and women from a range of ethnicities and cultures, with diverse personal and professional experiences and philosophies. This evolution in the make-up of college faculty, which continues today, necessarily influenced what students were learning and broadened the question of what they were expected to know. College writing, like colleges themselves, began to undergo a process of change. It was no longer possible, and it can be argued that it was no longer desirable, to find a single, monolithic definition of college writing.

These changes in how college writing is defined have been reinforced and validated by changes in our understanding of what it means
to write. When universities first began accepting students from a wider
range of social and economic background, English A and courses at
other universities modeled after English A were designed for the purpose of standardizing students' writing. It was assumed that there was a
single, correct way to write (and speak) that required mastery of specific
forms and phrasings that were familiar to the upper class. Instructors
concentrated their efforts and students' attention on the production of
"correct," daily themes that were written on assigned subjects, often
without revising, and with few reader's comments along the way.

The influence of American cultural diversity on college writing,
along with teaching experiences and research in the discipline of Composition that coalesced in the 1960s, provides evidence that writing is
much more complicated than the production of a daily theme and attention to sentence correctness would suggest. Each piece of writing–whatever the writer's cultural background–grows from a complex interplay of
the writer's thoughts, conversations, reflections, and readings. Writing is
not simply the act of recording completed ideas that have been stored in
our heads. It is a creative process, one that takes place over time and
is influenced by a vast number of experiences and reader reactions. It is
easy to see the final product, the finished text of writing, but what it took
to produce that text is, in large part, invisible. We can find evidence of a
writer's creative process in the visible form of drafts and notes. Yet, most
of the evolution of a piece of writing remains invisible in the thoughts
and feelings that occurred as the writer produced his or her work.

Traditionally, the final product has received all of the attention of
writing instruction. Yet the larger part of writing, what takes place on
the way to producing a finished text, holds the most influence over
one's development as a writer, beginning long before one sits down to
work on a particular task, long before one enters college. Consider, for
example, the relationship between the language or languages you
spoke before entering college and the language you are expected to use
in the classroom. Let's say you learned to speak English after years of
speaking Spanish or Tagalog or Cambodian in your home with your
parents and siblings; this will, by necessity, influence the way you hear
American academic language and what you feel about college writing
in English. If your first language is English, you did not learn it in the
context of a university, with all the expectations and qualifications that
come with writing for a college professor. Whatever languages you
speak and write, you have also had personal experiences with learning

and textbooks and classrooms and teachers that influence–in positive and negative ways–any writing that you produce.

Writing Log Entry 7

Finding Similarities and Differences in Writers' Experiences

Get together with one other person in the class and either exchange responses to *Writing Log Entry 6*, or read them aloud to each other. Once you have listened to and/or read each other's writing, write a response (Entry 7) to what the other person has written, about the way his or her experience strikes you as familiar or not. How is it like or unlike your own experience? What surprised or confused you? Tell the writer your reactions, feelings, and thoughts about the experience he or she described. Be sure to exchange one more time so that you can read the response you have written to each other's original entry.

✻ *Negotiating College Writing Standards*

At this point, you may be feeling skeptical about the picture of college writing that we have been outlining. To say that there is no longer a single standard for college writing and that your own personal and cultural experience should powerfully influence your writing may contradict your own experience and the very fact that you may be required to take your present writing course. Although college writing and our understanding of it has evolved in the ways we have described, college writing does continue to be influenced by its origins as a means of achieving uniformity and standardization. You may know from first-hand experience that colleges do, indeed, create standards and maintain expectations for students. Writing placement tests that students take before coming to campus or soon after, writing achievement or exit exams that occur before graduation, and required and recommended writing courses, provide evidence that college faculty continue to expect students to write in a particular way. And because tests and requirements vary from college to college, it's clear that expectations vary, that what is valued on one campus may not seem to be what is valued elsewhere.

Just as your college developed, and may still be developing, its curricular requirements over time–through weeks and weeks of faculty discussion and debate–it also developed a set of values about student writing, about how writing should be measured and taught, about what forms of writing should be emphasized. As the writing requirements and curriculum at your school evolved, faculty had to answer questions like these: How many terms of writing courses should be required? How should placement in writing courses be determined? What kinds of courses should be available–expository, creative writing, autobiography? Should students receive academic credit or grades for writing courses? Answers to these questions and to other questions specific to your school indicate that while college writing now has a much broader definition than it had in the 1870s, the tradition of creating and maintaining standards continues, even as it is significantly influenced by cultural diversity and individual creativity. Indeed, one of the purposes of *Shoptalk* is to help you, as a student, negotiate the demands of college writing standards and requirements, using, to your advantage, what we have come to know about the nature of writing and the development of writing abilities.

Writing Log Entry 8

Writing Requirements at Your School

What are the writing requirements of your school? How did you find out about these requirements and your school's writing courses? What seem to be the standards and expectations for college writing at your school? How do you know?

�֍ *Writing Outside of the English Department or Writing Program*

The expectations and standards that we have described so far develop inside English departments or writing programs and university curriculum committees. But there are other parts of the university that will affect you as a writer, if they haven't already. Each discipline at a university–each area of research and teaching–has its own set of writing standards called *conventions*. These conventions can apply to a range of writing concerns, from small, sentence-level issues to larger issues about essay structure, to an even larger concern with what subjects are interesting to write about. For example, conventions vary from discipline to discipline about the use of the first person ("I"), the value of passive voice ("The investigator argues . . ." versus "It is argued by the investigator . . ."), the use of abstracts or summaries at either the beginning or end of a piece of writing, the value of citing current sources, historical facts, or newly created experiences. As with the general writing standards set by your school, these conventions have evolved after years of discussion and debate. They are closely tied to the nature of a particular discipline and to what those who practice it value intellectually. In fact, this tie is so close that when individual members of a discipline refocus their attention and reevaluate their scholarly practices two things happen. First, established disciplines enlarge or change their conventions. Second, when the refocusing is too significant, then new or sub-disciplines evolve with new sets of writing conventions: psychology splits into cognitive and behavioral; sociology divides into quantitative analysis and qualitative analysis; English studies becomes literature and composition.

❋ Connections Between Personal Style and Disciplinary Conventions

What happens when a writer's personal style, one shaped by a lifetime of personal writing experiences, cultural influences, and creative tastes, meets up with the conventions and expectations of college writing in a variety of disciplines? Sometimes a writer's stylistic preferences and the conventions of a discipline fit nicely together: a tendency for writing long, complex sentences that include lots of highly descriptive illustrations and repeat one's main points may be a style that adapts comfortably to a literature assignment. But the same style may conflict loudly with the conventions of a scientific report where sentences are expected to be brief, illustrations kept concise, and repetitions deleted.

While it is not necessary or desirable for writers to strip themselves of their particular preferences in terms of writing style, it is useful to develop a sharpened awareness of which stylistic features they seem to favor most and, at the same time, to become familiar with the expected or favored conventions of the various disciplines for which they are assigned to write. With such knowledge, writers are better equipped to see the way their own stylistic preferences connect to and perhaps complement the general features of disciplinary style. They are then more likely to notice, also, ways they might modify their style as needed.

Writing Log Entry 9

Disciplinary Writing Conventions and Personal Style

What experiences have you had in writing essays or reports in those high school or college courses where writing was not the subject of study? What seemed to be the valued conventions of that discipline, and how did you find out about them? Did the conventions seem to fit comfortably with your way of writing? How did you feel that you had to adapt your own writing style to the conventions? How successful were you? How did you determine this success?

❧ *What, Then, Is College Writing?*

Rather than attempt to take you through the writing conventions of each discipline, we will use the writing assignments in *Shoptalk* to provide the guidance you will need for any college writing situation. Although, as we have discussed, the nature of college writing is evolving and different disciplines have some differing expectations, all college writing has certain expected, identifiable features.

First, college writing is *explicit*–that is, it spells out a particular focus or point of view or position–and it is *reflective*–that is, it takes some material, text, experience, or phenomenon and analyzes or interprets it.

Contrast these features with those expected in "creative" writing. The focus or point of your story or poem is intended to be implicit rather than explicit. A great deal is left open for interpretation. Readers are expected to draw their own conclusions from a story or poem or play. A college essay, on the other hand, must make its meaning known explicitly. Readers of college essays expect to know exactly where the writer stands, what position he or she is taking, and what specific points he or she is making.

It is the reader who must work hard to analyze and interpret the language of the story or poem; in a college essay, the writer is expected to do all the work. Whatever subject a college writer addresses, he or she not only records information or tells what happened, but also must reflect on and analyze in some way the material presented. The various terms often used to categorize different kinds of essays–proposal, compare and contrast, interpretation, argument–actually classify the kinds of reflective attention and analysis a writer can give any subject. What such classifications don't do is indicate the explicit purpose for which a particular writer is writing. It is only in the course of maintaining and developing some kind of reflective attention that writers clarify for their readers what they have to say and why.

Writers must also make critical choices about the kind of information that will hold the most value for their particular readers and to which they will give their reflective attention–what material they will analyze and use in the course of making their purpose clear and convincing. College writing, like all non-fiction writing, is informed by one or more of the following:

1. analysis and interpretation of recollections and memories from personal experience

2. analysis and interpretation of information gathered from conversations and observations

3. analysis and interpretation of readings and information from written texts.

Using these three sources, writers can effectively write for any number of purposes to make any number of points. The purpose the writer selects may depend on his or her personal interest in a particular topic, the audience he or she is addressing, and externally imposed requirements or limitations.

As you progress through the assignments in the book, you will create essays in whatever form is appropriate to your purposes for writing. However, each essay you write must meet the following general expectations: *all college writing conveys an explicit point by means of analyzing and reflecting on one (or more) of the three kinds of information: recollection and memory; observation and conversation; and written texts. Your means of analysis and reflection, as well as your choice of information, is influenced by the conventions and expectations of the discipline within which you are writing, the purpose for which you are writing, and your own creative, cultural, and individual experiences.*

C H A P T E R

4

DISCOVERING AND
CREATING YOUR ESSAY

✳ *Writing to Find Meaning*

"I've gone to the store—be back in half an hour." When you write a note like this, you use writing to record and convey information. To produce this kind of writing, you usually compose quickly and without much thought since you already know what you want to say. However, most of the writing you will do in college involves you not merely in recording something you already know, but in using written language to help you figure out what you want to say—even to help you figure out what you don't yet know. The process of putting your thoughts into words can actually help you to create new thoughts.

When any of us write, the words we put on a sheet of paper or computer screen have emerged from a long journey, most of which has taken place without our awareness. Before we write—or even speak—we experience a sense of wanting to say something, a physical or emotional desire to express a thought. We have what has been called a "felt sense" of our thoughts even before we may be able to articulate them in words.

Finding words for our "felt sense" is a natural process that often happens so quickly we are unaware of it. Sometimes, however, the process is slower, and we may notice that we shuttle back and forth between our sense of what we want to say and the words we're finding. In speaking, this process usually takes place quickly; as we express ourselves, our minds select and reject several possible words or phrases instantaneously. We cannot write as quickly as we speak, so in writing, we may be more aware of this shuttling process. As the match between our sense of what we want to say and the words we choose becomes closer, we may become more conscious of our choices. Much of the time, in both speaking and writing, we find the words we're seeking. But sometimes we pause, rephrase an idea, or reject a statement altogether. When we write, these pauses can seem to bog down our progress as we struggle to find words to capture what we are feeling and thinking. It is then that writers are likely to complain, "I know what I want to say. I just can't write it!"

Yet, something powerful is happening during this struggle. As we reject words, selecting only those that come closest to our sense of what we are trying to say, we are taking something that is vague and intangible and crystallizing it into visible, written language. This is a complicated process. We make connections between our initial, felt sense, and the words we use; we create new thoughts that wouldn't have existed had we not attempted to represent our ideas and feelings in words. When we find just the right word or phrase, when we reach an "I got it!" moment, we are experiencing the power of language to help us find meaning. We discover we can learn from our own writing.

✖ *Exploring with Freewriting*

One of the difficulties of writing is that, since it is slower than speaking, we have more time to get in our own way. That is, we may tend to criticize our work before we've even figured out what we're going to say. In the process of shuttling back and forth between our felt sense and the words we write, we may pause so long debating our choice of words that we lose our train of thought. Or we may think ahead to how a reader may view our writing, worrying whether we have said something "correctly" to such an extent that we can't concentrate on the meaning we are creating.

There is a writing technique called "freewriting" that we have incorporated extensively into the writing tasks assigned in *Shoptalk*. Many writers say it is the most useful strategy they know for generating writing. Freewriting takes advantage of the meaning-making power of written language by removing the blocks that can keep you from letting words guide you; it focuses your attention on whatever felt sense is emerging as you write. When you freewrite, you are able to shut out the critic in your head who distracts you from thinking about what you are writing with worries about how you are writing. Rather than pushing ahead, following the ideas you are generating, the critic nags at you to pause and rewrite, edit, cross out, get a cup of coffee—anything that will prevent you from attentively and insistently writing to capture what it is you want to say. Freewriting allows you to silence that critic.

The rules of freewriting are simple:

1. Write without stopping.

    Keep your pen, pencil, or cursor moving, even if you write, "I'm stuck, I'm stuck, I'm stuck," or "What'll I say? What'll I say?" until you find you've moved on to saying something else.

2. Do not reread or correct what you are writing.

    There will be time, later, for rereading, revising, editing, or discarding what you've written; while you are freewriting just keep the flow of thought pouring onto the page.

Freewriting is a way of brainstorming, of free-associating. It allows you to listen only to the words appearing on the page and not to the critic in your head who may want you to pause and make judgements. At first, it may seem like a difficult task to write without worrying about writing well; but with practice, it becomes easier, and, as you will see, because it helps you to generate writing, to get your ideas down, freewriting is a powerful technique for developing your abilities as a writer.

❧ *Invisible Writing*

One way to encourage yourself to freewrite and to ensure that you will not pause to reread as you are composing is to try "invisible writing." You can do invisible writing by hand or at the computer. To invisible write by hand, you will need a ballpoint pen with no ink left in the cartridge and a piece of carbon paper placed between two sheets of paper. When you write with the empty pen on the top sheet of paper, you will not be able to see what you are writing, but the carbon sheet will imprint your words on the bottom page. At the computer, you simply need to darken the screen so that you cannot see the words you are composing. Because there is no chance for rereading, invisible writing may focus your attention, force you to concentrate on meaning making, even more than regular freewriting.

❧ *Focused Freewriting*

Most of the time, writers do not compose an entirely free-associative kind of freewriting. Freewriting, in which you write anything at all that is on your mind, is the way you are likely to write in a journal or perhaps, in a letter to someone you know well. It is the best way to get feelings, first impressions, initial thoughts down on paper. However, even in entirely free-associative freewriting, our natural tendency is to focus on particular subjects or ideas, to follow our lines of thinking in particular directions.

Just as you can use freewriting to explore and create ideas, you can also use it to focus on any specific ideas you find interesting. Often, writers begin their freewriting in this way, with the intention of focusing on a particular subject. So, rather than writing anything that comes to mind, you write anything that comes to mind on a certain question or subject you wish to examine. This kind of writing is called "focused freewriting." You may have already been using focused freewriting as wrote the **Writing Log** entries so far in this book. On the other hand, you may have been letting your critic interrupt your writing process, and if so, you can now start composing the **Writing Log** entries as focused freewriting.

The idea you begin with in focused freewriting provides you with both a starting place and a reference point as you compose–nonstop–without your critic's nagging interference. Focused freewriting can help you explore an idea, expanding your sense of what that idea is, refining your understanding of it, or seeing connections between this idea and others.

Writing Log Entry 10

Trying Freewriting and Invisible Writing and Thinking about the Two

Freewrite for six or seven minutes. You don't have to write quickly, just steadily, without pausing to reread or make changes as you write. Write anything at all that comes to you.

Now try out invisible freewriting by hand or at the computer for six to seven minutes. As with any freewriting, you may write on whatever comes to mind.

Take a few minutes, when you have finished your invisible writing but have not yet looked at what you have written, to write about the process of invisible writing. How did it compare with your regular writing process and with that of freewriting? What surprised you or frustrated you about each?

Now read what you wrote during the invisible writing. Are you surprised by what you wrote? Does the structure or style in the invisible writing seem different from that of the freewriting? At what point in each piece of writing, if at all, did your sentences and ideas hang together? Did you write things that you wouldn't have predicted?

❧ *Rereading and Refocusing*

The techniques you have just learned–freewriting, invisible writing, and focused freewriting–help writers to compose, to generate writing. (You can also do an invisible, focused freewrite.) These ways of writing depend, in part, on the strategy of not pausing to reread so that you do not disrupt your concentration on meaning making. They require you to hold off on rereading until you've got some of your ideas onto the page. During invisible writing, you may have found it frustrating to be unable to do the glancing, casual rereading that is usually part of writing. During freewriting you may have had to consciously resist the urge to stop and reread as you wrote.

As you become accustomed to freewriting and focused freewriting, you will become familiar with this process of quickly generating material–and only then, rereading it. For, rereading is a significant part of the larger writing process.

At the beginning of this chapter, we described composing, how writers shuttle back and forth between their sense of what they want to say and the words they are selecting. As writers compose, the words we choose generate more words. After we have produced some writing, we then reread what we have written. Our rereading reminds us of both what we have already said and what we still want to say. In response to what we see we have said, we write more.

Just as the ability to freewrite can help you to get your thoughts onto the page, the ability to reread effectively what you have written can help you to write more. If you are actively engaged in the reading, paying attention to the meaning, to what you have written, rather than how you have written it (there will be plenty of time for that later), you can use your reading to help you generate more writing. You can reread with an eye to what more you have to say, to what direction your writing seems to be going, to what questions your writing seems to raise, and so on.

❧ *Writing Essays with This Book*

Each essay you write as you proceed through *Shoptalk* will evolve from writing that you generate over the course of several chapters. As you complete the reading and the **Writing Log** entries, you will also be creating material from which to draw as you move toward developing an essay. We have already introduced you to several strategies that will help you to move forward through the discovery and creation of your essay: *freewriting, focused freewriting,* and *rereading.* In the last part of this chapter, you will begin to use these strategies to move your writing from an initial exploration to an essay that is focused and purposeful by doing the **Perspectives and Focusing** activities. In the two chapters that follow, we will describe **Response** activities for getting valuable feedback on your work-in-progress as you revise, and guidelines for **Editing and Proofreading** that you can use to make your essay appropriate for your audience.

All of the essays you will be asked to write in *Shoptalk* will be instances of college writing: writing that reflects on and analyzes information in order to convey an explicit purpose or meaning to a reader. As the summary at the end of Chapter 1 indicated, the assignments in *Shoptalk* will help you to gain experience writing from each of the three main sources of information available to college writers: for Essays 1 and 2, your sources of information will be your interpretations and analysis of your own remembered experiences; Essays 3 and 4 will draw on information you gather from other people; and Essay 5 will emerge from your reading and interpretation of academic texts.

Essay 1

Select from your recollections and memories some experiences, attitudes, or personal knowledge about writing that you would like to reflect on more extensively. Your *Writing Log* entries provide an initial source for these recollections; discussions you've had in class or outside of class may trigger some relevant memories as well. As you have been reading *Shoptalk,* you have already begun think about college writing, your own college writing history, and your feelings, attitudes, and beliefs about writing.

Next, use the Perspectives and Focusing activities to analyze and interpret these reflections, and determine an explicit purpose or meaning for your essay. The essay you eventually write will use your recollections to make and support a particular point or points about writing, college writing, or yourself as a writer.

WRITING ESSAY 1

Notice an important distinction we are making: Your first essay emerges from your reflections on these recollected experiences; it is not a narrative of your personal experiences. Such a narrative, like the story by one of the authors of this book in Chapter 2, does not include the kind of sustained reflective analysis or explicit meaning that is required of college writing. Your experiences and thoughts are a source of information, a place to find an issue to explore, questions to answer, and, moreover, a purpose for writing.

We intentionally designed the **Writing Log** entries so that, in the process of completing them, you would be using the source of information appropriate to the essay you would be writing in that section of the book. Consequently, the **Writing Log** entries you have already completed have fixed your attention on a variety of topics, all emerging from your own personal experiences with writing and language. Now, using freewriting to explore and analyze your thinking and what you have written in the **Writing Logs,** we ask you to look for connections, surprising perspectives, particular sets of belief or opinion, or other points from which your essay might develop. It is the writer's own evolving point of view and desire to be heard that allows an essay to achieve interest and purpose for both the writer and reader. By rereading your **Log** entries, listening carefully for what they say to you and for how they reverberate in relation to one another, you can begin to find your own emerging essay.

DEMONSTRATIONS FROM STUDENTS AND PROFESSIONALS

At this point, as you set off to start your first essay, you may be concerned about what your essay should look like. What we are asking you to do is to find your own purpose for writing, one that matters to you. And because the purpose you select will determine, to a large extent, what your essay will look like, no one else's essay can possibly provide you with a "model" for your own. Rather than modeling the way the assignment "should" be done, we will let students' own writing and some professional essays jump start your thinking and, we hope, convince you that what we are asking you to do is well within your range of capability and interest. We encourage you to look at the student and professional demonstrations with an analytic eye, to see what you can learn about your own evolving essay from the choices that these writers have made.

You will find **Student Demonstrations** throughout the parts of the book titled "Discovering and creating your essay." Some of the demonstrations are quotations taken from students' **Writing Log** entries or from exploratory writing; others are sections or paragraphs from students' drafts. We have tried to include enough of their writing to give you a sense of the explicit, reflective qualities in their essays. These demonstrations represent the voices of other students who have already completed the writing assignments you are working on now. They offer you moral support in the best way they can, by telling you and showing you how they handled some of the writing issues you are now facing.

As you begin working on your first essay you might refer to these demonstrations from students, as well as to the **Professional Demonstration Essays** that appear at the end of this chapter (and will for each essay assignment) and the questions we have included. Along with the activities we include to help you generate and focus your essay, the demonstrations can give you a sense of the wide range of options available to you when you write from your own personal learning and writing experiences and the wide variety of ways that writers' ideas and purposes can emerge from their recollected experiences.

DISCOVERING AND CREATING YOUR ESSAY

The **Perspectives and Focusing** activities you will begin in this chapter will help you to generate and focus ideas for Essay 1. As you create these writings, you will be moving from initially random and exploratory thoughts on paper, toward writing that is more focused and intentional. If you allow your ideas and your essay to develop in this way, giving yourself space and time to explore and expand your ideas early on, you can build a foundation for making the final draft of the essay interesting, purposeful, and complete.

In the first set of activities, "Taking on different perspectives," we ask you to try out various perspectives from which to reflect on your **Writing Log** entries about experiences with writing. You may find that the differences among these perspectives seem slight, but we urge you to let your mind stay open and flexible. Don't limit yourself and your power to create by resisting the possibility of seeing various perspectives and points of view.

Keep in mind that what you have written so far in your **Writing Log** serves only as a starting point for the creation of your essay. In other words, your essay is not a recollection or a memory. Rather, its purpose will emerge from your reflections on and analysis of your recollections and memories about writing. By asking you to look for connections, contradictions, similarities, and congruencies among your recollections, the **Perspectives** activities promote the kind of analysis and reflection that is necessary for producing a college essay. You may or may not want to proceed through these activities in the order they appear. You may want to use them in an order and at a time that seems most appropriate to your needs as you write. Your instructor may also have some advice for you.

The second set of activities, "Focusing your direction," provides a series of writing prompts that will help you find direction in the thoughts you have recorded in your reflective writing. Having analyzed your recollections from the vantage of a number of perspectives you may begin to feel a center from which to write. The **Focusing** activities offer you some tools for moving closer and closer to this "felt sense" of your ideas as they come together, rereading your words and quickly writing again, using each successive piece of writing as the inspiration from which to move ahead.

By the end of this chapter then, you will have had the opportunity to generate a first, exploratory draft and then a second, more focused draft using recollection and memory to express an explicit purpose. We strongly recommend that before you begin, you read through all of the activities carefully in order to get a clear sense of how they work. Although you may find that you can strengthen your essay by including support from sources other than memory and recollection, such as what other people have said in conversation or in print, your personal experience provides the primary information source for this essay.

TAKING ON DIFFERENT PERSPECTIVES

PERSPECTIVES: *Questions and Connections*

Reread all the **Writing Log** entries you have done so far. Jot down notes about any connections or relationships you see among them. You might consider some of these questions: Can you make some connections between your memories of writing experiences and your starting point as you begin this course? What links do you notice among the writing memories? Do the writing courses that exist on your campus meet your expectations for what college writing should be? How do your expectations, hopes, and fears about college writing fit with the expectations for writing implied by the writing requirements at your school? What questions arise for you from the similarities and differences between your experiences and those of other students? Are there one or more **Writing Log**

entries that seem particularly intriguing to you about which you may
have more to say?

Student Demonstration
PERSPECTIVES: *Questions and Connections*
Example 1

Throughout my whole life, whenever I have completed
something whether it be a paper or scoring the winning
point in a basketball game I felt as if I didn't adequately do everything in my power to make it complete.
This thought somehow transfers into a feeling of self-
consciousness while writing a paper. Due to this self-
consciousness I start writing my paper several different
times because I have told myself that it is not correct.
Once I am able to get past this, I can finish my paper. I
turn it in with a feeling that dominates my mind that I
can do better. Why am I creating this imaginary problem
with every paper that I write?

Example 2

I enjoy the movement of writing, the feel of the pen
on the paper, the way it looks, and the outlet it gives
me for my feelings. On the other hand, I cannot get over
my feelings of resentment toward all the times that I
struggled for days to get a paper finished for a class. I
find that my negative feelings toward writing have accumulated over the years from the multitudes of bad experiences I have had. My feelings on writing have ranged from
pain to being terrified to even feeling like writing had
complete control over my life and I was never going to
gain the control myself.

The feelings of having writing central in my life came
from when my father would help me with my English papers.
My father taught me many things about writing, but while
doing it he made me hate it. He used to stay up with me to
all hours helping me revise my papers. It's like I was
scared that my father would no longer love me if the paper
was not well-written.

PERSPECTIVES: *Conflicting Points of View*

The experiences on which we base our beliefs are never entirely consistent; sometimes they are positive and other times not. So, implicit in your various **Writing Log** entries there are, most likely, two or more conflicting points of view on writing. For example, from one perspective in your experience writing may be fun, engaging, rewarding. From the point of view of another experience writing may be a valuable private respite from the world. From still another, you may see anger toward writing that is required by someone else and that is difficult and painful to create. These different viewpoints emerge from your writing memories, from your hopes, fears, and expectations, even from your response to your classmates' writing.

In this freewriting exploration, identify what points of view emerge from your **Writing Log** entries and then listen to them as if to the distinct voices of individuals who maintain singular perspectives. Write out a conversation among these voices. If the individuals who contain these voices were to sit together at a crowded college pub and discover that they are enrolled in the college writing class you find yourself in today, what might they say to one another?

PERSPECTIVES: *Metaphoric Thinking*

One way to explore an object or a concept is by making a comparison between it and something else that is equally or more familiar to you. In fact, the creative part of our brain makes such comparisons all the time. When we see something for the first time or encounter a new idea, we think about it, metaphorically, we try to understand it in relation to other things and ideas that are familiar to us. Sometimes this comparison allows us to categorize successfully and sometimes not. Either way, when we use this strategy intentionally, we are often surprised at the way our understanding expands, at the way new perspectives on the concept or object emerge.

Reread the **Perspectives** writing you have done so far and identify a concept or object that appears in or is suggested by the writing. Make three comparisons between the original concept or object and something else that, somehow, it reminds you of (writing in school is like . . .; using computers to write is like . . .; school newspapers are like . . ., etc.). Then, explain each comparison, freewriting for a few minutes about how the comparison works and what the comparison shows you about the concept or object that you might not have otherwise noticed.

Student Demonstration

PERSPECTIVES: *Metaphoric Thinking*

Example 1

Sometimes trying to start a writing assignment is like learning how to ride a bike for the first time. You keep trying and trying but you can't get it perfect on the first try.

This comparison makes me think how difficult it is for me sometimes to get started with an idea when I am assigned an assignment. I usually have about 15 different papers, all with ideas that are different or rearranged, but not one of them is what I want. This is like riding a bike because you keep falling off, or messing up, and each time you get on the bike it is new time. You won't get it right unless you practice for awhile.

FOCUSING YOUR DIRECTION

FOCUSING: *Questions and Connections*

What connections can you make among your explorations? Write three or four sentences of questions or observations emerging from the **Perspectives** activities.

Student Demonstration

FOCUSING: *Questions and Connections*

Example 1

How can I resolve my conflict between wanting to learn more about and improve my writing and wanting to give up because my skills have not developed yet? I'm excited about my English class, but my writing isn't very impressive, and I don't think any English class can help me. For me, writing a great essay is like finding a rose in a weed patch.

Example 2

I hate any writing that has to do with school. School writing is laborious and has too many rules to follow. Is college writing something that you can learn to do even if you hate it?

Example 3

> American lifestyle kills muses, therefore I highly doubt that in the "noodle factory-like" universities there is space for creation—maybe for learning, but even that is questionable. It is not the mistake of a teacher or a writing program, and that's where it all interconnects. Thousands and thousands of little connections at work together along with my own.

FOCUSING: *Writing More*

Use a statement or question that you wrote above (in Questions and Connections) as a focus from which to begin, and from which to guide, this freewriting. Push yourself to write two or three pages. The only parameters are those set by the sentences you have already written. Use the statement as a taking off point as well as a thought to return your attention to as you generate more writing.

FOCUSING: *Rereading and Writing Again*

Reread the pages you have written; while doing so, underline sentences or sections of your writing that jump out at you in some way, the ones that catch your eye and stay with you. Find a sentence or two that you like or that seems important to you or that seems to get at something that you don't completely understand, something you might want to reflect on further, or something that you feel is worth telling others. With three or four of these sentences in mind, write several more pages of focused freewriting.

FOCUSING: *Rereading, Reseeing, and Rewriting*

Together, all of the writing you have done so far makes up an initial, exploratory draft. Like most exploratory writing, it is somewhat random and disconnected, especially at first. But the more writing you do, dropping some ideas, adding and developing others, the more focused and full of direction it becomes.

Reread all the pages you have written in these activities, paying particular attention to the focused freewriting at the end. Ask yourself what explicit purpose for writing emerges from the first draft. That is to say, what is it that you are writing about and to what end?

With this subject and purpose in mind, and with all of the writing you have done so far at hand, write a second draft. Unlike writing your exploratory draft, you will try to begin this second draft with a sense of purpose and with some ideas about how the recollections and memories you have recorded and reflected on can help you to accomplish that purpose. Because the value of the writing you have done for your exploratory first-draft is in the analysis and reflection that it allowed you to do, you may or may not use sections of it in your second draft. What you will use, however, are the ideas it produced, the connections it uncovered, the purpose it sharpened.

Student Demonstration
REFLECTIVE ANALYSIS OF RECOLLECTION AND MEMORY
Example 1

My inspiration to write hero stories is based on my hobby of comic book collecting. When I first started reading comic books, it was because I really did not enjoy reading long, boring pictureless books.

I was never comfortable with my reading because I was always slower than the other kids. So to catch up with their pace, I would skip a few lines or even a few pages. As I read more comic books, my vocabulary increased and my confidence in writing interesting papers was raised.

I also gained the ability to write from emotion. Before I started reading comic books, I would attempt to be too analytical, exposing as little of myself as I could. Comic book writers have captivated my attention by putting in the heros' emotions and feelings. Reading comics has opened up my imagination and helped me enjoy writing that includes personal experience and emotions.

Example 2

I remember as a child when my mother and I would go places that required her to sign papers, and she didn't have the skills to. So she would always have to take someone with her. It hurts me to know that I have learned this skill that she always wanted. It was difficult for me to write about my mother's experience because it really hurts me to know that my mother does not know how to read or write and that if it hadn't been for my mother and father coming to the U.S. I have probably would not have received

much of an education myself and would have probably been
married now with kids like my cousins who live where my
parents once lived.

❧ *Professional Demonstration Essays*
QUESTIONS TO CONSIDER AS YOU READ THESE ESSAYS

During the process of drafting your first essay, it may be helpful to
read the demonstration essays that follow. These essays emerge from a
writer's experiences with writing; each essay takes its shape and direction from the particular recollections of the writer and the purpose he or
she has determined for it. Any one of these essays might have begun as
yours will, with a writer reflecting on a particular experience in school
or at home, noting a particular change in feelings about writing, admiring the way someone else writes or makes others feel with writing. The
writers then stood back from those initial recollections or feelings, and
analyzed them for repeated behaviors, points of conflict, or particular
moments that could be understood or interpreted in particular ways.
From this analysis grew the writer's own purpose or reason for writing—
to show something particular about him or herself or someone else, to
make an argument, to make a comparison, or to show a change. Whatever the purpose, just like your essay, each demonstration essay relies on
the writer's own personal experience as a primary source of information.
Each one uses this information to illustrate the point the writer wants to
make, to support the claims that the writer is proposing.

By looking closely at how these writers have used recollection and
memory to support and extend the purpose for which they are writing,
you may gain insight for your own essay. You might, for example, notice
how the writers have integrated their experience into their essays, using
it to illustrate the purpose for which they are writing. Use the following
questions to help you examine each demonstration essay in more detail:

1. In a sentence or two, how would you summarize the explicit purpose
    of each essay? Another way of thinking about this would be to imag-
    ine that you were to ask the writer what the essay was about and
    then ask, "So what?" How might he or she answer?

2. How do the writers make their points explicit? What are the sen-
    tences or parts of the essay that make this happen for the reader?

3. How do the writers use information from recollection and memory
    to support or illustrate the purpose of their essays? How is this infor-
    mation integrated into the text and used as a point of authority?

꧁꧂

From Outside, In*

Barbara Mellix

1   Two years ago, when I started writing this paper, trying to bring order out of chaos, my ten-year-old daughter was suffering from an acute attack of boredom. She drifted in and out of the room complaining that she had nothing to do, no one to "be with" because none of her friends were at home. Patiently I explained that I was working on something special and needed peace and quiet, and I suggested that she paint, read, or work with her computer. None of these interested her. Finally, she pulled up a chair to my desk and watched me, now and then heaving long, loud sighs. After two or three minutes (nine or ten sighs), I lost my patience. "Looka here, Allie," I said, "you too old for this kinda carryin' on. I done told you this is important. You wronger than dirt to be in here haggin' me like this and you know it. Now git on outta here and leave me off before I put my foot all the way down."

2   I was at home, alone with my family, and my daughter understood that this way of speaking was appropriate in that context. She knew, as a matter of fact, that it was almost inevitable; when I get angry at home, I speak some of my finest, most cherished black English. Had I been speaking to my daughter in this manner in certain other environments, she would have been shocked and probably worried that I had taken leave of my sense of propriety.

3   Like my children, I grew up speaking what I considered two distinctly different languages–black English and standard English (or as I thought of them then, the ordinary everyday speech of "country" coloreds and "proper" English)–and in the process of acquiring these languages, I developed an understanding of when, where, and how to use them. But unlike my children, I grew up in a world that was primarily black. My friends, neighbors, minister, teachers–almost everybody I associated with every day–were black. And we spoke to one another in our own special language: *That sho is a pretty dress you got on. If she don' soon leave me off I'm gon tell her head a mess. I was so mad I could'a*

*Mellix, Barbara. "From Outside, In" originally appeared in *The Georgia Review*, Volume XLI, No. 2 (Summer 1987), © 1987 by The University of Georgia, © 1987 by Barbara Mellix. Reprinted by permission of Barbara Mellix and *The Georgia Review*.

pissed a blue nail. He all the time trying to low-rate somebody. Ain't that just about the nastiest thing you ever set ears on?

4   Then there were the "others," the "proper" blacks, transplanted relatives and one-time friends who came home from the city for weddings, funerals, and vacations. And the whites. To these we spoke standard English. "Ain't?" my mother would yell at me when I used the term in the presence of "others." "You *know* better than that." And I would hang my head in shame and say the "proper" word.

5   I remember one summer sitting in my grandmother's house in Greeleyville, South Carolina, when it was full of the chatter of city relatives who were home on vacation. My parents sat quietly, only now and then volunteering a comment or answering a question. My mother's face took on a strained expression when she spoke. I could see that she was being careful to say just the right words in just the right way. Her voice sounded thick, muffled. And when she finished speaking, she would lapse into silence, her proper smile on her face. My father was more articulate, more aggressive. He spoke quickly, his words sharp and clear. But he held his proud head higher, a signal that he, too, was uncomfortable. My sisters and brothers and I stared at our aunts, uncles, and cousins, speaking only when prompted. Even then, we hesitated, formed our sentences in our minds, then spoke softly, shyly.

6   My parents looked small and anxious during those occasions, and I waited impatiently for our leave-taking when we would mock our relatives the moment we were out of their hearing. "Reeely," we would say to one another, flexing our wrists and rolling our eyes, "how dooo you stan' this heat? Chile, it just too hy*ooo*-mid for words." Our relatives had made us feel "country," and this was our way of regaining pride in ourselves while getting a little revenge in the bargain. The words bubbled in our throats and rolled across our tongues, a balming.

7   As a child I felt this same doubleness in uptown Greeleyville where the whites lived. "Ain't that a pretty dress you're wearing!" Toby, the town policeman, said to me one day when I was fifteen. "Thank you very much," I replied, my voice barely audible in my own ears. The words felt wrong in my mouth, rigid, foreign. It was not that I had never spoken that phrase before–it was common in black English, too–but I was extremely conscious that this was an occasion for proper English. I had taken out my English and put it on as I did my church clothes, and I felt as if I were wearing my Sunday best in the middle of the week. It did not matter that Toby had not spoken grammatically correct English. He was white and could speak as he wished. I had something to prove. Toby did not.

8   Speaking standard English to whites was our way of demonstrating that we knew their language and could use it. Speaking it to standard-English-speaking blacks was our way of showing them that we, as well as they, could "put on airs." But when we spoke standard English, we acknowledged (to ourselves and to others–but primarily to ourselves) that our customary way of speaking was inferior. We felt foolish, embarrassed, somehow diminished because we were ashamed to be our real selves. We were reserved, shy in the presence of those who owned and/or spoke *the* language.

9   My parents never set aside time to drill us in standard English. Their forms of instruction were less formal. When my father was feeling particularly expansive, he would regale us with tales of his exploits in the outside world. In almost flawless English, complete with dialogue and flavored with gestures and embellishment, he told us about his attempt to get a haircut at a white barbershop; his refusal to acknowledge one of the town merchants until the man addressed him as "Mister"; the time he refused to step off the sidewalk uptown to let some whites pass; his airplane trip to New York City (to visit a sick relative) during which the stewardesses and porters–recognizing that he was a "gentleman"–addressed him as "Sir." I did not realize then–nor, I think, did my father– that he was teaching us, among other things, standard English and the relationship between language and power.

10   My mother's approach was different. Often, when one of us said, "I'm gon wash off my feet," she would say, "And what will you walk on if you wash them off?" Everyone would laugh at the victim of my mother's "proper" mood. But it was different when one of us children was in a proper mood. "You think you are so superior," I said to my oldest sister one day when we were arguing and she was winning. "Superior!" my sister mocked. "You mean I am acting 'biggidy'?" My sisters and brothers sniggered, then joined in teasing me. Finally, my mother said, "Leave your sister alone. There's nothing wrong with using proper English." There was a half-smile on her face. I had gotten "up-pity," had "put on airs" for no good reason. I was at home, alone with the family, and I hadn't been prompted by one of my mother's proper moods. But there was also a proud light in my mother's eyes; her children were learning English very well.

11   Not until years later, as a college student, did I begin to understand our ambivalence toward English, our scorn of it, our need to master it, to own and be owned by it–an ambivalence that extended to the public-school classroom. In our school, where there were no whites, my teachers taught standard English but used black English to do it. When

my grammar-school teachers wanted us to write, for example, they usually said something like, "I want y'all to write five sentences that make a statement. Anybody git done before the rest can color." It was probably almost those exact words that led me to write these sentences in 1953 when I was in the second grade:

> The white clouds are pretty.
> There are only 15 people in our room.
> We will go to gym.
> We have a new poster.
> We may go out doors.

12   Second grade came after "Little First" and "Big First," so by then I knew the implied rules that accompanied all writing assignments. Writing was an occasion for proper English. I was not to write in the way we spoke to one another. The white clouds pretty; There ain't but 15 people in our room; We going to gym. We got a new poster; We can go out in the yard. Rather I was to use the language of "other": clouds *are, there are, we will,* we *have,* we *may.*

13   My sentences were short, rigid, perfunctory, like the letters my mother wrote to relatives:

> Dear Papa,
> How are you? How is Mattie? Fine I hope. We are fine. We will come to see you Sunday. Cousin Ned will give us a ride.
>
> > Love,
> > Daughter

The language was not ours. It was something from outside us, something we used for special occasions.

14   But my coloring on the other side of that second-grade paper is different. I drew three hearts and a sun. The sun has a smiling face that radiates and envelops everything it touches. And although the sun and its world are enclosed in a circle, the colors I used–red, blue, green, purple, orange, yellow, black–indicate that I was less restricted with drawing and coloring than I was with writing standard English. My valentines were not just red. My sun was not just a yellow ball in the sky.

15   By the time I reached the twelfth grade, speaking and writing standard English had taken on new importance. Each year, about half of the newly graduated seniors of our school moved to large cities–particularly in the North–to live with relatives and find work. Our English teacher constantly corrected our grammar: "Not 'ain't, but 'isn't.'" We seldom

wrote papers, and even those few were usually plot summaries of short stories. When our teacher returned the papers, she usually lectured on the importance of using standard English: "I *am;* you *are;* he, she, or it *is*," she would say, writing on the chalkboard as she spoke. "How you gon git a job talking about 'I is,' or 'I isn't' or 'I ain't?'"

16   In Pittsburgh, where I moved after graduation, I watched my aunt and uncle–who had always spoken standard English when in Greeleyville–switch from black English to standard English to a mixture of the two, according to where they were or who they were with. At home and with certain close relatives, friends, and neighbors, they spoke black English. With those less close, they spoke a mixture. In public and with strangers, they generally spoke standard English.

17   In time, I learned to speak standard English with ease and to switch smoothly from black to standard or a mixture, and back again. But no matter where I was, no matter what the situation or occasion, I continued to write as I had in school:

Dear Mommie,

How are you? How is everybody else? Fine I hope. I am fine. So are Aunt and Uncle. Tell everyone I said hello. I will write again soon.

                                                                   Love,
                                                                   Barbara

COLLEGE BRINGS ALIENATION FROM FAMILY, FRIENDS*

John Gonzales

My decision to chase a dream, return to college at age 24 and take the liberal arts courses that will help me become a journalist has forced me to be two people. One face is for family and longtime friends, another is for my classes and college friends.

My homeboys have not read Marx, Nietzsche or Freud. They do not care to probe the economics behind their being paid less, despite working more, than their fathers. They don't want to hear about the Oedipus complex or the nature of good and evil. For them, intellectual theories are elaborate, unnecessary attempts to explain the inexplicable. Ideas do not feed their families and only seem to highlight the fact that I have begun to change. "That's enough. Don't read any more. I don't understand a word you're saying," Fidel, my *compadre,* said after I responded to his request to read him a paragraph from one of my textbooks. He had telephoned while I was doing homework and jibed, "What the hell are you studying now?"

I also stumble to explain my studies to my parents. My father had a sixth-grade education. My mother earned her GED 15 years after leaving high school. I often reluctantly hand them my term papers they ask to see, knowing they won't truly comprehend them. After a careful reading, my mother's usual response: "You write so beautifully, *mijo.* I didn't really understand all the words you used but we can just tell how educated you are."

A senior at the University of Southern California, receiving a bachelor's degree in journalism and political science this May, I painfully realize the downside to education, a subtle alienation from friends and loved ones. I understand more clearly why Latinos approach higher learning with trepidation. For beyond the barriers of low income and racism lies another fight, the struggle to blend old and new identities.

It is not that education is discouraged; my family is proud of me and would be crushed if I were to quit. But disproportionately few Latinos

---

*Gonzales, John. "College Brings Attention from Family, Friends." *The Los Angeles Times* 26 January 1996. Reprinted by permission.

acquire higher learning and those who do often must balance an incompatible past and future.

I envision my old friends and new friends at my graduation party. Would they eat, drink and laugh together or huddle in separate groups? Which group would I join? Who am I?

That is why many promising Latinos I know who attend college choose to major in business or other fields with more easily identifiable rewards for their parents and themselves. "I'm learning how to start and manage a restaurant," is certainly something my father, a part-time contractor, would grasp more clearly than the abstract knowledge I've obtained.

Noble careers that require no college sometimes seem even more attractive. My aunt, mother of an army sergeant, beams with pride at family gatherings when she recalls my cousin's boot-camp graduation. Yet my mother struggles to explain the value of my work as a journalist. Amid the music, food and drink of the get-together, a reporter is not a craftsman with words, not a guardian of democracy, not a voice against society's ills. Instead, journalists are perceived as the intrusive talking heads on the 11 o'clock news, the Latino ones pretentiously pronouncing their surnames with forced accents.

For other Latinos I know studying philosophy, sociology and literature, the struggle to retain identity is similar. In this political climate of Proposition 187, the demise of the Great Society and threats to affirmative action, analytical, creative Latino minds are needed more than ever. But the sacrifices are great indeed.

A WAY OF WRITING*

William Stafford

A writer is not so much someone who has something to say as he is someone who has found a process that will bring about new things he would not have thought of if he had not started to say them. That is, he does not draw on a reservoir; instead, he engages in an activity that brings to him a whole succession of unforeseen stories, poems, essays, plays, laws, philosophies, religions, or–but wait!

Back in school, from the first when I began to try to write things, I felt this richness. One thing would lead to another; the world would give and give. Now, after twenty years or so of trying, I live by that certain richness, an idea hard to pin, difficult to say, and perhaps offensive to some. For there are strange implications in it.

One implication is the importance of just plain receptivity. When I write, I like to have an interval before me when I am not likely to be interrupted. For me, this means usually the early morning, before others are awake. I get pen and paper, take a glance out of the window (often it is dark out there), and wait. It is like fishing. But I do not wait very long, for there is always a nibble–and this is where receptivity comes in. To get started I will accept anything that occurs to me. Something always occurs, of course, to any of us. We can't keep from thinking. Maybe I have to settle for an immediate impression: it's cold, or hot, or dark, or bright, or in between! Or–well, the possibilities are endless. If I put down something, that thing will help the next thing come, and I'm off. If I let the process go on, things will occur to me that were not at all in my mind when I started. These things, odd or trivial as they may be, are somehow connected. And if I let them string out, surprising things will happen.

If I let them string out. . . . Along with initial receptivity, then, there is another readiness: I must be willing to fail. If I am to keep on writing, I cannot bother to insist on high standards. I must get into action and not let anything stop me, or even slow me much. By "standards" I do not mean "correctness"–spelling, punctuation, and so on. These details become mechanical for anyone who writes for a while. I am thinking about

*Stafford, William. "A Way of Writing." From *Field* #2, Spring 1970. Copyright Oberlin College Press. Reprinted with permission.

such matters as social significance, positive values, consistency, etc. I resolutely disregard these. Something better, greater, is happening! I am following a process that leads so wildly and originally into new territory that no judgment can at the moment be made about values, significance, and so on. I am making something new, something that has not been judged before. Later others–and maybe I myself–will make judgments. Now, I am headlong to discover. Any distraction may harm the creating.

So, receptive, careless of failure, I spin out things on the page. And a wonderful freedom comes. If something occurs to me, it is all right to accept it. It has one justification: it occurs to me. No one else can guide me. I must follow my own weak, wandering, diffident impulses.

A strange bonus happens. At times, without my insisting on it, my writings become coherent; the successive elements that occur to me are clearly related. They lead by themselves to new connections. Sometimes the language, even the syllables that happen along, may start a trend. Sometimes the materials alert me to something waiting in my mind, ready for sustained attention. At such times, I allow myself to be eloquent, or intentional, or for great swoops (Treacherous! Not to be trusted!) reasonable. But I do not insist on any of that; for I know that back of my activity there will be the coherence of my self, and that indulgence of my impulses will bring recurrent patterns and meanings again.

This attitude toward the process of writing creatively suggests a problem for me, in terms of what others say. They talk about "skills" in writing. Without denying that I do have experience, wide reading, automatic orthodoxies and maneuvers of various kinds, I still must insist that I am often baffled about what "skill" has to do with the precious little area of confusion when I do not know what I am going to say and then I find out what I am going to say. That precious interval I am unable to bridge by skill. What can I witness about it? It remains mysterious, just as all of us must feel puzzled about how we are so inventive as to be able to talk along through complexities with our friends, not needing to plan what we are going to say, but never stalled for long in our confident forward progress. Skill? If so, it is the skill we all have, something we must have learned before the age of three or four.

A writer is one who has become accustomed to trusting that grace, or luck, or–skill.

Yet another attitude I find necessary: most of what I write, like most of what I say in casual conversation, will not amount to much. Even I will realize, and even at the time, that it is not negotiable. It will be like practice. In conversation I allow myself random remarks–in fact, as I recall, that is the way I learned to talk–so in writing I launch many expendable efforts. A result of this free way of writing is that I am not writing for others, mostly; they will not see the product at all unless the activity eventuates in something that later appears to be worthy. My guide is the self, and its adventuring in the language brings about communication.

This process-rather-than-substance view of writing invites a final, dual reflection:

1. Writers may not be special–sensitive or talented in any usual sense. They are simply engaged in sustained use of a language skill we all have. Their "creations" come about through confident reliance on stray impulses that will, with trust, find occasional patterns that are satisfying.

2. But writing itself is one of the great, free human activities. There is scope for individuality, and elation, and discovery, in writing. For the person who follows with trust and forgiveness what occurs to him, the world remains always ready and deep, an inexhaustible environment, with the combined vividness of an actuality and flexibility of a dream. Working back and forth between experience and thought, writers have more than space and time can offer. They have the whole unexplored realm of human vision.

꙰

ANOREXIA: THE CHEATING DISORDER*

Richard Murphy

> I wanted to pray. A part of me would not let myself ask Him for help. I did it to myself. God understood my confusion. I tried to figure out why it was happening to me, and how. It only happens to weak girls, girls who have no self-control, girls who are caught up with society's standards–not me. But was I one of them? It was happening to me, just like the cases I read about in magazines.

This is the first paragraph of an essay I received from a young woman purporting to describe her own experience with anorexia nervosa. Before I had finished reading one page, I suspected it was plagiarized. I cannot easily explain my hunch. Something canned about the writing, its confessional sentiment exactly like the cases in the magazines. I ran a quick search through the *Magazine Index* in the library and then through recent issues of *Teen, McCall's, Glamour*, and *Mademoiselle*. In a half-hour, I had six articles: "Anorexia Nearly Killed Me," "Starving Oneself to Death," "Starving for Attention," "Two Teens," "My Sister and I," and "One Teen's Diet Nightmare." I did not accuse the student of plagiarism on the evidence of this search, but I decided to talk with her before I would comment on or evaluate her paper. I guessed that in our talk she would reveal that she had copied her essay or in some other way falsified it. She did.

I am not inquiring here into the causes of plagiarism among students nor describing how teachers ought to respond to it. I am simply telling two stories in order to convey something of its perversity.

Several years before I received the anorexia paper, a student submitted a brief analysis of James Joyce's "The Dead." As I was reading it, the paper tripped some wire in my mind. It seemed both accomplished and incompetent, full of discontinuities like those in the following two sentences:

---

*Murphy, Richard. "Anorexia: The Cheating Disorder." From *College English* December 1990. Copyright 1990 by the National Council of Teachers of English. Reprinted with permission.

The physical movement of the main character, Gabriel Conroy, from a house in the western part of the city eastward to a hotel at the very center expresses in spatial terms his commitment to the ways and the doom of his fellow Dubliners. His spiritual movement westward, in our imaginative vision, symbolizes his supremeness of that doom through recognition of its meaning and acceptance of this truth of his inward nature.

Much of the first sentence here is sensible; the character's physical movement expresses his commitment. It is also syntactically sophisticated. The grammatical subject, "movement," is sustained through five prepositional phrases before its meaning is completed by the verb "expresses." The verb itself is modified by a prepositional phrase ("in spatial terms") that parallels and reiterates the adjective "physical." The second sentence, however, is nonsense. The grammatical kernel (movement symbolizes supremeness) is unintelligible. The pronoun sequence creates nothing but blur (his-our-his-that-its-this-his). One sentence, then, is substantial and coherent. The next is gummed with vagueness. So stark is the contrast between the two that it was difficult for me to imagine the same person writing both.

When I had assigned the paper, I explicitly restricted the use of secondary sources. I asked students to select a short reading from the literature we had been studying and to write an essay defining and explaining what they considered its central aesthetic purpose. I asked them to write about the work only as it presented itself to them in their reading. They were not to read or refer to any critical or historical background discussions of it.

In spite of the assignment's restriction, however, parts of this student paper about Gabriel Conroy seemed to me surely to have been copied. I scanned several library collections of critical essays on Joyce, browsed in longer works that made reference to *Dubliners,* and then, without having found anything but still persuaded the paper was plagiarized, asked the student to come to my office to talk with me.

"Before I give you credit for this paper," I said, "I need to ask a couple of questions: Did you use any outside materials when you wrote this? Did you read any books or articles about Joyce or about this story?"

To both of these questions he answered, "No," simply and firmly. But the look on his face was perplexed, and I realized once again how difficult it is to confront plagiarism without proof, how important it is not to accuse a student of cheating without sufficient cause. I hurried to soften the impression that I thought he had cheated by saying that my reason for asking was the strange inconsistency in the paper between specific recounting of the story line and abstract discussion of thematic issues. I was trying to understand the combination, I said, and I thought that perhaps he had looked at some outside sources which had influenced what he wrote. He still looked puzzled, but said, "No," again, and our brief conference ended.

Plagiarism irritates, like a thin wood splinter in the edge of one's thumb. With any sort of reasonable perspective, I realize that one student's possibly copying part of one paper on James Joyce is a small matter. In a typical semester, I teach 120 students and read perhaps 600 student papers. In a typical day, I have two classes to prepare and teach, committee meetings to attend, conferences with individual students, the utility bill to pay, a child to pick up from a Cub Scout meeting. But everything I touch rubs the sliver in my thumb and sets its irritation pulsing. As much as I try, I cannot ignore it.

So when I happened to be sitting in a colleague's office, waiting for her to finish a phone call, my eye seized upon the book of Joyce criticism on her shelf. I had to look. It took only a moment. The phrases of the student's jumbled sentences were everywhere. I borrowed the book, took it back to my office, double-checked its lines with the lines of the paper, and then went again to the library.

I wanted to verify that our library collection contained the book and thus that it had actually been available to the writer. It was checked out. "To whom?" I asked. The circulation clerk said that library policy prohibited his divulging that information, but if I wished I could have the book recalled. I did, and reconciled myself to waiting several days for it to arrive.

In order to make the story complete, I have to explain some of the mixture of my feeling during this episode. Though I should not have had time to play detective, I made room among all the duties of my life to pursue this student. I was thrilled by the chase. When I happened on those sentences in my colleague's office, I was exhilarated. They promised the solution to a puzzle that had eluded me. They reinforced my sense of judgment and my sense of self-satisfaction at the thought that, in a small way, I was preserving the integrity of the university.

I was also dismayed, however, and angry at what I came to feel as the obligation to play out this scene, at my exhilaration, at the student's distortion of our whole working relationship. When I thought about his voice, about his poise in denying that he had used any outside sources, I thought too about the other 119 students and wondered what his cheating meant about them. When I went into class in the following days and watched their faces, I realized that I had lost some of my faith in them.

For no more reason than my experience with him, I found myself wondering what the rest of them had copied.

The recall notice came shortly afterward. I hurried to the library to pick up the book. When I could not find the sentences I was looking for, I first imagined that I had inadvertently recalled the wrong book. Then I thought that perhaps this was a different edition. I walked away from the circulation desk flipping the pages and wondering–through the electronic gate at the library door, out through the foyer past the philodendrons in their huge pots, onto the columned porch–and then I saw it. The gap in the pagination, page 98 followed immediately by page 113, and, in the fold of the binding so neatly done as to be almost invisible, the seven razor-bladed stumps.

He still denied it, first in my office, then in the Dean of Students' office, sitting with his legs crossed in an upholstered armchair next to a whirring tape recorder. He began by denying that he had even used the book, then that he had damaged it in any way; he went so far as to say that he had noticed the missing pages and reported them to the library himself. He hadn't wanted to be blamed, he said. What kind of person did we think he was, he asked, how did we suppose he had been brought up? He was offended at the very thought of it. But when I finally left the hearing room, he admitted to the Dean both that he had copied and that he had cut out the pages he had used. Within the week he was suspended from the university.

Nearly every year I encounter students who cheat in their writing. Their stories are all different, and all the same: they were worried about their school work, rushed, unclear about the assignment, afraid. My stories are all different, and all the same: an intuition, some feeling on the surface of the page, something about the dye of the ink that whispers this is counterfeit currency; the excitement of judicial self-satisfaction, the slanderous suspicion that all students are cheating. Though particularly vivid, my experience with the *Dubliners* paper is like all the others, obsessive and bilious. Like all the others, it has nothing whatever to do with what the job of teaching should be.

"Did this really happen?" I asked my student when we met to talk about her essay on anorexia. She was already nodding yes when I thought that I shouldn't seem rude in my disbelief. "I mean," I said, trying to make the edge of my question sharp, "I mean, did this happen the way you tell it here?"

"Yes," she nodded again. "Why do you ask?"

"Well, I don't know exactly." I looked up from the paper at her face, then back down to the typed page. "It's sort of vague in places, as if . . . I don't know . . . as if you didn't remember what happened in your own story."

Now she was shaking her head. "I don't know what you mean."

She played the correct gambit–my move, force me to commit myself. But I didn't want to move yet. I was after proof, and I needed to go after it slowly. This was a parody of a writing conference. I was asking her about the details of her story, trying to appear helpful, as if I were attempting to help her revise, when in fact I was trying to tease out the insincerity of her paper.

"I mean, I'm sort of confused by your essay," I said. "In the part here on page three where you say you ran to the bathroom to vomit–'I would run to the toilet to vomit, screaming the entire way' and 'The vomiting ceased after awhile'–when did that happen? Did that happen before you went to the hospital or after?"

"After."

"And here where you say, on page two, that your father stroked your hair and rubbed behind your ears, and then on the next page you say that your father was a monster who yelled at you and forced food down your throat constantly. Are you talking about what caused your anorexia or what happened afterward?"

She didn't answer this question at all, just sat there looking at me; so I tried a different tack.

What struck me as I read and reread her paper were the seams, the joints, where the parts were pushed together with no bonding. She is lying in a hospital bed staring at the ceiling tiles. She is trying to listen to the doctor talk to her. She is using and abusing a whole series of diet plans. She is flipping through a magazine looking at the pictures of models. She is taking a laxative every night before she goes to bed. She is listening to her father tell her that she is going home.

The effect on me was two-fold. I thought that the details she included were completely credible: only a person who had lain in a hospital bed would think to mark off the ceiling tiles; only a girl whose father actually rubbed behind her ears would think to mention that specific caress. At the same time, the vague and abrupt transitions between these highly individual details seemed to me understandable only if I assumed that she had copied them in fragments from a magazine memoir. My guess was that she had taken them from an article that was too long to copy in its entirety and so had included just selected parts in her essay.

"Did you write this?" I finally asked unexpectedly. I did not plan to say it like that, but I couldn't seem to approach the real point of my questions by just skirting the issue.

Her face looked so blank that I immediately switched to a different question. "Is this story really about you?"

She paused for a moment and then asked quietly, "What would happen if it weren't?"

I told her that I could not accept such a paper since the assignment was to write about a personal experience of her own. I told her, too, that it would help explain the vagueness I had been trying to point out to her: if she wrote the paper about someone else's experience, then she would be likely to leave gaps in the story that she couldn't fill.

"What grade would I get on it if it were about someone else?" she asked. To pin me down.

"I wouldn't grade it at all. I wouldn't give you any credit for doing it. It's not the assignment."

"OK," she said. "It's not about me. It's about a friend of mine."

My reaction to this admission was complicated. I had been expecting it, in fact working toward it, trying to get her to tell me where the paper had come from. I was glad finally to have its pretense uncovered but disappointed because I knew immediately that I would have to accept this substitute explanation though I didn't believe it either. I was sorry I had not been able to find the magazine story that provided the actual source of her paper and so would have to settle for this second lie about its roots. And I was angry at the whole situation: at the wasted time in the library, at the wasted conference with her, at my own inability to define the fakery of the piece, and at her apparent inability to see the purpose of our work together. I wanted her to write truthfully about her own experience and to use my responses, along with others', to help her convey the meaning of that experience more surely and vividly. As it was, her paper seemed just a hoax.

The deep flux of such feeling is just one of the dimensions for me of the problem of plagiarism. Another is the comic peculiarity of my claiming to be committed to helping students learn but sometimes spending large chunks of everyone's time trying to corner them in a fraud. Then there is the distance, the surprising separation I discover in such situations between myself and students. Because I assume their good will and candor and my own, both their cheating and my response to it shock me. I take for granted that we are working together and thus am amazed each time at the unimagined distance between us.

But even if I had expected the fakery of the anorexia paper, I would not have been prepared for what happened. Even if I had remembered the pages sliced out of the book of Joyce criticism and the self-righteous posturing of that frightened student writer trying to elude me, I would not have anticipated the journal of the woman who had told me that her essay on anorexia was not really about herself but about her friend.

I gave her a zero on the paper. She completed the rest of the semester's assignments, and at the end of the term, as required, she turned in a binder containing all her work for the course. As I was rereading her finished essays and the background notes and drafts she had made while working on them, I came upon the following entries in her journal:

> Feb. 7. My roommates and I did watch the Miss America pageant. I believe pageants are my favorite programs to watch. They are so inspiring. But sometimes that can make you sick.
> Feb. 21. The title of Miss America is such a distinguished title. Who ever is chosen for this honor represents the dreams of millions of young girls.
> Feb. 22. My next paper I am writing about when I had anorexia. The thought of going all through that again scares me but I think it would be a good experience to write about.
> Feb. 22. Skinny. Healthy. Slim. Muscle. Diets. Firmness. Roundness. All thoughts of women in today's society. Is this such a healthy attitude to have? Women can be obsessed with these listed thoughts to the point of worshipped, slimness, firmness, healthiness etc.–
> Feb. 22.
>> . . . It really hurt.
>> "You're fat" my brother said to me.
>> I looked in the mirror.
>> You're fat I said to myself.
>
> March 1. Blindness is a scary experience or at least it was for me. I haven't experienced blindness but something close to it. The world diminishes. Your only hope is through touch.
> March 2. Scared and alone. I laid in my hospital bed. I wanted to pray. I thought prayer would make me feel closer to the only friend I had left. My situation had done this to me. I thought it only happened to weak girls, girls who have no self-control, girls concerned w/society.

These journal entries astonished and appalled me. Their sincerity was unmistakable. These were not descriptions of a friend's experience. These were not fragments copied from the pages of a popular magazine. They were threads of memory–a brother's teasing, a father's touch. As closely as I can reconstruct it, she and I met in conference to discuss her essay on anorexia nervosa March 12, eighteen days after she began writing it, thirty-three days after she had begun to remember in her journal about her feelings that led both to her sickness and to her writing.

What must she have been thinking as I began to ask her those strange questions in our conference? At what point did she catch a glimmer of what I was really doing there? And when she saw it–if she saw it– what must she then have thought about it all–the course, me, the whole project of learning in school? What calculation, what weariness with it all, must have led her to deny her own paper? "Is this paper about you?" I asked her.

"No," she said.

I did not mean for it to come to this.

5

RESPONSE AND COLLABORATION

❧ *Reviewing Your Writing Journey So Far*

Congratulations! You have traveled the first part of the journey of writing an essay; you have created both an exploratory draft and a more focused second draft. Many writers consider the work you have just completed to be the most difficult part of essay writing—getting through the initial drafts and writing out the thoughts that will lead to a finished essay. Because this journey is one you will be making again and again as you write more essays for this course and others, it should prove helpful to review the road you took to get here.

As you read and responded to the first four chapters of this book, you wrote informally, producing *Writing Log* entries, whose primary value was not the form or style in which they were written, but the content of what they said. Writing in this reflective way you could remember and record a number of past experiences and think about your own understanding of those experiences.

Then, after collecting several reflective writings, you began to identify connections among them, to locate places where your words and ideas in one piece might be said to intersect with words and ideas in your other writings. During this process of making connections, you could find questions, conflicts, contradictions, and associations suggested to you by your own writing. We asked you to reflect further, to continue writing and observing your own evolving thoughts as you found points of connection emerging from your memories and reflections. Over time, your cumulative process of exploring and focusing, exploring and focusing again, helped move your writing toward what will finally become an analytic, reflective essay that conveys an explicit purpose to the reader. Most writers contend that they do not know exactly what it is they want to say until they find their ideas developing in their drafts.

The section of the writing journey you just went through is sometimes referred to as "prewriting" to indicate that a writer usually generates material in fragments before he or she writes a more coherent draft. Composing a first draft is often called "drafting" or simply, "writing" and the work you do after you've written the first draft is then called "revising." While the term "prewriting" may serve as a useful reminder of how much informal writing must be done in the course of creating a formal essay, it also seems to suggest that "real" writing doesn't begin until you are writing a whole draft. But this exploratory and reflective writing is not really "pre" anything–it is not so much a stage before the real writing begins as it is the real writing. That is, your draft emerges out of this informal writing; it is not essentially separate from the essay itself. Informal writing that helps the writer to make meaning–to generate, sort, resort, and expand ideas–is not confined to a distinct stage in the larger task of essay writing; it goes on throughout the whole process of writing a formal essay. By writing and rewriting, reading and rewriting, a writer moves slowly, and often painstakingly, toward an increasingly clearer expression of meaning.

❧ *Time for a Reader's Response*

Writers do not usually go through this process entirely alone. Yet, so far, one distinctive feature of the reflective and draft writing you have done is that you were not expected to consider anyone outside yourself as you wrote. In most of the *Writing Log* entries you could write without concern for how another reader might understand them. There is an advantage to composing in this way, for it can allow you to listen carefully to your own developing ideas as you write toward a draft. And, as you did this, as your draft emerged from the pieces of writing you composed, the things you wanted to say–the things you will want your reader to hear–are likely to have become more clear to you. Thoughtful, engaged rereading of your own drafts helps you to hear the developing meaning in your writing.

Once a good part of that meaning becomes clear to you, you may be ready to collaborate or work together with readers, getting their perspective on what you have written. Ultimately, all college writing is written to be shared with other readers. And, that purpose presents another challenge for writers.

No matter how perceptive a reader you are of your own drafts, you are necessarily limited by what you know. A writer is intimately connected to the feelings, thoughts, and experiences that lie behind his or her words. A writer reading his or her own draft can use this knowledge easily to fill in gaps or untangle confusions that another reader might find in the draft. Since, as we discussed earlier, readers of college essays expect to be able to know exactly where the writer stands, the essay needs to speak for itself, to be clear to another reader who does not have access to your private history and knowledge. So, there is great value in having someone other than yourself, someone who doesn't have the inside line, read your draft and provide response to what you have written.

There is another benefit of getting readers' responses to your work-in-progress. Readers bring their own experience and understanding to bear on what they read. The opportunity to hear how several readers make sense of one's writing allows a writer to view his or her work from the outside, from the perspective of other readers who may have a variety of ways of responding to the same, developing essay.

Notice that we have used the word, "response," rather than "evaluation" or "judgment." In the process of reading your drafts your readers may not be able to keep themselves from saying, "I really liked this part," or "I think this is great"–the kind of response that writers usually feel ready to hear. We do not ask you to refrain from this kind of positive response since it may encourage your fellow writers to keep going through the sometimes difficult task of expanding and finishing an essay. But we want to caution you that evaluating an early draft is premature. At this point the work is not complete; any critical evaluation would be unfairly offered. What the work is ready for and what will be most useful to the writer are readers' responses in which they share with you how they read your draft, pose questions they have, say back to you what they understand, and so on.

Imagine yourself having a discussion with friends. You offer your point of view or you tell a story, and then you wait for your friends to respond to what you have said, to the content. You wouldn't expect your friends to evaluate how you presented your point of view or told your story, to say, "Your argument was confusing," or "I don't like the way you organized your sentences." A draft, like a conversation, is an opportunity for readers or listeners to respond to what you have said. They might continue the conversation by picking up on a certain comment you made; they might laugh at humorous words or lines, agree or disagree with you, ask for more information, or add some of their own. This kind of response allows you to continue the conversation, to fill in information, or simply to know which of your words got through; it allows you to hear back how someone outside yourself understands what you have said.

❀ *Making Use of Readers' Responses*

Because our individual experiences, affinities, knowledge, and interests come into play as we read any text, it is particularly useful to have the opportunity for several different readers to respond to your work-in-progress. Your readers are there to provide response rather than advice on or evaluation of your work, and from these responses you, as the writer, can return to your draft with a broader understanding of how different readers make sense of and react to what you have written. Some readers may have questions to which you wish to respond as you revise. Others may be confused by something in your draft, and this information may affect your next draft. Readers may point out sections of the essay that they were especially drawn in by or that they found particularly intriguing, and this information may also help you as you continue working. If someone disagrees with your argument, you may become aware that there are some points that you haven't yet said, or that the order of your comments has been confusing or misleading. You may find that your argument is convincing for some readers and not for others, and this may help you direct the way you address your audience as you revise. Readers' comments may influence what you decide to expand on and what you decide needs to be deleted, the order in which you structure your essay, and what details you wish to include.

It is worth noting that this chapter is titled, "Response and Collaboration." When you ask someone to read your work as it is evolving, that person has the opportunity to collaborate with you, to think about your topic, to talk over your ideas. Most writing outside of school settings is highly collaborative. In the workplace it is rare for someone to write without feedback, and it is extremely common for two or more people to work together on a particular piece of writing. The assignments in this text are designed as single-author pieces of writing. But the response strategies we ask you to try out allow you to have some experience with the collaborative nature of writing and with supportive, nonjudgmental feedback.

❀ *The Writer's Responsibility*

In conversation, if a friend says that she didn't understand a sentence or was offended by your slang, you usually don't abandon the whole idea you were trying to express. More likely you will pause and reconsider what you have said, perhaps rephrase your idea or elaborate to make it more understandable for your friend. Similarly, readers' responses of the kind we are outlining here are not criticisms of your work but are simply that: readers' responses. As the writer, you have the opportunity to develop your own writing as you choose. Often readers' responses are useful to writers in surprising ways; sometimes they can help you to re-see what had already seemed to be quite clear and thought-out, or help you to view your work in a new way. Your responsibility to yourself as a writer is to take in as much response to your work as you can, and after your responders have run out of things to say, to ask for specific responses to aspects of your draft you have questions about or you want to do more work on. Your job is to listen attentively and openly, without interrupting your responders to explain what you meant. If you don't help them out or immediately answer questions for them, you are likely to get more response.

✷ *The Responder's Responsibility*

Up to this point the predominant focus of attention in *Shoptalk* has been on college writing. But without readers who are knowledgeable of and comfortable with academic conventions and expectations and who can respond to writing as academic readers, college writing cannot really exist. That is to say, college writing looks and sounds like it does, in large part, because there are readers who expect it to, and who will, ultimately, evaluate and grade it on these bases. Keep in mind that these judgments are an end point, one preceded by a reader's response to the writing. And it is this response that we will focus on now.

Sometimes, students new to college writing feel tongue-tied when asked to read and respond to one anothers' essay drafts. These same students are then surprised by the shear amount of response that their instructors can generate to the same drafts that left them virtually speechless. The significant difference here between the students and the instructors is that the latter have spent a great deal of time becoming familiar with and internalizing the language and conventions of the academic culture and, in the course of reading countless essays, have also tuned in to their own response to the writing. In addition to helping you to become better college writers, we hope this book will also provide you with an apprenticeship in becoming an academic reader.

Although all of us are used to responding to each other's spoken language, most people do not have experience responding in nonjudgmental ways to writing. *When you respond to a work-in-progress your job is not to give advice or to evaluate the writing. Your job is to tell how you read the draft, to ask the questions you have, to give the writer as clear a picture as you can of what you understand and connect to in the text.* When it is your turn to respond to a classmate's work you cannot respond "incorrectly" if you read and listen carefully and try to give the responses you really have. What are your questions? What strikes you about the text? What do you want to know more about?

Because, as we have said, response is such an important part of the process of writing, in this chapter we have included some guidelines: 1. sources from whom you might receive response to your writing; 2. specific ways of responding to any work-in-progress and to writing that relies on personal experience and recollections as its source of information. You may refer to these guidelines any time you are called upon to give supportive, useful feedback to another writer's work.

✳ *Sources from Whom You Can Get Response to Drafts*

Before thinking about *how* one might respond to your draft, it is useful to identify *who* might be doing so–the people who can read what you have written and respond to it in the ways we will later review. These individuals or groups of individuals provide important information about the clarity, focus, development, credibility, and tone of your essay by explaining how they are understanding and reacting to your emerging work. And the more of such information you collect, the more effectively you will be able to revise. While you may not always have the opportunity to use all of these sources for every essay, over the course of the term, you should become familiar with the advantages of using each of them and comfortable with using them all.

RESPONSE FROM ONE OTHER PERSON IN CLASS

One excellent source of response to a draft is the intensely focused response of a single individual, someone in your class who is also drafting an essay. The two of you will be familiar with the context in which the essay is being written and with *Shoptalk* as well as any particular ways that your instructor is using *Shoptalk* or adapting the assignment. At the same time, you will each be able to concentrate your response skills on just one draft, providing a full and unhurried response.

The particular individual with whom you exchange drafts could vary as the term progresses. This change in readers will provide you with equally varied responses. Sometimes you might want to work with a friend who knows you and your writing style and can, therefore, make some assumptions based on this familiarity; sometimes it can be helpful to work with someone you know only in the context of class and who hasn't any additional information about you, who must rely solely on the draft.

IN-CLASS RESPONSE IN GROUPS OF THREE TO FIVE

Your instructor may ask you to form groups that remain a permanent part of your class for the entire term. Or you may form new groups several times during the course. It is even possible to form new groups for each essay. Often, when groups last for several weeks or months, the individuals in the groups find they become used to working together in ways that help their ability to respond to each other's writing. Once you become familiar with nonevaluative ways of responding, even in a group of new people, you will find that response–both giving response and receiving it–is not something fearful. It is a positive way to learn about other people's experiences and ideas and to communicate your own ideas and experience to others.

You may decide to divide up the ways of responding among the members of the group so that each draft is assured of getting all the different forms of response, or you may just let the response evolve more spontaneously. It is a good idea to allow time for the writer to make some notes to help him or her remember the responses. It is also useful for each member of the group to write down one or more responses for the writer.

RESPONSE FROM SOMEONE OUTSIDE OF CLASS

Individuals who are not directly connected to your writing class can give you a clear sense of how your draft is working on its own. They can offer responses that tell you whether or not the draft, so far, can be read and understood without the special information available to students enrolled in your class who are writing the same assignment.

If your school has a Writing Center or Writing Lab, take your draft to a tutor for response. You may want have some questions in mind for the tutor, something that will help to focus your discussion of the essay.

If your school does not have a Writing Center, seek out a friend who is not in the class, someone who is not as familiar with your work and ideas as your classmates. You may want to identify specific parts of your essay on which you need feedback. You might show your friend the "ways of responding" as a guide.

✖ *Four Ways of Responding*

The four ways of responding described below can be used as you work on any of the writing assignments in this book and will be valuable for getting response to other writing you do as well. The ways of responding are arranged here in the order you might use them as your essay evolves and as you get more and more feedback. Don't be dismayed by the length of the list. As you will see, some ways of responding are already familiar to you; you already do them quite naturally, but you may not have thought of them as "response"; some require more time and are more involved than others; some could be incorporated into one another. Once you and your classmates become comfortable with responding in these ways, you will be able to read and give your feedback to each other's work quite spontaneously, probably without referring much to this outline. For now, try out each kind of response to get used to the way it works. The four ways of responding you will be learning are: **listening, reporting, elaborating,** and **questioning.** This outline describes each form of response and provides you with specific techniques for each one.

LISTENING

The first kind of response most writers need is simply to be heard, to know that someone is really listening and taking in what they have written. This form of response is critical to all the other forms; it is the foundation for your ability to be a helpful responder.

LISTENING 1: RECEIVING

Listen carefully to the essay as it is read. Respond without words. Your job is to receive the writing, to take it in, and to have any reactions you naturally have. That is, you might find yourself nodding in agreement or smiling or feeling sad but you will not, at this time, articulate your response in words. Simply say "thank you" to the writer for reading, or clap for the writing if you are in a larger group. The writer has had an attentive audience hear what she or he has to say.

LISTENING 2: ECHOING

Use the writer's own words as your response. As you hear the piece of writing again or read it to yourself, jot down or underline words and phrases that stand out for you, that strike you in some way. Without using any other words, repeat the writer's words you have noted. By echoing back the writer's own words, you are letting the writer know what especially got through to you.

REPORTING

Next, the writer can benefit from knowing how different readers understand his or her writing. Your job in reporting is to report on your own reading of the text. You cannot know with certainty exactly what the writer intended, but you are an authority on your own reading. The following are strategies for reporting your reading to the writer.

REPORTING 1: MAIN POINTS

List for the writer what seem to you to be the main points he or she is making in the draft. What seem to be the main ideas that are included so far in what you have read?

REPORTING 2: FOCUS

What do you feel is the focus for the whole essay, so far? Is the writer's purpose or reason for writing explicit and clear? How does the essay accomplish this? You might come up with a title that, for you, represents the heart of what the draft seems to be saying.

REPORTING 3: SUMMARY

Give a summary of what you read. The summary gives more detail than the list of Main Points, but of course it doesn't include everything. You might summarize by writing down a few sentences that elaborate your understanding of each main point or by recording what you remember from the piece without looking at it.

REPORTING 4: STORY OF YOUR OWN READING

Tell the writer what you thought and what you felt as you heard or read the piece of writing. The idea is to try to tell the story of what happened to you, in you, as you read or listened. The story of your own reading is not a summary or an analysis; it is a narrative of what went through your mind and what feelings you had at specific points as you read or heard the draft.

ELABORATING

In the next kind of response, you move beyond your immediate reaction to the text to make connections between your own experience and knowledge and what you have read. Elaborating helps you provide the writer with a broader understanding of his or her material since different readers will make different connections to and have different commentary on what the writer has said.

ELABORATING 1: CONNECTIONS

What does the writing connect to in your own experience? What have you read that corroborates what has been said? What can you add to the points the writer has made? What further examples can you think of? In what ways do you agree with the piece of writing? What parts of the writing do you particularly agree with or feel particularly connected to?

ELABORATING 2: CONTRADICTIONS

Is there anything in the piece of writing that contradicts your own experience or something you have read? What alternative perspectives can you offer on the points the writer has made? What is there in the piece of writing with which you disagree? Is there something that seems to you to be left out of the piece?

QUESTIONING

Finally, it is valuable to ask the questions you have about a work-in-progress. Don't hold back on any questions that come to you, for it will be useful to the writer to know what questions the piece, in its current version, raises for different readers.

QUESTIONING 1: WHAT I'D LIKE TO HEAR MORE ABOUT

Ask the writer about any aspect of the writing you would like to hear more about. The writer may choose to include some of this material or may choose not to add this information in subsequent versions of the piece depending on his or her purpose and the audience for whom the writing is intended.

QUESTIONING 2: WHAT I DON'T YET UNDERSTAND

Ask the writer for clarification of any points, ideas, words, or phrases that you have questions about. Again, the writer may find that in the next draft she or he wants to make some changes as a result of the questions she or he was asked.

QUESTIONING 3: THE WRITER ASKS YOU QUESTIONS

At this point, the writer can ask for comments about any aspect of the draft she or he wants response to that doesn't seem to have been addressed. Again, the feedback is a nonjudgmental form of response.

✳ *Responding to the Writer's Use of Information from Recollection and Memory: Questions for Response*

The ways of responding we have listed above can be applied to any draft. Some additional response, specific to the kind of information you have incorporated into your essay, can also be helpful. One of the lessons you learn as you write college essays is how to use the information available to you most convincingly, effectively, and appropriately. The following are some questions your responders might ask to help you determine how well you have used recollection and memory, the information source for Essays 1 and 2.

Before answering the following questions about how the writer has used information in the essay, responders should first remind themselves of what they found to be the essay's explicit purpose or meaning. Keeping that purpose in mind, give the writer your sense of how he or she used recollection and memory in the draft.

1. How are instances of recollection and memory used in relation to the purpose of the essay?

2. What claims or observations does the writer make based on his or her information? Tell the writer what makes his or her claims convincing for you. Tell the writer any claims that feel unconvincing to you. What would make these claims more convincing for you?

3. Where does recollection and memory appear in the essay? Tell the writer what seems to you to be the purpose for which each instance of recollection or memory is presented. Are there further details you would like to know? Are there some details that you could not connect to the purpose of the essay?

4. How are the recollections cited? Is there more you would like to know about the context of the recollections, about when and where the event took place? (Note that an explanation appears in the next chapter about how to cite or reference personal experience information.)

✻ *A Reminder for the Writer as You Turn to Revision*

Once you have received a complete response to your draft, it's time for you to use this response, along with your own response to your writing, to revise, expand, develop, refine, and complete the draft. You may want to remind yourself of ways of using the responses you've received by taking another look at "Making use of readers' responses" and "The writer's responsibility" in this chapter.

C H A P T E R

6

EDITING, PROOFREADING, AND FINAL REFLECTIONS

❧ *Reading Your Penultimate Draft for Surface Presentation*

While you have been drafting and revising your essay, we have been encouraging you to focus on the meaning and purpose you are developing rather than on the way you are presenting your ideas. When writers turn to editorial and proofreading concerns too soon, focusing on spelling or punctuation or word usage, they can easily lose track of their thoughts. Giving over attention to word choice or syntax or spelling rather than to the ideas he or she is on the verge of making and finding, a writer may even block his or her own ability to write. But once the writer has revised to the point that the ideas are expressed in ways readers can understand, then attention to usage or format or spelling is not only appropriate, it is necessary.

Although your ideas have been the main focus of your drafting process so far, at the same time, you have been making choices about what words to use, the order of your sentences and paragraphs, and so on. Your attention to meaning, however, has kept you from debating over surface-level concerns like individual word order or punctuation choices or correct spelling. Having gone through the work of the previous chapters, at this point you can take time to focus on these secondary concerns and on the overall presentation of your essay.

As we discussed earlier, the nature of language used in college is in flux, and what constitutes "standard" English is evolving, but academic readers who read college essays do have expectations that you can meet by reviewing the surface presentation of your essay. Your essay may not be read as seriously as it might otherwise be if it does not meet these expectations. (The rather complex issue of English conventions is a topic we will examine further in Part Two of this text.) If a word is misspelled, for instance, readers may still be able to understand the intended meaning. However, academic readers—and you, yourself, are now becoming an academic reader—expect words to be spelled correctly in college writing, and they notice when they are not. Readers take their attention away from the ideas in the text and, however briefly, focus attention on the misspelled word. We believe that when readers do this, your essay may not be getting as good a reading as it would without the reader's shift of attention.

Spelling is a particularly easy surface feature to address since it is one of the few editing concerns that has only one right answer. That is, since English spelling was standardized in the eighteenth century, there is only one way (or a preferred and a second way!) for any word in English to be spelled. Although we recommend that you compose your draft on, or at some stage enter the draft into, a computer using a program that has a spell check, you will not always be able to rely on someone else, or technology, for all decisions about spelling. Your spell check will not recognize some words and will not correct for words that are misused.

Along with spelling, there are several other surface features that seem to disturb academic readers, to take their attention away briefly from the meaning of your text. These are not necessarily the most important surface features, and for some readers, other constructions sometimes may be more distracting.

To ensure that your ideas are taken seriously and are as available as possible to academic readers, it is useful to be familiar with which usage and textual features are most likely to disrupt your readers' attention from the meaning of your essay, and what strategies you can apply to edit and proofread for these concerns. What follows is a discussion of potential distractions for academic readers and some suggestions for helping writers make choices about editing and proofreading in light of how academics read student texts.

✵ *Usage Distractions for Academic Readers and Suggestions for Writers*

Most sentence level "distractions" would not be noticed at all, or would not disturb most academics, if they occurred in speech rather than in writing. Indeed, the first five distractions we describe are silent in speech, even if you are reading aloud from a written text. Following these, we give a brief description of the audible distractions (7–9) that might hinder your readers' progress through your essay. It is our experience that although there are other editing issues, some of which we will address in other chapters in this text, a college writer who learns to "correct" for these nine distractions will appear to be writing "standard" enough English to receive a good reading, that is, a reading as good as anyone else might receive from an academic reader. Your instructor may suggest you buy a handbook to supplement your dictionary as a resource for the many other usage issues that occur in conventional, standard English.

SILENT DISTRACTIONS

1. SPELLING

Academic *readers* often make severe judgments about writers' abilities based on the correctness of their spelling. It is common for readers to assume that an inordinate number of misspellings indicates laziness or irresponsibility in the writer. The assumption that writers just don't care is especially strong when they misspell common words (for example, "alot" instead of "a lot;" "there" when it should be "their" or "they're"; "it's" when it should be "its") or make common errors, ones that readers have seen so many times that they become pet peeves or annoyances. *Writers* can correct spelling errors using a spell check on the computer or a good dictionary. In fact, because spell checkers can't identify homonyms (a spell checker will find that "threw" is spelled correctly even if you really mean to use "through") or misplaced words ("She it the one who threw it."), it is important to have a dictionary on hand too.

Some people who have good visual memories are adept at spelling. Others, including many famous writers, need to look up words before letting a piece of writing stand on its own. If spelling is not particularly easy for you, you will need to take time to look up longer or uncommon words in a dictionary.

2. TYPOS

Like spelling errors, typos may be used by *readers* to make a quick determination of your skill and the commitment you have to your writing. *Writers* can locate some typos using a spell check; others will get by since they may be correctly spelled words, but not the words you intended. One useful strategy for "seeing" typos is to read your essay from the end, moving word by word backwards through the text. This process can help highlight the typos for you. Final versions of essays need to be proofread for typing mistakes. If you notice a mistake just as you are turning in a final version of a paper, it is always better to correct it than to have a perfectly neat paper.

3. CAPITALIZATION

Capitalization has virtually no effect on the *reader's* understanding of a text but a misplaced capital, or a missing one, sends a distress signal to an academic reader that may take his or her attention away from your essay. Because capitalization errors are often the result of a typing mistake, it is important for *writers* to check that words that need capitals, like names of people or places and first words of sentences, are capitalized, and that words that don't need capitals are not capitalized. Reading the essay backwards word by word is often a useful strategy for finding missing capitalizations too.

4. FORMATTING

Like spelling, typos, and capitalization, formatting has no effect on meaning. However, academic *readers* expect paragraph indentations and will be disturbed if your whole essay appears in one paragraph. It is a matter of *writer's* choice where to break paragraphs. Two page and single sentence paragraphs are unusual but are not incorrect. The general wisdom about paragraphing is that when you move on, in some way or degree, to a new topic, it is time for a new paragraph. Reread any chapter of this text (or any other academic text) to get a sense of paragraphing.

Other usual formatting issues are that most academic papers are double spaced, typed, have standard one-inch margins, use average size type, and are presented on standard weight, white, 8-½ × 11 inch paper. Academic papers are expected to look alike.

5. POSSESSIVES

We have listed possessives under silent distractions because the proofreading concern we want to highlight regarding possessives is the apostrophe ('). In speech, we may or may not hear the "s" signifying the possessive in "the boy's bike" or "the boys' bikes." Nevertheless, in college writing, *readers* expect the apostrophe to appear, standing for "belongs to." While checking for possessives, the *writer* should look for missing instances as well as for any apostrophes that appear in the text unnecessarily. Apostrophes are only used in forming contractions (like can't or wouldn't) and for possessives. No apostrophe should appear where a plural is intended except if it is a plural possessive.

6. SENTENCE BOUNDARIES

When we speak it is often not possible and it is certainly not necessary to identify where one sentence ends and the next begins. Like the first four distractions, sentence boundaries are of concern only to *readers,* not to listeners. Sentence boundaries seem to matter a great deal to academic readers even though, like the other silent distractions, they usually have no effect on one's ability to understand a text. In editing one's own essay, the *writer* should know that there are only two possible inconsistencies in the category of sentence boundaries: 1) fragments, in which you write part of a sentence but punctuate it as if it is a complete sentence, and 2) fused or run-on sentences, in which you write two sentences together but punctuate as if you have written one sentence. Under certain circumstances–for emphasis–fragments are acceptable, though usually student writing is expected to be free of fragments; fused and run-on sentences are not acceptable in college writing, although long, correctly punctuated sentences are sometimes valued as part of a particularly "academic" style.

We know of no fully reliable rule for what makes a complete sentence in English. The general formula is that one needs a subject and a predicate, the person or thing the sentence is about and a description of that subject's action or state of being. "He stands" is a complete sentence, but "standing, idly by the streetlight, the sirens blaring, the horns honking" is not a complete sentence because there is no subject; you're left to say, "Who is standing, idly . . . ?" "The quiet, long-haired boy in the front of the line," is also an incomplete sentence because there is no predicate. You're left to say, "What about 'the quiet, long-haired boy . . . ?' Our favorite test for complete sentences is to imagine that the sentence is all someone said when he walked into the room; would the sentence make some kind of complete sense or would you ask the kind of questions the fragments in the example above provoke?

It is difficult to notice fragments because they are usually made complete by attaching them to the previous or preceding sentence. So, when you are writing, you make that connection in your mind. Run-on or fused sentences are a little more difficult to detect, and it is our experience that they occur in student writing less frequently than fragments. If you have two complete sentences, you can either divide them up with a period (.) or you can join them together with a semicolon (;) or a comma and a conjunction such as "and," "or," and "but." You can't join two sentences together with a comma (,). The best technique we know of for checking sentence boundaries is to read a paper, sentence by sentence, backward. If you start with the last sentence of the essay, then read the next to last, and so on, you will be able to focus on sentence completeness without being influenced by the meaning of the text.

AUDIBLE DISTRACTIONS

7. AGREEMENT

The meaning of a sentence is rarely affected by the convention of agreement but nonstandard agreement is a particularly powerful distraction for academic *readers*. Agreement means that there is consistency within a sentence. The main parts of the sentence are either both plural or both singular. The form of the verb depends on whether the sentence contains a singular or plural subject. In the same way, singular or plural pronouns match singular or plural antecedents. To meet the expectations of academic readers you will need to check for both subject/verb agreement and pronoun/antecedent agreement.

Using a handbook is often a useful way for *writers* to check for agreement. In general, you will need to review each sentence first to see that the form of the verb matches that of the subject: In the sentence, "Each student has a notebook," the singular subject "student" matches the verb form "has." In the sentence, "Students take tests in chemistry," the plural subject "Students" matches the verb form "take." Second, you will need to see that in a sentence the antecedent, which is the word a pronoun refers to, is plural if the pronoun is plural, and singular if the pronoun is singular. In the sentence, "Musicians must practice if they want to become accomplished performers," the plural pronoun, "they" matches the plural antecedents, "Musicians" and "performers." In the sentence, "A musician must practice if he or she wants to become an accomplished performer," the singular pronouns "he or she" match the singular antecedents "musician" and "performer." Again, agreement is a convention of standard college writing that you may need to give attention to when you make the presentation of your essay conform to the expectations of academic readers.

8. TENSE

The academic *reader* who encounters a surprising, nonstandard tense shift in a college essay will, as with the other audible distractions, still be able to understand what is being said. He or she may pause to reflect on the writer's language history or background, surmising that this is a speaker of other languages besides English or other dialects besides the standard one. Even if the writer's background or history is the subject of the essay, the academic reader will expect the writer's knowledge of other languages and dialects to remain invisible in the finished text. (We believe that, at this time, the academic world is biased in favor of the standard form, although this bias is undergoing debate and change.)

In editing and proofreading, the *writer* will want to focus, again, on the verbs in the sentences, perhaps using a handbook to help. Are the verbs in their standard form? Is the tense consistent within sentences or paragraphs and, when there is a tense change, does it make sense in the context of the rest of the paragraph or essay? We will say more about tense and agreement in the next section of the book.

9. WORD CHOICE

The final audible distraction is word choice or diction. Academic *readers* find a wide range of language and diction acceptable. But they expect words to be used in conventional ways. As a *writer*, you may want to review your draft for the accuracy and appropriateness of the words, something that is not always easy to distinguish. We advise you to choose words from your own vocabulary, which is enormous, rather than use a thesaurus to find unfamiliar words that you may not be able to use conventionally. We also encourage you to ask others if you are unsure of the choice you have made; be sure to ask for their explanation, not just their decision. Word choice options include not only replacing words that are used incorrectly, but finding the most precise words to express your ideas and reach your audience.

ADDITIONAL DISTRACTIONS

CITING INFORMATION FROM RECOLLECTION AND MEMORY

Whatever the explicit purpose or meaning you have determined for your first essay, you have developed or supported it with information from your personal recollections and memories. Sometimes, in order to make this information more authoritative and credible or because it would be dishonest not to, writers cite their sources. They might include a direct naming of their source within the body of their writing or an internal reference to an actual date or a place. For example, you might find it necessary to indicate the original source of your own words or phrases: "How many times have I said to my own friends the words that my Dad used to repeat to me, 'The squeaky wheel gets the grease.'" Or you might need to cite something you yourself wrote in the past: "In writing the 'Farewell to the Counselors' speech (Camp Trefoil, August 1996), I found myself surprisingly able to find words that never would have come to me had I been writing for school."

Keep in mind that the purpose of citations is to indicate what words or ideas you have borrowed or built on (even if the first ones were your own) and to establish your own authority as someone who understands the value of knowledge and information that is passed on from person to person or place to place.

❧ *Additional Advice for Editing and Proofreading*

In addition to the particular strategies we have mentioned already, we find that it is always helpful to read your draft aloud, slowly, paying attention to agreement, tenses, and word choice. And finally, because the distractions we identified may or may not be immediately visible to you in your draft, it is advisable to get some help in locating points where some changes in the draft may be warranted. As we suggested, all of the distractions call for decisions to be made by the writer. While some distractions, like spelling and formatting, may present only one option for the writer, most editorial concerns can be resolved in a variety of ways. When you are editing and proofreading someone else's text, do not make any changes on the draft. Your job will be to locate any places where you feel there may be distractions about which the writer will then make an editorial decision. The key here is not to correct one another's essays, but to identify places where the writer may want to consider editing. Discuss the places you marked in each other's essays. If possible, exchange with someone else in class so that you have more than one other reader's review.

All of these distractions for academic readers that we have listed force a cautionary stance on writers which is in direct opposition to the open stance of generating writing. That is why it is important to treat the distractions as the most superficial part of writing. Nevertheless, you may find that focus on the surface features of the text will allow you to fine-tune your presentation in ways that make your meaning even more available to readers.

❧ *A Final Rewrite*

Rewrite your essay one last time including all the editorial and proofing changes. You may find that some editorial changes lead you to further revision, as well.

Writing Log Entry 11

On Writing Essay 1

Write a page about what it was like to have written your first essay. What were the most freely flowing parts of the writing for you? Where did you get bogged down? What do you hope a reader will take from your essay? What did you learn that you might take with you to your next essay assignment?

7

WRITING TO LEARN
Writing a Second Essay from Recollection and Memory

❧ *Reconsidering the Process of Writing*

As you worked your way through the first six chapters of this text, you directed your attention to your past and present experiences with writing and college writing, and to the relationships among these experiences. We limited your choice of subjects for Essay 1, so, in the process of composing, you were necessarily reflecting on and trying out the assertions we were making about writing and its power to help one make and find meaning. Because you had already read several chapters by the time you started Essay 1, you had been thinking and writing about college writing and your own experiences for at least a few days or weeks. Using the exploratory writing and the responses you received to your work-in-progress, you composed an essay that drew on your own experience and observations: an essay that had an explicit purpose, that expressed your perspectives on a subject that emerged from your thinking about writing. While you knew your essay was going to have something to do with writing, college writing, or your writing experiences, you also had to make the subject your own; you had to come up with your own purpose or reason for writing.

We imagine that the kinds of writing you were asked to do in the Perspectives and Focusing for Essay 1 were somewhat unfamiliar to you; you may have felt awkward writing them—not sure where you were headed or why. In fact, your first essay may have left you feeling rather ambivalent or even doubtful about the exploratory activities to which we have introduced you. Your essay may have had a good foundation of details and examples, but the focus of the essay, because it was yours to find, may have never become as clear as you (or your instructor) would have liked. At this point, let us reassure you that each time you complete an essay for *Shoptalk*, this kind of exploratory writing will become more familiar, the results less unexpected. And each time you succeed in finding your own purpose for writing, that process, too, will become easier and more familiar.

Because personal knowledge can provide valuable information for all college writing, the second essay will give you another opportunity to reflect on and analyze your own experience. However, while you will still write from personal experiences, this time you are no longer limited to the subject of writing; your essay may come from recollections and interpretations of **any** of your experiences. Again you will use informal writing to explore and focus in on your material, to make connections, observations, and interpretations, to learn what it is your experiences may be urging you to write, and to choose among these possibilities for a topic and a purpose for writing. Again, we remind you that this essay is based on your analysis of your experience and recollection. Your reflection on your experiences, the conclusions you reach, provide you with a purpose for writing, an explicit meaning to convey. As in Essay 1, the story or stories you have to tell are your data from which you will argue or explain or interpret and so on.

The choice of what you will write about for Essay 2 may seem so wide open as to be somewhat daunting, but zeroing in on such a seemingly unrestricted assignment provides valuable experience of the way writers actually work. Although some professional writing is the result of an assignment, the vast majority of it is created out of an individual's desire to express an opinion, to answer a question, provide some information, propose a solution to a problem, and so on. Most writing evolves out of the writer's urge to say something.

It is true that the "urge to say something" is not the initial reason most students write. When you first enroll in some courses, you may feel you have no personal interest in the subject of study. You may be taking the course because you are required to; it may seem you have no apparent reason for caring intellectually or personally about the assignments you are given. Further, most school writing assignments are contrived for the purposes of instruction. This text, too, asks you to go through a writing process that is somewhat artificial; you are doing assignments that we have designed in a very particular way with particular intentions in mind.

While all work in school is in one sense an exercise, you will also find that some—perhaps, a great deal—of your work in college, will genuinely cause your world and your awareness to expand, will be meaningful not only for the skills or credentials it gives you to use in the future, but for the experience it gives you now, in the present. To take full advantage of this experience requires making every subject you study, to some degree, your own, investing some of yourself in the assignments and the issues they raise.

The power that writing has to help writers create or discover their personal connection with subjects is the same power that helps them to figure out what they want to say or to make sense of what they don't initially understand. In this sense, writing is a primary way to learn. The first exploratory activities for Essay 2 provide ways for using writing to learn, to think about and learn from new material you are studying and from any of your own experiences. The activities will help you to begin focusing in on a subject to examine in an essay.

When you scroll through your memory for experiences that might serve as the catalyst for this next essay, consider especially those that are in some ways still unresolved, or those that have stayed with you, or that you find yourself thinking about. They need not seem important from the outside, or they may be. You can use these assignments to think about things you are actually interested in thinking about. Working writers begin at this point, knowing they have something that, for them, needs to be written.

Essay 2

Select from your recollections and memories any experience or set of experiences from which you would like to begin writing. Then, use the Perspectives and Focusing activities to analyze and interpret the experience(s) you chose and to find an explicit purpose or meaning you wish to convey to the reader. You might convince or persuade someone of something, inform or instruct someone about an issue or topic, explain or interpret something you saw or read, answer a question you have about something, or center on any other purpose that is appropriate to your interests and personal knowledge of the subject. In your essay, the details of your experience or experiences will provide you with a means of supporting and developing your purpose.

WRITING ESSAY 2

As with Essay 1, the Perspectives and Focusing activities are designed to help you find your topic and your angle into it; the Response guidelines can help you revise, and the Editing and Proofreading suggestions should be useful toward ensuring that your essay is ready to stand on its own. Most of the activities below will be familiar to you from your work on Essay 1. However, because you must find your own subject for this second essay, we have included several additional Perspectives to help you zero in on your subject. As in Essay 1, you may find that you can strengthen your essay by including information from what others have said in conversation or in print, but the primary source of information for this essay is your own experience.

At this point, or perhaps, after you have begun exploring your own thinking, take some time to review the professional demonstration essays at the end of the chapter. These essays demonstrate some ways that writers have used their personal experiences and recollections as a source for writing about various subjects for a variety of purposes. We have also included several student demonstrations selections in the section of this chapter on "Discovering and creating your essay."

DISCOVERING AND CREATING YOUR ESSAY
TAKING ON DIFFERENT PERSPECTIVES
PERSPECTIVES: *Tapping into Your Experiences*

Make a list of experiences that you remember. You might recall events that stand out for you this year and in the past few years. You might recall back into your childhood for events that you remember. To help jog your memory you might think of times when you were most happy or most sad or most apprehensive or when something changed for you. Just a word or two to represent the event is enough. The list is just for you, so do not censor yourself; make as long a list as you can.

Student Demonstration
PERSPECTIVES: *Tapping into Your Thinking*
Example 1

```
1. Pajama Gammy-gam

2. CIF finals—how to resolve bad feelings with J.W.

3. Lyp-sync party—why did I go?

4. Problems of getting my new car
```

5. Handling fears about attending college

6. My goal of having a "celebrity party" like Angela's

7. What to do about procrastination; how to organize

8. Gospel choir play at church—how Denise is like me

PERSPECTIVES: *Tapping into Your Thinking*

Quickly list what is on your mind right now. What questions and issues are you thinking about or struggling with? You might reflect on experiences at home, at school, or in the community; movies or plays you have recently seen; places you have visited; people in your life. Don't feel that the list must be remarkable in any way other than that it provides a quick snapshot of your mind.

PERSPECTIVES: *Your State of Mind*

By process of elimination, cross out items on each list that you do not feel like writing about today. Don't cross out the item so completely that you can't read it; the list may be useful to you for future writings. You can make your decisions on any basis you choose, narrowing down to the two or three items on each list that currently look most inviting, perhaps, that seem to be the richest experiences or the most compelling thoughts, topics that you would not mind giving a few minutes of your attention to, today.

Eliminate all but two items on each list. Write briefly, and freely, for 5–10 minutes, about each topic. This writing is intended to explore your knowledge, feelings, state-of-mind about each item.

Reread your two brief writings and select the one about which you have the most interest, the most curiosity, the greatest feeling, the most to say, or even the greatest confusion.

PERSPECTIVES: *What You Know, Need to Know, Could Never Know*

Thinking about the subject you have chosen, freewrite a page or so in response to each of the following questions:

1. What do you know about the subject you have selected? Describe it in detail. Tell about your current feelings and understanding of the subject.

2. What is the story of this subject or your story about it? Tell the story.

3. What do you feel you need to know about yourself or others in relation to the subject? Why do you need to know these things—to what end?

4. What are the kinds of things that you could never understand about the subject and what would prevent that understanding?

PERSPECTIVES: *Questions and Connections*

Reread the Perspectives writings you have completed. Jot down some notes about the connections you can make among them and questions they raise. For example: Do the limitations of your understanding in any way explain your feelings or beliefs about the topic? Do you suspect that as you come to learn more about yourself and others in relation to the topic your feelings will change as well? Do any of the three writings seem particularly intriguing to you and leave you wanting to say more?

PERSPECTIVES: *Contradictions and Points of View*

The experiences on which we base our beliefs are never entirely consistent; sometimes they are positive and other times not. So, implicit in your various writings there are, most likely, two or more conflicting points of view on the subject. These different viewpoints emerge from your memories, expectations, or the various contexts in which you have experienced this topic.

In this exploration, identify what points of view emerge from your writings and then listen to them as if to the distinct voices of individuals who maintain singular perspectives. Write out a conversation among these voices.

Student Demonstration

PERSPECTIVES: *Conflicting Points of View*

Person A: "Sometimes I feel as though my parents can be too overprotective and that they make certain rules just to make my life miserable!"

Person B: "That's not true. Your parents are looking out for your best interests. They don't want to see you get into a bad situation."

Person A: "I know they care; but they must realize that I'm 19 years old . . . they've raised me to have good judgement. I feel I should have the freedom to make most of my own decisions."

Person B: "The only way you'll be able to make most or all of your decisions is to have your own career, home, car, and money. Otherwise, your parents have authority over you."

Person A: "So, just because my parents support me financially means I have to do what makes them happy all the time?"

Person B: "No, it means you owe them some amount of respect, because sometimes you don't realize how many sacrifices they've made just for you."

Person A: "Sometimes I wish I wasn't an only child, because all the pressure from my parents is placed on me."

Person B: "You can feel blessed that you're an only child because you are your parents' number one priority. If you had other sib lings, then you might be complaining about unfairness and lack of attention."

Person A: "I wish my parents wouldn't breathe down my back so much!"

Person B: "You're lucky you have two parents who are willing to put their time and energy into making you a decent member of society. They obviously show that they care enough to catch you before you fall. So you had better appreciate it now. The person who you become will exist because of the fact that you had loving parents who did actually care."

PERSPECTIVES: *Metaphoric Thinking*

Reread the Perspectives you have done so far, and identify a concept or an object that appears in or emerges from the writing. Make three comparisons between the original concept or object and something else that it somehow reminds you of. Then, explain each comparison, freewriting for a few minutes about how the comparison works and what this comparison shows you about the concept or object that you might not otherwise have noticed.

FOCUSING YOUR DIRECTION

FOCUSING: *Questions and Connections*

What connections can you make among the Perspectives you have written? Write three or four sentences about the connections that you see emerging. What can you say about the subject and its importance to you? Instead of making a statement, you might also put these thoughts in the form of a question.

FOCUSING: *Writing More*

Use the statement or question that you wrote above as a focus from which to begin freewriting. Push yourself to write 2 or 3 pages. The only parameters are those set by the sentences you have already written.

FOCUSING: *Rereading and Writing Again*

Reread the pages you have written; while doing so, underline sentences or sections of your writing that jump out at you in some way. Find a sentence or two that seem significant to you or that raise some question for you that you might want to reflect on further, or something that you feel is worth telling others. With 3 or 4 of these sentences in mind, write several more pages of focused freewriting.

FOCUSING: *Rereading, Reseeing, and Rewriting*

Together, all of the writing you have done so far makes up your exploratory draft for Essay 2. Like the exploratory draft of Essay 1, this draft was initially somewhat random and disconnected. But the more writing you did, the more focused and full of direction the draft became.

Reread all the pages you have written in these activities, paying particular attention to the focused freewriting at the end. Ask yourself what explicit purpose for writing emerges from this first draft. What is it that you are writing about and to what end?

With this subject and purpose in mind, and with all of the writing you have done so far at hand, write a second draft. Unlike writing your exploratory draft, you will begin this second draft with a sense of purpose and some idea about how the recollections and memories you have recorded and reflected on can help you to accomplish that purpose.

Student Demonstration

REFLECTIVE ANALYSIS OF RECOLLECTION AND MEMORY

Example 1

Three years ago I saw a play that told the story of a young African-American girl named Denise. At the beginning, Denise was a typical, playful nine-year old who was innocent and very obedient to her parents. Throughout the play, Denise's character began to change as she reached her pre-teen years. She became more disobedient because she felt as though she had been too sheltered growing up and was never free to make her own judgements and decisions. When Denise's behavior became out-of-control, her parents set stricter and stricter rules. But they never explained to her why they were doing so, expecting her to follow the rules anyway. Yet the more guidelines that were set, the more Denise would break them.

I wanted to tell about this play to explain how it helped me understand my own experiences and why communication between parent and child is so important. Parents need to find a balance between giving a child a certain amount of freedom and setting rules and guidelines that point the child down the right path. Attending the play, I found that many of my own experiences compared with those of the character of Denise. As an adolescent I was what you'd call a "goody-two shoes." I was very obedient and never got into major trouble. There were only rare instances when I would get out of line. Once I reached my early teenage years, I didn't become quite as rebellious, mischievous, and disobedient as Denise. I just started to question why I couldn't go outside to play with friends before I did my homework; why I couldn't wear make-up; why I couldn't spend the night at my friend's house anymore; and why I had to do so many chores around the house.

Example 2

It is not easy to talk with your child about politics. Should you as a parent even do it? Is it healthy for the development of the child? What if you lived behind the Iron Curtain where every wall had ears and every neighbor was willing to turn you in? During that dark period of time in my home country many parents did not even dare to try to bring up these topics. Some of them agreed with the political system, some were stupid enough not to realize the flaws. Many people did not want to play with their children's minds. Life was difficult enough. "Let the children believe the official version; forget the doubles-peak!" they thought. But my parents were different.

In the middle of my seventh grade year my parents assumed that I was mature enough to hold a family secret, which if told to the wrong people could destroy us all. I remember that afternoon vividly: my parents excited, their

cheeks flushed, opening their deepest secrets, tearing down
the good old lies. They told me everything, after we had
turned the water and television on real loud. They showed me
all the bent titles which they had been hiding in the second
row in their library. That night I could not sleep. I had to
think, compare what I had been told by teachers for all
those years, to what my parents said. All that information I
had learned, all that waste. Did they all know it was false?
Did they just play the game? Or did they not know? That
question sat on my head as big as a spider.

GETTING RESPONSE TO ESSAY 2

Your sources for getting response to the draft of Essay 2, as with all
of the essays you will write, are another individual in your class, a
group of classmates, and someone outside of class–a friend or a tutor
in the writing center. Using the four ways of responding first described
in Chapter 5 (listening, reporting, elaborating, and questioning), you
can get information and reaction from one or more of these sources.
Remember that as a responder your job is to give as clear a picture as
you can of how you read the draft; your job is not to evaluate or judge
but to respond. The writer's job is to take in as much response as
possible. Both giving response and receiving it is a positive way to
learn about other people's experiences and ideas and to communicate
your own.

FOUR WAYS OF RESPONDING
LISTENING

The first kind of response most writers need is simply to be heard, to
know that someone is really listening and taking in what they have written. This form of response is critical to all the other forms; it is the foundation for your ability to be a helpful responder.

LISTENING 1: RECEIVING

Listen carefully to the essay as it is read. Respond without words.
Your job is to receive the writing, to take it in, to have any reactions you
naturally have. That is, you might find yourself nodding in agreement
or smiling or feeling sad but you will not, at this time, articulate your

response in words. Simply say "thank you" to the writer for reading, or clap for the writing if you are in a larger group. The writer has had an attentive audience hear what she or he has to say.

LISTENING 2: ECHOING

Use the writer's own words as your response. As you hear the piece of writing again or read it to yourself, jot down or underline words and phrases that stand out for you, that strike you in some way. Without using any other words, repeat the writer's words you have noted. By echoing back the writer's own words, you are letting the writer know what especially got through to you.

REPORTING

Next, the writer can benefit from knowing how different readers understand his or her writing. Your job in reporting is to report on your own reading of the text. You cannot know with certainty exactly what the writer intended, but you are an authority on your own reading. The following are strategies for reporting your reading to the writer.

REPORTING 1: MAIN POINTS

List for the writer what seem to you to be the main points he or she is making in the draft. What seem to be the main ideas that are included so far in what you have read?

REPORTING 2: FOCUS

What do you feel is the focus for the whole essay, so far? Is the writer's purpose or reason for writing explicit and clear? How does the essay accomplish this? You might come up with a title that, for you, represents the heart of what the draft seems to be saying.

REPORTING 3: SUMMARY

Give a summary of what you read. The summary gives more detail than the list of Main Points, but of course it doesn't include everything. You might summarize by writing down a few sentences that elaborate your understanding of each main point or by recording what you remember from the piece without looking at it.

REPORTING 4: STORY OF YOUR OWN READING

Tell the writer what you thought and what you felt as you read the piece of writing. The idea is to try to tell the story of what happened to you, in you, as you read. The story of your own reading is not a summary or an analysis, it is a narrative of what went through your mind and what feelings you had at specific points as you read or heard the draft.

ELABORATING

In the next kind of response, you move beyond your immediate reaction to the text to make connections between your own experience and knowledge and what you have read. Elaborating helps you provide the writer with a broader understanding of his or her material since different readers will make different connections to and have different commentary on what the writer has said.

ELABORATING 1: CONNECTIONS

What does the writing connect to in your own experience? What have you read that corroborates what has been said? What can you add to the points the writer has made? What further examples can you think of? In what ways do you agree with the piece of writing? What parts of the writing do you particularly agree with or feel particularly connected to?

ELABORATING 2: CONTRADICTIONS

Is there anything in the piece of writing that contradicts your own experience or something you have read? What alternative perspectives can you offer on the points the writer has made? What is there in the piece of writing with which you disagree? Is there something that seems to you to be left out of the piece?

QUESTIONING

Finally, it is valuable to ask the questions you have about a work-in-progress. Don't hold back on any questions that come to you, for it will be useful to the writer to know what questions the piece, in its current version, raises for different readers.

QUESTIONING 1: WHAT I'D LIKE TO HEAR MORE ABOUT

Ask the writer about any aspect of the writing you would like to hear more about. The writer may choose to include some of this material or may choose not to add this information in subsequent versions of the piece depending on his or her purpose and the audience for whom the writing is intended.

QUESTIONING 2: WHAT I DON'T YET UNDERSTAND

Ask the writer for clarification of any points, ideas, words or phrases that you have questions about. Again, the writer may find that in the next draft she or he wants to make some changes as a result of the questions she or he was asked.

QUESTIONING 3: THE WRITER ASKS YOU QUESTIONS

At this point, the writer can ask for comment about any aspect of the draft she or he wants response to that doesn't seem to have been addressed. Again, the feedback is a non-judgmental form of response.

❋ *Responding to the Writer's Use of Information from Recollection and Memory: Questions for Response*

The following are some questions your responders might ask to help you determine how well you have used recollection and memory, the primary information source for Essay 2. Before answering these questions about how the writer has used information in the essay, responders should first remind themselves of what they found to be the essay's explicit purpose or meaning. Keeping that purpose in mind, give the writer your sense of how he or she used recollection and memory in the draft.

1. How are instances of recollection and memory used in relation to the purpose of the essay?

2. What claims or observations does the writer make based on his or her information? Tell the writer what makes his or her claims convincing for you. Tell the writer any claims that feel to you unconvincing. What would make these claims more convincing for you?

3. Where does recollection and memory appear in the essay? Tell the writer what seems to you to be the purpose for which each instance of recollection or memory is presented. Are there further details you

would like to know? Are there some details that you could not connect to the purpose of the essay?

4. How are the recollections cited? Is there more you would like to know about the context of the recollections, about when and where the event took place? (Note that an explanation appears in the next chapter about how to cite or reference personal experience information.)

✳ *Editing and Proofreading the Penultimate Draft of Essay 2*

When you have revised your essay enough that it begins to feel complete and you are near to having a penultimate draft, you are ready to edit and proofread. In order to make the process easier, we will repeat for each essay in the textbook the list of silent and audible distractions. We have also included the description of some additional distractions that can occur in essays whose primary source of information is recollection and memory.

Remember that all of the distractions call for decisions to be made by the writer. So if you are editing and proofreading someone else's text, do not make any changes on the draft. Your job will be to locate any places where you feel there may be a possible reader's distraction about which the writer will then make an editorial decision.

SILENT DISTRACTIONS

1. SPELLING

Academic *readers* often make severe judgements about writers' abilities based on the correctness of their spelling. It is common for readers to assume that an inordinate number of misspellings indicates laziness or irresponsibility in the writer. The assumption that writers just don't care is especially strong when they misspell common words (for example, "alot" instead of "a lot;" "there" when it should be "their" or "they're," "it's" when it should be "its") or make common errors, ones that readers have seen so many times that they become pet peeves or annoyances. *Writers* can correct spelling errors using a spell check on the computer or a good dictionary. In fact, because spell checkers can't identify homonyms (a spell checker will find that "threw" is spelled correctly even if you really mean to use "through") or misplaced words ("She it the one who threw it."), it is important to have a dictionary on hand too.

Some people who have good visual memories are adept at spelling. Others, including many famous writers, need to look up words before letting a piece of writing stand on its own. If spelling is not particularly easy for you, you will need to take time to look up longer or uncommon words in a dictionary.

2. TYPOS

Like spelling errors, typos may be used by *readers* to make a quick determination of your skill and the commitment you have to your writing. *Writers* can locate some typos using a spell check; others will get by since they may be correctly spelled words, but not the words you intended. One useful strategy for "seeing" typos is to read your essay from the end, moving word by word backwards through the text. This process can help highlight the typos for you. Final versions of essays need to be proofread for typing mistakes. If you notice a mistake just as you are turning in a final version of a paper, it is always better to correct it than to have a perfectly neat paper.

3. CAPITALIZATION

Capitalization has virtually no effect on the *reader's* understanding of a text but a misplaced capital, or a missing one, sends a distress signal to an academic reader that may take his or her attention away from your essay. Because capitalization errors are often the result of a typing mistake, it is important for *writers* to check that words that need capitals, like names of people or places and first words of sentences, are capitalized, and that words that don't need capitals are not capitalized. Reading the essay backwards word by word is often a useful strategy for finding missing capitalizations too.

4. FORMATTING

Like spelling, typos, and capitalization, formatting has no effect on meaning. However, academic *readers* expect paragraph indentations and will be disturbed if your whole essay appears in one paragraph. It is a matter of *writer's* choice where to break paragraphs. Two page and single sentence paragraphs are unusual but are not incorrect. The general wisdom about paragraphing is that when you move on, in some way or degree, to a new topic, it is time for a new paragraph. Reread any chapter of this text (or any other academic text) to get a sense of paragraphing.

Other usual formatting issues are that most academic papers are double spaced, typed, have standard one-inch margins, use average size type, and are presented on standard weight, white, 8-$\frac{1}{2}$ × 11 inch paper. Academic papers are expected to look alike.

5. POSSESSIVES

We have listed possessives under silent distractions because the proofreading concern we want to highlight regarding possessives is the apostrophe ('). In speech, we may or may not hear, the "s" signifying the possessive in "the boy's bike" or the boys' bikes." Nevertheless, in college writing, *readers* expect the apostrophe to appear, standing for "belongs to." While checking for possessives, the *writer* should look for missing instances as well as for any apostrophes that appear in the text unnecessarily. Apostrophes are only used in forming contractions (like can't or wouldn't) and for possessives. No apostrophe should appear where a plural is intended except if it is a plural possessive.

6. SENTENCE BOUNDARIES

When we speak, it is often not possible and it is certainly not necessary to identify where one sentence ends and the next begins. Like the first four distractions, sentence boundaries are of concern only to *readers,* not to listeners. Sentence boundaries seem to matter a great deal to academic readers even though, like the other silent distractions, they usually have no effect on one's ability to understand a text. In editing one's own essay, the *writer* should know that there are only two possible inconsistencies in the category of sentence boundaries: 1) fragments, in which you write part of a sentence but punctuate it as if it is a complete sentence and 2) fused or run-on sentences, in which you write two sentences together but punctuate as if you have written one sentence. Under certain circumstances–for emphasis–fragments are acceptable, though usually student writing is expected to be free of fragments; fused and run-on sentences are not acceptable in college writing, although long, correctly punctuated sentences are sometimes valued as part of a particularly "academic" style.

We know of no fully reliable rule for what makes a complete sentence in English. The general formula is that one needs a subject and a predicate, the person or thing the sentence is about and a description of that subject's action or state of being. "He stands" is a complete sentence, but "standing, idly by the streetlight, the sirens blaring, the horns honking" is not a complete sentence because there is no subject; you're left to say, "Who is standing, idly . . .?" "The quiet, long-haired boy in the front of the line," is also an incomplete sentence because there is no predicate. You're left to say, "What about 'the quiet, long-haired boy . . .'?" Our favorite test for complete sentences is to imagine that the sentence is all someone said when he walked into the room; would the sentence make some kind of complete sense or would you ask the kind of questions the fragments in the example above provoke?

It is difficult to notice fragments because they are usually made complete by attaching them to the previous or preceding sentence. So, when you are writing, you make that connection in your mind. Run-on or fused sentences are a little more difficult to detect, and it is our experience that they occur in student writing less frequently than fragments. If you have two complete sentences, you can either divide them up with a period (.) or you can join them together with a semicolon (;) or a comma and a conjunction such as "and," "or," and "but." You can't join two sentences together with a comma (,). The best technique we know of for checking sentence boundaries is to read a paper, sentence by sentence, backward. If you start with the last sentence of the essay, then read the next to last, and so on, you will be able to focus on sentence completeness without being influenced by the meaning of the text.

AUDIBLE DISTRACTIONS

7. AGREEMENT

The meaning of a sentence is rarely affected by the convention of agreement but non-standard agreement is a particularly powerful distraction for academic *readers*. Agreement means that there is consistency within a sentence. The main parts of the sentence are either both plural or both singular. The form of the verb depends on whether the sentence contains a singular or plural subject. In the same way, singular or plural pronouns match singular or plural antecedents. To meet the expectations of academic readers you will need to check for both subject/verb agreement and pronoun/antecedent agreement.

Using a handbook is often a useful way for *writers* to check for agreement. In general, you will need to review each sentence first to see that the form of the verb matches that of the subject: In the sentence, "Each student has a notebook," the singular subject "student" matches the verb form "has." In the sentence, "Students take tests in chemistry," the plural subject "students" matches the verb form "take." Second, you will need to see that in a sentence the antecedent, which is the word a pronoun refers to, is plural if the pronoun is plural, and singular if the pronoun is singular. In the sentence, "Musicians must practice if they want to become accomplished performers," the plural pronoun, "they" matches the plural antecedents, "musicians" and "performers." In the sentence, "A musician must practice if he or she wants to become an accomplished performer," the singular pronouns "he or she" match the singular antecedents "musician" and "performer." Again, agreement is a convention of standard, college writing that you need to give attention to when you are making the presentation of your essay conform to the expectations of academic readers.

8. TENSE

The academic *reader* who encounters a surprising, nonstandard tense shift in a college essay will, as with the other audible distractions, still be able to understand what is being said. He or she may pause to reflect on the writer's language history or background, surmising that this is a speaker of other languages besides English or other dialects besides the standard one. Even if the writer's background or history is the subject of the essay, the academic reader will expect the writer's knowledge of other languages and dialects to remain invisible in the finished text. (We believe that, at this time, the academic world is biased in favor of the standard form, although this bias is undergoing debate and change.)

In editing and proofreading, the *writer* will want to focus, again, on the verbs in the sentences, perhaps using a handbook to help. Are the verbs in their standard form? Is the tense consistent within sentences or paragraphs and, when there is a tense change, does it make sense in the context of the rest of the paragraph or essay? We will say more about tense and agreement in the next section of the book.

9. WORD CHOICE

The final audible distraction is word choice or diction. Academic *readers* find a wide range of language and diction acceptable. But they expect words to be used in conventional ways. As a *writer*, you may want to review your draft for the accuracy and appropriateness of the words, something that is not always easy to distinguish. We advise you to choose words from your own vocabulary, which is enormous, rather than use a thesaurus to find unfamiliar words that you may not be able to use conventionally. We also encourage you to ask others if you are unsure of the choice you have made; be sure to ask for their explanation, not just their decision. Word choice options include not only replacing words that are used incorrectly, but finding the most precise words to express your ideas and reach your audience.

ADDITIONAL DISTRACTIONS

1. CITING INFORMATION FROM RECOLLECTION AND MEMORY

Whatever the explicit purpose or meaning you have determined for your second essay, you have developed or supported it with information from your personal recollections and memories. Sometimes, in order to make this information more authoritative and credible or because it would be dishonest not to, writers cite their sources. They might include a direct naming of their source within the body of their writing or an internal reference to an actual date or a place. For example, you might find it necessary to indicate the original source of your own words or phrases: "How many times have I said to my own friends the words that my Dad used to repeat to me, 'The squeaky wheel gets the grease.'" Or you might need to cite something you yourself wrote in the past: "In writing the 'Farewell to the Counselors' speech (Camp Trefoil, August 1996), I found myself surprisingly able to find words that never would have come to me had I been writing for school."

Keep in mind that the purpose of citations is to indicate what words or ideas you have borrowed or built on (even if the first ones were your own) and to establish your own authority as someone who understands the value of knowledge and information that is passed on from person to person or place to place.

❊ *A Final Rewrite*

Rewrite your essay one last time, carefully including all the editorial and proofing changes. You may find that some editorial changes lead you to further revision, as well.

Writing Log Entry 12

Reflections on Writing Essay 2

Write a page about what it was like to have written a second essay from personal recollection and interpretations. What were the most freely flowing parts of the writing for you? Where did you get bogged down? How was this experience different or not from the writing of the first essay?

❊ *Professional Demonstration Essays for Essay 2*
SOME QUESTIONS TO CONSIDER

As you brainstorm your own ideas for Essay 2, and as you begin the process of exploring and drafting, you might refer to these demonstration essays, noticing the range of options available when one writes from personal experience. You can find in the Demonstration Essays a variety of ways writers integrate personal experience into their essays, analyzing and interpreting their experiences, identifying for themselves an explicit purpose for which they want to write, then using the experiences to illustrate and support that purpose.

Beginning from subjects they know and care about, the writers set out to evaluate, explain, make comparisons, or present arguments to their readers. Though the topics and purposes of these essays make them appear very different from one another, they are similar in the sense that each one relies primarily on the writer's own experience as a source of information, illustration, and support. Use the following questions to help you examine each demonstration essay in more detail:

1. In a sentence or two, how would you summarize the explicit purpose of each essay? Another way of thinking about this would be to imagine that you were to ask the writer what the essay was about and then ask, "So what?" How might he or she answer?

2. How do the writers make their points explicit? What are the sentences or parts of the essay that make these points available to the reader?

3. How do the writers use information from recollection and memory to support or illustrate the purpose of their essays? How is this information integrated into the text and used as a source of authority?

THE ANDROGYNOUS MAN*

Noel Perrin

1   The summer I was 16, I took a train from New York to Steamboat Springs, Colo., where I was going to be assistant wrangler at a camp. The trip took three days, and since I was much too shy to talk to strangers, I had quite a lot of time for reading. I read all of *Gone With the Wind.* I read all of the interesting articles in a couple of magazines I had, and then I went back and read all the dull stuff. I also took all the quizzes, a thing of which magazines were fuller then than now.

2   The one that held my undivided attention was called "How Masculine/Feminine Are You?" It consisted of a large number of inkblots. The reader was supposed to decide which of four objects each blot most resembled. The choices might be a cloud, a steam-engine, a caterpillar and a sofa.

3   When I finished the test, I was shocked to find that I was barely masculine at all. On a scale 1 of to 10, I was about 1.2. Me, the horse wrangler? (And not just wrangler, either. That summer, I had to skin a couple of horses that died–the camp owner wanted the hides.)

4   The results of that test were so terrifying to me that for the first time in my life I did a piece of original analysis. Having unlimited time on the train, I looked at the "masculine" answers over and over, trying to find what it was that distinguished real men from people like me–and eventually I discovered two very simple patterns. It was "masculine" to think the blots looked like man-made objects, and "feminine" to think they looked like natural objects. It was masculine to think they looked like things capable of causing harm, and feminine to think of innocent things.

5   Even at 16, I had the sense to see that the compilers of the test were using rather limited criteria–maleness and femaleness are both more complicated than that–and I breathed a hugh sigh of relief. I wasn't necessarily a wimp, after all.

6   That the test did reveal something other than the superficiality of its makers I realized only many years later. What it revealed was that there

---

is a large class of men and women both, to which I belong, who are essentially androgynous. That doesn't mean we're gay, or low in the appropriate hormones, or uncomfortable performing the jobs traditionally assigned our sexes. (A few years after that summer, I was leading troops in combat and, unfashionable as it now is to admit this, having a very good time. War is exciting. What a pity the 20th century went and spoiled it with high-tech weapons.)

7   What it does mean to be spiritually androgynous is a kind of freedom. Men who are all-male, or he-man, or 100% red-blooded Americans, have a little biological set that causes them to be attracted to physical power, and probably also to dominance. Maybe even to watching football. I don't say this to criticize them. Completely masculine men are quite often wonderful people: good husbands, good (though sometimes overwhelming) fathers, good members of society. Furthermore, they are often so unself-consciously at ease in the world that other men seem to imitate them. They just aren't as free as androgynes. They pretty nearly have to be what they are; we have a range of choices open.

8   The sad part is that many of us never discover that. Men who are not 100% red-blooded Americans—say those who are only 75% red-blooded—often fail to notice their freedom. They are too busy trying to copy the he-men ever to realize that men, like women, come in a wide variety of acceptable types. Why this frantic imitation? My answer is mere speculation, but not casual. I have speculated on this for a long time.

9   Partly they're just envious of the he-man's unconscious ease. Mostly they're terrified of finding that there may be something wrong with them deep down, some weakness at the heart. To avoid discovering that, they spend their lives acting out the role that the he-man naturally lives. Sad.

10   One thing that men owe to the women's movement is that this kind of failure is less common than it used to be. In releasing themselves from the single ideal of the dependent woman, women have more or less incidentally released a lot of men from the single ideal of the dominant male. The one mistake the feminists have made, I think, is in supposing that all men need this release, or that the world would be a better place if all men achieved it. It wouldn't. It would just be duller.

11   So far I have been pretty vague about just what the freedom of the androgynous man is. Obviously it varies with the case. In the case I know best, my own, I can be quite specific. It has freed me most as a parent. I am, among other things, a fairly good natural mother. I like the nurturing role. It makes me feel good to see a child eat—and it turns me to mush to see a 4-year-old holding a glass with both small hands, in order to drink. I even enjoyed sewing patches on the knees of my daughter Amy's

Dr. Dentons when she was at the crawling stage. All that pleasure I would have lost if I had made myself stick to the notion of the paternal role that I started with.

12   Or take a smaller and rather ridiculous example. I feel free to kiss cats. Until recently it never occurred to me that I would want to, though my daughters have been doing it all their lives. But my elder daughter is now 22, and in London. Of course, I get to look after her cat while she is gone. He's a big, handsome farm cat named Petrushka, very unsentimental though used from kittenhood to being kissed on the top of the head by Elizabeth. I've gotten very fond of him (he's the adventurous kind of cat who likes to climb hills with you), and one night I simply felt like kissing him on the top of the head, and did. Why did no one tell me sooner how silky cat fur is?

13   Then there's my relation to cars. I am completely unembarrassed by my inability to diagnose even minor problems in whatever object I happen to be driving, and don't have to make some insider's remark to mechanics to try to establish that I, too, am a "Man With His Machine."

14   The same ease extends to household maintenance. I do it, of course. Service people are expensive. But for the last decade my house has functioned better than it used to because I have had the aid of a volume called "Home Repairs Any Woman Can Do," which is pitched just right for people at my technical level. As a youth, I'd as soon have touched such a book as I would have become a transvestite. Even though common sense says there is really nothing sexual whatsoever about fixing sinks.

15   Or take public emotion. All my life I have easily been moved by certain kinds of voices. The actress Siobhan McKenna's, to take a notable case. Give her an emotional scene in a play, and within ten words my eyes are full of tears. In boyhood, my great dread was that someone might notice. I struggled manfully, you might say, to suppress this weakness. Now, of course, I don't see it as a weakness at all, but as a kind of fulfillment. I even suspect that the true he-men feel the same way, or one kind of them does, at least, and it's only the poor imitators who have to struggle to repress themselves.

16   Let me come back to the inkblots, with their assumption that masculine equates with machinery and science, and feminine with art and nature. I have no idea whether the right pronoun for God is He, She, or It. But this I'm pretty sure of. If God could somehow be induced to take that test, God would not come out macho and not feminismo, either, but right in the middle. Fellow androgynes, it's a nice thought.

WHAT ARE FRIENDS FOR?*

Marion Winik

I was thinking about how everybody can't be everything to each other, but some people can be something to each other, thank God, from the ones whose shoulder you cry on to the ones whose half-slips you borrow to the nameless ones you chat with in the grocery line.

Buddies, for example, are the workhorses of the friendship world, the people out there on the front lines, defending you from loneliness and boredom. They call you up, they listen to your complaints, they celebrate your successes and curse your misfortunes, and you do the same for them in return. They hold out through innumerable crises before concluding that the person you're dating is no good, and even then understand if you ignore their good counsel. They accompany you to a movie with subtitles or to see the diving pit at Aquarena Springs. They feed your cat when you are out of town and pick you up from the airport when you get back. They come over to help you decide what to wear on a date. Even if it is with that creep.

What about family members? Most of them are people you just got stuck with, and though you love them, you may not have very much in common. But there is that rare exception, the Relative Friend. It is your cousin, your brother, maybe even your aunt. The two of you share the same views of the other family members. Meg never should have divorced Martin. He was the best thing that ever happened to her. You can confirm each other's memories of things that happened a long time ago. Don't you remember when Uncle Hank and Daddy had that awful fight in the middle of Thanksgiving dinner? Grandma always hated Grandpa's stamp collection; she probably left the windows open during the hurricane on purpose.

While so many family relationships are tinged with guilt and obligation, a relationship with a Relative Friend is relatively worry-free. You don't even have to hide your vices from this delightful person. When you slip out Aunt Joan's back door for a cigarette, she is already there.

*Winik, Marion. "What are Friends For?" From *Telling*. Copyright © 1994 by Marion Winik. Reprinted by permission of Villard Books, a division of Random House, Inc.

Then there is that special guy at work. Like all the other people at the job site, at first he's just part of the scenery. But gradually he starts to stand out from the crowd. Your friendship is cemented by jokes about coworkers and thoughtful favors around the office. Did you see Ryan's hair? Want half my bagel? Soon you know the names of his turtles, what he did last Friday night, exactly which model CD player he wants for his birthday. His handwriting is as familiar to you as your own.

Though you invite each other to parties, you somehow don't quite fit into each other's outside lives. For this reason, the friendship may not survive a job change. Company gossip, once an infallible source of entertainment, soon awkwardly accentuates the distance between you. But wait. Like School Friends, Work Friends share certain memories which acquire a nostalgic glow after about a decade.

A Faraway Friend is someone you grew up with or went to school with or lived in the same town as until one of you moved away. Without a Faraway Friend, you would never get any mail addressed in handwriting. A Faraway Friend calls late at night, invites you to her wedding, always says she is coming to visit but rarely shows up. An actual visit from a Faraway Friend is a cause for celebration and binges of all kinds. Cigarettes, Chips Ahoy, bottles of tequila.

Faraway Friends go through phases of intense communication, then may be out of touch for many months. Either way, the connection is always there. A conversation with your Faraway Friend always helps to put your life in perspective: when you feel you've hit a dead end, come to a confusing fork in the road, or gotten lost in some crackerbox subdivision of your life, the advice of the Faraway Friend–who has the big picture, who is so well acquainted with the route that brought you to this place– is indispensable.

Another useful function of the Faraway Friend is to help you remember things from a long time ago, like the name of your seventh-grade history teacher, what was in that really good stir-fry, or exactly what happened that night on the boat with the guys from Florida.

Ah, the Former Friend. A sad thing. At best a wistful memory, at worst a dangerous enemy who is in possession of many of your deepest secrets. But what was it that drove you apart? A misunderstanding, a betrayed confidence, an unrepaid loan, an ill-conceived flirtation. A poor choice of spouse can do in a friendship just like that. Going into business together can be a serious mistake. Time, money, distance, cult religions: all noted friendship killers. You quit doing drugs, you're not such good friends with your dealer anymore.

And lest we forget, there are the Friends You Love to Hate. They call at inopportune times. They say stupid things. They butt in, they boss you around, they embarrass you in public. They invite themselves over. They take advantage. You've done the best you can, but they need professional help. On top of all this, they love you to death and are convinced they're your best friend on the planet.

So why do you continue to be involved with these people? Why do you tolerate them? On the contrary, the real question is, What would you do without them? Without Friends You Love to Hate, there would be nothing to talk about with your other friends. Their problems and their irritating stunts provide a reliable source of conversation for everyone they know. What's more, Friends You Love to Hate make you feel good about yourself, since you are obviously in so much better shape than they are. No matter what these people do, you will never get rid of them. As much as they need you, you need them too.

At the other end of the spectrum are Hero Friends. These people are better than the rest of us, that's all there is to it. Their career is something you wanted to be when you grew up—painter, forest ranger, tireless doer of good. They have beautiful homes filled with special handmade things presented to them by villagers in the remote areas they have visited in their extensive travels. Yet they are modest. They never gossip. They are always helping others, especially those who have suffered a death in the family or an illness. You would think people like this would just make you sick, but somehow they don't.

A New Friend is a tonic unlike any other. Say you meet her at a party. In your bowling league. At a Japanese conversation class, perhaps. Wherever, whenever, there's that spark of recognition. The first time you talk, you can't believe how much you have in common. Suddenly, your life story is interesting again, your insights fresh, your opinion valued. Your various shortcomings are as yet completely invisible.

It's almost like falling in love.

꧁꧂

HOW IT FEELS TO BE OUT OF WORK*

Jan Halvorsen

Layoffs, unemployment and recession have always affected Walter Cronkite's tone of voice and the editorial page. And maybe they affected a neighborhood business or a friend's uncle. But these terms have always been just words, affecting someone else's world, like a passing ambulance. At least they were until a few weeks ago, when the ambulance came for me.

Even as I sat staring blankly at my supervisor, hearing, "I've got bad news: we're going to have to let you go," it all still seemed no more applicable to my daily life than a "60 Minutes" exposé. I kept waiting for the alternative–"but you can come back after a couple of months," or "you could take a salary cut, a different position," or even, "April fool." But none of these came. This was final. There was no mistake and no alternative.

You find yourself going back over it in your idle moments. There wasn't so much as a "Thank you" for the long nights working alone, the "Sure, no problem, I'll have it tomorrow," the "Let me know if I can help," the "I just went ahead and did it this weekend" and, especially, for the "You forgot to tell me it changed! Oh, that's all right, I'll just do it over. No big deal."

No big deal. How it all echoes through your evenings and awakens you in the morning. The mornings are probably the worst–waking up with a habitual jar, for the first two weeks, thinking, "I'm late!" Late for what? The dull ache in your lower stomach reminds you: late for nothing.

Again, you face the terms. "Loss of self-esteem and security, fear of the future, stress, depression." You wonder dully if eating a dozen chocolate-chip cookies, wearing a bathrobe until 4, combing your hair at 5, cleaning behind the stove (twice) and crying in an employment-agency parking lot qualify as symptoms of stress or maybe loss of self-esteem. Fighting with your spouse/boyfriend? Aha–tension in personal relationships.

The loss of a job is rejection, resulting in the same hurt feelings as if a friend had told you to "bug off." Only this "friend" filled up 40 to 60 (or more) hours of your week. Constant references to the staff as "family"

---

*Halvorsen, Jan. "How It Feels to be Out of Work." *Newsweek* (1975). Copyright *Newsweek* magazine. Reprinted by permission.

only accentuate the feeling of desertion and deception. You picture your-self going home to your parents or spouse and being informed, "Your ser-vices as our daughter/my wife are no longer required. Pick up your baby pictures as you leave."

Each new affirmation of unemployment renews the pain: the first trip to the employment agency, the first friend you tell, the first interview and, most dreaded of all, the first trip to the unemployment office.

Standing in line at the unemployment office makes you feel very much the same as you did the first time you ever flunked a class or a test—as if you had a big red "F" for "Failure" printed across your fore-head. I fantasize myself standing at the end of the line in a crisp and effi-cient blue suit, chin up, neat and straight as a corporate executive. As I move down the line I start to come unglued and a half hour later, when I finally reach the desk clerk, I am slouching and sallow in torn jeans, ten-nis shoes and a jacket from the Salvation Army, carrying my worldly be-longings in a shopping bag and unable to speak.

You do eventually become accustomed to being unemployed, in the way you might accept a bad limp. And you gradually quit beating yourself for not having been somehow indispensable—or for not having become an accountant. You tire of straining your memory for possible infractions. You recover some of the confidence that always told you how good you were at your job and accept what the supervisor said: "This doesn't reflect on your job performance; sales are down 30 per cent this month."

But each time you recover that hallowed self-esteem, you renew a fight to maintain it. Each time you go to a job interview and give them your best and they hire someone else, you go another round with yourself and your self-esteem. Your unemployment seems to drag on beyond all justification. You start to glimpse a stranger in your rearview mirror. The stranger suddenly looks like a bum. You look at her with clinical curios-ity. Hmmm. Obviously in the chronic stages. Definitely not employable.

We unemployed share a social stigma similar to that of the rape vic-tim. Whether consciously or subconsciously, much of the work-ethnic-driven public feels that you've somehow "asked for it," secretly wanted to lose your job and "flirted" with unemployment through your attitude—probably dressed in a way to invite it (left the vest unbuttoned on your three-piece suit).

SATISFACTION

But the worst of it isn't society's work-ethnic morality; it's your own, which you never knew you had. You find out how much self-satisfaction was gained from even the most simple work-related task: a well-worded letter, a well-handled phone call–even a clean file. Being useful to yourself isn't enough.

But then almost everyone has heard about the need to be a useful member of society. What you didn't know about was the loneliness. You've spent your life almost constantly surrounded by people, in classes, in dorms and at work. To suddenly find yourself with only your cat to talk to all day distorts your sense of reality. You begin to worry that flights of fancy might become one way.

But you always were, and still are, stronger than that. You maintain balance and perspective, mainly through resorting frequently to sarcasm and irreverence. Although something going wrong in any aspect of your life now seems to push you into temporary despair much more easily than before, you have some very important things to hang on to–people who care, your sense of humor, your talents, your cat and your hopes.

And beyond that, you've gained something–a little more knowledge and a lot more compassion. You've learned the value of the routine you scorned and the importance of the job you took for granted. But most of all, you've learned what a "7.6 per cent unemployment rate" really means.

❧

THE BLACK WRITER AND THE SOUTHERN EXPERIENCE*

Alice Walker

1 My mother tells of an incident that happened to her in the thirties during the Depression. She and my father lived in a small Georgia town and had half a dozen children. They were sharecroppers, and food, especially flour, was almost impossible to obtain. To get flour, which was distributed by the Red Cross, one had to submit vouchers signed by a local official. On the day my mother was to go into town for flour she received a large box of clothes from one of my aunts who was living in the North. The clothes were in good condition, though well worn, and my mother needed a dress, so she immediately put on one of those from the box and wore it into town. When she reached the distribution center and presented her voucher she was confronted by a white woman who looked her up and down with marked anger and envy.

2 "What'd you come up here for?" the woman asked.

3 "For some flour," said my mother, presenting her voucher.

4 "Humph," said the woman, looking at her more closely and with unconcealed fury. "Anybody dressed up as good as you don't need to come here *begging* for food."

5 "I ain't begging," said my mother; "the government is giving away flour to those that need it, and I need it. I wouldn't be here if I didn't. And these clothes I'm wearing was given to me." But the woman had already turned to the next person in line, saying over her shoulder to the white man who was behind the counter with her, "The *gall* of niggers coming in here dressed better than me!" This thought seemed to make her angrier still, and my mother, pulling three of her small children behind her and crying from humiliation, walked sadly back into the street.

6 "What did you and Daddy do for flour that winter?" I asked my mother.

7 "Well," she said, "Aunt Mandy Aikens lived down the road from us and she got plenty of flour. We had a good stand of corn so we had plenty

---

*Walker, Alice. "The Black Writer and the Southern Experience" from *In Search of our Mothers' Gardens: Womanist Prose,* copyright © 1983 by Alice Walker, reprinted by permission of Harcourt Brace & Company.

of meal. Aunt Mandy would swap me a bucket of flour for a bucket of meal. We got by all right."

8   Then she added thoughtfully, "And that old woman that turned me off so short got down so bad in the end that she was walking on *two* sticks." And I knew she was thinking, though she never said it: Here I am today, my eight children healthy and grown and three of them in college and me with hardly a sick day for years. Ain't Jesus wonderful?

9   In this small story is revealed the condition and strength of a people. Outcasts to be used and humiliated by the larger society, the Southern black sharecropper and poor farmer clung to his own kind and to a religion that had been given to pacify him as a slave but which he soon transformed into an antidote against bitterness. Depending on one another, because they had nothing and no one else, the sharecroppers often managed to come through "all right." And when I listen to my mother tell and retell this story I find that the white woman's vindictiveness is less important than Aunt Mandy's resourceful generosity or my mother's ready stand of corn. For their lives were not about that pitiful example of Southern womanhood, but about themselves.

10   What the black Southern writer inherits as a natural right is a sense of *community*. Something simple but surprisingly hard, especially these days, to come by. My mother, who is a walking history of our community, tells me that when each of her children was born the midwife accepted as payment such home-grown or homemade items as a pig, a quilt, jars of canned fruits and vegetables. But there was never any question that the midwife would come when she was needed, whatever the eventual payment for her services. I consider this each time I hear of a hospital that refuses to admit a woman in labor unless she can hand over a substantial sum of money, cash.

11   Nor am I nostalgic, as a French philosopher once wrote, for lost poverty. I am nostalgic for the solidarity and sharing a modest existence can sometimes bring. We knew, I suppose, that we were poor. Somebody knew; perhaps the landowner who grudgingly paid my father three hundred dollars a year for twelve months' labor. But we never considered ourselves to be poor, unless, of course, we were deliberately humiliated. And because we never believed we were poor, and therefore worthless, we could depend on one another without shame. And always there were the Burial Societies, the Sick-and-Shut-in Societies, that sprang up out of spontaneous need. And no one seemed terribly upset that black sharecroppers were ignored by white insurance companies. It went without saying, in my mother's day, that birth and death required assistance from the community, and that the magnitude of these events was lost on outsiders.

12   As a college student I came to reject the Christianity of my parents, and it took me years to realize that though they had been force-fed a white man's palliative, in the form of religion, they had made it into something at once simple and noble. True, even today, they can never successfully picture a God who is not white, and that is a major cruelty, but their lives testify to a greater comprehension of the teachings of Jesus than the lives of people who sincerely believe a God *must* have a color and that there can be such a phenomenon as a "white" church.

13   The richness of the black writer's experience in the South can be remarkable, though some people might not think so. Once, while in college, I told a white middle-aged Northerner that I hoped to be a poet. In the nicest possible language, which still made me as mad as I've ever been, he suggested that a "farmer's daughter" might not be the stuff of which poets are made. On one level, of course, he had a point. A shack with only a dozen or so books is an unlikely place to discover a young Keats. But it is narrow thinking, indeed, to believe that a Keats is the only kind of poet one would want to grow up to be. One wants to write poetry that is understood by one's people, not by the Queen of England. Of course, should she be able to profit by it too, so much the better, but since that is not likely, catering to her tastes would be a waste of time.

14   For the black Southern writer, coming straight out of the country, as Wright did—Natchez and Jackson are still not as citified as they like to think they are—there is the world of comparisons; between town and country, between the ugly crowding and griminess of the cities and the spacious cleanliness (which actually seems impossible to dirty) of the country. A country person finds the city confining, like a too tight dress. And always, in one's memory, there remain all the rituals of one's growing up: the warmth and vividness of Sunday worship (never mind that you never quite believed) in a little church hidden from the road, and houses set so far back into the woods that at night it is impossible for strangers to find them. The daily dramas that evolve in such a private world are pure gold. But this view of a strictly private and hidden existence, with its triumphs, failures, grotesqueries, is not nearly as valuable to the socially conscious black Southern writer as his double vision is. For not only is he in a position to see his own world, and its close community ("Homecomings" on First Sundays, barbecues to raise money to send to Africa—one of the smaller ironies—the simplicity and eerie calm of a black funeral, where the beloved one is buried way in the middle of a wood with nothing to mark the spot but perhaps a wooden cross already coming apart), but also he is capable of knowing, with remarkably

silent accuracy, the people who make up the larger world that surrounds and suppresses his own.

15   It is a credit to a writer like Ernest J. Gaines, a black writer who writes mainly about the people he grew up with in rural Louisiana, that he can write about whites and blacks exactly as he sees them and *knows* them, instead of writing of one group as a vast malignant lump and of the other as a conglomerate of perfect virtues.

16   In large measure, black Southern writers owe their clarity of vision to parents who refused to diminish themselves as human beings by succumbing to racism. Our parents seemed to know that an extreme negative emotion held against other human beings for reasons they do not control can be blinding. Blindness about other human beings, especially for a writer, is equivalent to death. Because of this blindness, which is, above all, racial, the works of many Southern writers have died. Much that we read today is fast expiring.

17   My own slight attachment to William Faulkner was rudely broken by realizing, after reading statements he made in *Faulkner in the University,* that he believed whites superior morally to blacks; that whites had a duty (which at their convenience they would assume) to "bring blacks along" politically, since blacks, in Faulkner's opinion, were "not ready" yet to function properly in a democratic society. He also thought that a black man's intelligence is directly related to the amount of white blood he has.

18   For the black person coming of age in the sixties, where Martin Luther King stands against the murderers of Goodman, Chaney, and Schwerner, there appears no basis for such assumptions. Nor was there any in Garvey's day, or in Du Bois's or in Douglass's or in Nat Turner's. Nor at any other period in our history, from the very founding of the country; for it was hardly incumbent upon slaves to be slaves and saints too. Unlike Tolstoy, Faulkner was not prepared to struggle to change the structure of the society he was born in. One might concede that in his fiction he did seek to examine the reasons for its decay, but unfortunately, as I have learned while trying to teach Faulkner to black students, it is not possible, from so short a range, to separate the man from his works.

19   One reads Faulkner knowing that his "colored" people had to come through "Mr. William's" back door, and one feels uneasy, and finally enraged that Faulkner did not burn the whole house down. When the provincial mind starts out *and continues* on a narrow and unprotesting course, "genius" itself must run on a track.

20   Flannery O'Connor at least had the conviction that "reality" is at best superficial and that the puzzle of humanity is less easy to solve than that of race. But Miss O'Connor was not so much of Georgia, as in

it. The majority of Southern writers have been too confined by prevailing social customs to probe deeply into mysteries that the Citizens Councils insist must never be revealed.

21   Perhaps my Northern brothers will not believe me when I say there is a great deal of positive material I can draw from my "underprivileged" background. But they have never lived, as I have, at the end of a long road in a house that was faced by the edge of the world on one side and nobody for miles on the other. They have never experienced the magnificent quiet of a summer day when the heat is intense and one is so very thirsty, as one moves across the dusty cotton fields, that one learns forever that water is the essence of all life. In the cities it cannot be so clear to one that he is a creature of the earth, feeling the soil between the toes, smelling the dust thrown up by the rain, loving the earth so much that one longs to taste it and sometimes does.

22   Nor do I intend to romanticize the Southern black country life. I can recall that I hated it, generally. The hard work in the fields, the shabby houses, the evil greedy men who worked my father to death and almost broke the courage of that strong woman, my mother. No, I am simply saying that Southern black writers, like most writers, have a heritage of love and hate, but that they also have enormous richness and beauty to draw from. And, having been placed, as Camus says, "halfway between misery and the sun," they, too, know that "though all is not well under the sun, history is not everything."

23   No one could wish for a more advantageous heritage than that bequeathed to the black writer in the South: a compassion for the earth, a trust in humanity beyond our knowledge of evil, and an abiding love of justice. We inherit a great responsibility as well, for we must give voice to centuries not only of silent bitterness and hate but also of neighborly kindness and sustaining love.

PART TWO

FINDING YOUR PLACE IN LANGUAGE COMMUNITIES

Sources for Essays 3 and 4: Conversation and Observation

C H A P T E R

8

HOW WE ARE SITUATED
IN LANGUAGE

❧ *Integrating Others' Voices with Your Own*

In Part One of this book, we examined the value of personal knowledge–your own history as a writer and the assumptions about writing that have emerged from it. As you recalled events from your writing history, looking at the details of your recollections, you were not only analyzing yourself as a writer, but creating an essay whose purpose grew, in part, from your analysis. At the same time you recalled your experiences with school writing and with writing for different instructors in different courses.

When you worked on Essay 1, we directed your attention to a single source of information–personal experience–and to two areas of writing– your history as a writer and the history of college writing. We asked you to view these topics in isolation. That is, you focused your attention only on *your* perspective and *your* recollections of a diverse set of occurrences and requirements collectively called "college writing."

Whatever subject you chose for Essay 2, you again focused primarily on your own recollections and perceptions. You may have included references to other people's lives in both of these essays and some of your ideas may have come from recalling others' words and stories; yet your own experience was the primary source of information, yours was the voice heard most directly in the essay, and in this way it seemed to represent you, alone. However, in actuality, your voice represents more than just you, an individual person.

Your voice, the stories you choose to tell, the words you select, the way you put words together, emerge from thousands of competing and contributing voices that surround you. All of us find ourselves, each day, in numerous situations where others' words shape our views of reality and the way we use language. Examples of this interplay of language are easy to identify. Here are two that might occur at a movie theater.

Imagine, first, that you are standing in line at the theater. While you are waiting, you overhear a woman in an adjoining line review the film you are about to see. "The acting was really bad," you hear her say, "and half the time, I couldn't even follow the story line. Oh, and the ending–it's really lame." No matter how determined you are to tune out her opinion and have your own, you cannot "unhear" what she said. In some way her comments may stay with you as you watch the film and form your own judgments. Each judgment you make about the film may be, on some level, a response to her words.

Now imagine that during the film, a central character played by a popular, well-known actor uses a phrase such as, "Go ahead, make my day;" or "Hasta la vista, baby"; or "Show me the money." Though your attention was initially on the scene in which the actor uttered the phrase, you may leave the theater taking the phrase with you, and you may find yourself using it in your own, everyday life, a life that probably differs greatly from that of the movie character.

These two examples suggest that even though the thoughts you have and the words you use have been selected by you, and in that sense are yours, they emerge from a whirlwind of language of which we are all a part. In the first example, your thinking about the movie, even the way you perceive the film, may be influenced by the language you encountered as you waited in line. In the second example, language from one context–in this case the way it is used in a film–becomes adapted to your own personal context. We encourage you, as you develop as a writer, to pause and listen to some of these voices around you. You will find yourself growing more conscious of the interconnectedness of language use, the ways in which our individual perspectives are influenced by and in turn influence others' thoughts and words.

Writing Log Entry 1

Hearing the Same Story from Another Perspective

Think of a recent conversation or argument or experience you had. Write down the details of what happened. Who said what? Where were the points of disagreement and agreement?

Once you have recorded all you can recall, ask someone who was involved in this same experience or conversation or argument to recollect its details. Without interrupting or prompting the speaker, take notes on his or her recollection. Reread your notes and compare them to what you first wrote. What similarities and differences do you see?

✾ *What Does It Mean to Be Situated in Language?*

As a writer your words and voice belong to you and represent your individuality, and yet they also exist separately from you as part of a vast, verbal whirlwind of words and language: the stories, exclamations, commands, questions, statements, etc., within which we all live. This profusion of words and language circles around us, we take in some of it, and it influences the way we name and perceive the world. At the same time, none of us is merely an observer and absorber of language; we are all participants who adapt and filter language through our own experiences and thought processes. To varying degrees, our interaction with language has an effect on those around us, on others' thinking and on the words they use.

Moreover, this whirlwind of language is complex. It is not as if there is a single, generic language for all situations. Instead, we encounter many different language situations, each with differing characteristics and conventions. While the same words may be used, they will take on different emphases or meanings depending on the context. What is appropriate in one set of circumstances might be wildly inappropriate in another. Imagine walking into the operating room of a hospital while a team of doctors and nurses is undertaking a complicated surgical procedure. The whirlwind of language around you would be quite distinct from, for instance, the language you might hear if you walked into a session of the state legislature, or the language environment you would be part of at a baseball game. Now, imagine the still different whirlwind of language you would hear at a religious service; contrast that with the language arena you enter in a cafeteria at your school.

What makes the language of each of these circumstances distinct is the specialized vocabulary it includes, the tone the speakers use, and the purposes for which people are speaking: the variables comprising the language situation. As a speaker entering each circumstance, you will feel varying degrees of comfort or unfamiliarity, informality or distance. Speakers can give conscious attention to how they want to fit themselves into a particular language circumstance. Finding ways to fit themselves into the conversation, they effectively situate themselves in the language being used.

Consider this contrast: Were you to join the verbal exchange in the operating room, you might be a bit tongue-tied and unsure about where to jump in, both because you are unfamiliar with the language and because a misuse of language could possibly result in a life-threatening error. But in the cafeteria you are likely to feel relatively at ease adding to the conversation. Because you are familiar with the words, their particular uses, and the topics most frequently discussed, you can add to the conversation at the expected moments in the expected, appropriate ways.

In each of these examples, the familiarity or confusion you feel would also affect the authority with which you speak, authority that you need to situate yourself successfully in the conversation. To gain this authority, yours is not the only critical action to be accounted for. There must be a psychological shift in the people with whom you are speaking. Rather than seeing you as an outsider, disconnected from the conversation, they must perceive you as a member of the conversation and, consequently, award you the right to speak and to be heard.

In most language situations, this shift in perception is subtle. At the state legislature, for example, you would be formally called upon to speak, but in most situations you merely sense you are a member of the conversation through others' gestures, word choice, and mode of response. It is the difference between talking to someone whose arms are folded across his chest, who looks off in the distance, impatiently tapping his foot; and to someone who is looking you in the eye, perhaps leaning toward you slightly, nodding to draw out your comments.

Writing Log Entry 2

Speaking as an Authority

For this entry, gather some information from a classmate on a subject about which your classmate is an authority. First, jot down subjects about which *you* have some expertise. You may be an expert on certain academic subjects, sports, hobbies; you may know about certain cities, countries, languages; you may have specific life experiences or interests about which you know a great deal. After you have compiled your list, choose one subject, or ask the person you are working with to help you choose one to tell about.

Make notes as your classmate speaks on his or her subject. Find out as much as you can about the subject. When you have both spoken, reread your notes and write up the information. What did you learn from your classmate? What did you learn about speaking as an authority?

❉ *Establishing the Authority to Be Heard*

In significant ways, as a speaker, you influence this awarding of the right to speak and be heard. You can affect others' perceptions by identifying your own particular contribution to the on-going conversation. That is, to enter into the conversation and be situated in its language, you have to locate a position from which to speak that you will find authentic and personally valuable and that, at the same time, will hold the attention of those listening. The more authentically you are able to speak, the more effectively you will be able to do this.

If you tried to participate in the operating room conversation as if you were a full-fledged member of the surgical team, or if you stood up in the legislature posing as a senator, you might even be removed from these environments. But if you were to speak to the surgeons from a position you really hold, that of someone who has a particular interest in the surgery underway, or if in the state legislature you were able to provide, from your perspective as a student, a commentary on the bill under discussion, you would be helping to establish your authority to speak by participating from a position you actually hold.

In other situations, sitting in the school cafeteria, for instance, you don't have to give conscious attention to getting authority to speak. Your speaking privilege is much easier to establish because you have the same status as others involved in the conversation: you are all students at the same university.

Yet, any language situation may be uncomfortable at first. Even the most confident among us is likely to feel awkward engaging in conversation with surgeons in the fictional operating room we have mentioned. No matter how sure you are of yourself and what you want to say, it takes remaining in a particular setting for a while, listening to the conversation, and trying out your own responses, to overcome any initial feelings of being a bit out of place at first.

As a college writer working on any subject, you will be examining what perspectives you can offer to give authority to your voice, your words. In this language situation, as in all others, you learn to situate yourself, appropriately and authentically, in relation to the language community you enter.

Writing Log Entry 3

An Unfamiliar or Difficult Language Situation

Make detailed notes on a story that someone else tells you about a moment in which he or she felt awkward or ill-at-ease speaking or engaging in conversation. To help you think of a story you might share, make a list of moments, from school or personal experiences, in which you found yourself in an unfamiliar or difficult language situation. Choose one of the moments, perhaps the one you recall most vividly, to relate to another member of your class.

As your classmate shares the memory, jot down the places, participants, emotions, and events as quickly as you can. If there is information that you missed, ask questions so that you can get the whole story. Once you have each told your stories, take some time to reread your notes; write out, in a more narrative fashion, the story you were told.

9

FAMILIAR CIRCLES
OF COMMUNICATION

❊ *Authority in Language Close to Home*

Without necessarily giving conscious attention to it, you have been negotiating among various language situations all your life. Just now, you are getting used to the nature of the academic world, but before you came to the university, you had accumulated years of experience in meeting–with ease–the expectations of a wide range of language situations.

You were probably not surprised by our claim in the last chapter that most people occasionally feel awkward or out of place in new language situations. By contrast, you might think about the language that is most familiar to you, the language you speak and hear in your home or among your close friends. In communication with people who are closest to you, there may be times when you are concerned about how to approach a particular subject, times when you debate, inside yourself, about when would be the best moment to ask a specific question, times when you feel unable to say what you want to say. However, even on these occasions, when you find yourself searching for the best approach to take, your choices are part of a well-established pattern which is familiar to you.

Among the most familiar language situations are those that occur in one's family. Here, your right to speak, to engage in conversation, to make statements, ask questions, and so on, and the authority with which you do so, is closely tied to your role in the family and the relationships you have with other family members. Part of this role is defined by your position in the family as a son, daughter, mother, father, husband, wife, partner, brother, sister, cousin, or any other such role or position that remains constant, affecting, in predictable ways, how people in the family converse. For example, a parent might be expected to be the dominant member of a conversation with a child; an elder sibling might have more authority than the younger.

At the same time, while you continue in your role, circumstances change as you grow older or new members may come into the family, to some degree shifting the conversational structure. The effect of family history, ethnic and religious traditions, regional style, and economic influences help define particular family and speaking positions. Roles for women, children, eldest siblings, parents of the husband, and other specific positions may affect what the authority structure will be. The degree of responsibility, respect, and authority that your role holds was established with your entrance into, or the formation of, your family, and it evolves as you age and mature and as your family evolves.

Writing Log Entry 4

Authority in Family Structures

Ask a friend or classmate to describe for you the hierarchy in his or her family. Who are the most dominant and least dominant members of the family, and how is the authority established and demonstrated in language situations? Ask him or her to illustrate this with a conversation that actually occurred among family members. Take detailed notes.

❧ *Characteristics of Language Close to Home*

The familiar language we have been describing is spoken in circles of communication that begin, for a child, in the family of which she or he is a part. As soon as children form friendships, they become part of other close-to-home language circles as well. Although we have used the family to illustrate this kind of language, speaking patterns and relationships among close friends are similarly well-established and affected by a shared history. The language conventions we use at home and with close friends and the relationships we have established with people close to us are grounded in a history that reaches back much further than our own, individual lives. It reaches back to the way our grandparents spoke to our parents and our great grandparents spoke to them. This history reaches beyond the homes in which we have lived, to the homes of generations of individuals in our family and the families of our friends. It reaches through all of these individuals into the cultures they inhabited. And so, in one sense the language any of us uses close to home is like that of many others' from similar cultures and generations. But in another sense, each familiar, home language is unique, having evolved from the coming together of specific individuals in specific situations.

Consequently, though we can understand the conversation of people outside our own, close communication circle, our understanding is to some degree limited by the fact that the language we hear is embedded in years and years of circumstances and events that we have not shared. Any language that is close to home includes a kind of code, words or phrases that have particular meaning to the members of this family, to groups of friends, or to those who share a common history.

These codes become even more complex when we consider the possible influence of different languages or dialects. When members of a family speak different languages, sometimes with different levels of proficiency, a home language can become a unique combination of the historically original language of that family and the second or third languages that have been brought into the family more recently. To a certain extent, every family's language is such a combination, since different family members bring home with them particular "dialects" or slang from the communities they frequent outside the family. When a young teenager turns to his grandmother and says, "Rad" in response to her question, "How was the school party?" a cross-dialect code is being created, one whose success relies on each speaker understanding the others' ways of speaking, ways that might not be immediately or completely understood by a visitor to the family.

In fact, codedness is what distinguishes close-to-home languages from the languages of wider communication we will discuss in Chapter 10. Some close-to-home language is rich in metaphor and color; speakers refer to a whole sequence of shared experience in a few words, describing specific behavior or reflecting on a past event in a kind of shorthand. Over time, they may have created names for certain foods, games, moods, places, events, that are now part of an everyday vocabulary. This language is highly audience-specific; you have to be part of the group to fully understand it.

Writing Log Entry 5

Identifying Code Language

List some of the phrases, words, names, or references you use in any of your close communication circles that you expect others, outside that circle, may not understand or, at least, might not understand in the same way you do. Once you have your list, exchange with someone in the class, each of you writing out what you imagine to be the definitions of one another's words and phrases. Once you have done this, tell one another what the "real" definitions are and where they came from.

❧ *Language of Communities*

Imagine that the circles of communication through which we all move weave a continuum from the most narrow, audience specific, such as the language you have been thinking about in the last **Writing Log** entry, toward language that is used for the widest, most general instances of communication. Between these two extremes is the language of communities. Just as families and friendships establish some distinctive ways of communicating, the various communities of which we are a part create other circles of relatively familiar language.

Communities may be demarcated by distinct, physical objects or by more abstract, intangible qualities. For example, you may define a community by the streets that frame a particular neighborhood or by the man-made or naturally-formed structures that indicate its perimeters. A larger geographic area may also form a community. Community may also be defined more fluidly by cultural, ethnic, religious, socioeconomic, or lifestyle identifications.

Needless to say, communities are much larger and more diverse than families. But, like home and family, communities have some degree of constancy, and to some extent it is the language of communities that helps assure their continuance, that distinguishes and defines them.

The language of communities is both a consistent, historically embedded language and a fluid, evolving one. It carries the consistency provided by years of shared history and accumulated events. But it also reflects the fluidity of change, of people coming and going, of interaction from outside the community. This familiar language, rich with the code words of the history of its members, is also made more generic by the influence of the outside world.

Think about some of the communities of which you are a part. Depending on your life experience, you might identify a neighborhood, geographic area, ethnic group, religious affiliation, or lifestyle, as part of a distinctive community. Like your connection to family, your community connection has a certain degree of consistency to it, and yet, your relation to it may change at different times in your life. Like a family, the community, itself, undergoes change and development over time and yet keeps many of its distinctive, defining qualities.

Writing Log Entry 6

Communities Connected to Your Classroom

Choose one community you would want to tell about to another classmate. Interview someone in class about his or her community and the roles and characteristics of language in that community. Since one role of language in all communities is to pass on and preserve the stories of that community, ask your classmate, in particular, to think about and tell you one or more of the stories of his or her community, historically true stories as well as community legends or stories one might remember from childhood. Make notes on what you are told and what you learn.

❊ *Establishing Authority to Speak in Communities*

When you communicate with family or close friends, there is little need to "decode" your highly coded, familiar language; at the same time, your authority to speak is usually well-established, closely aligned with roles held in the family and with the speakers' shared history. The language situation in communities is more complex because the audience is more diverse in background and experience. Therefore, the extent to which you establish the right to speak and to be heard will vary from situation to situation and audience to audience. You enter into these conversations with some authority; as a member of the community, you are on equal footing with others in that group. But beyond that initial entry, your speaking privilege depends also on your becoming situated, finding a position from which to speak that will serve both you and the listener. Because you share knowledge with other members of the community about what this membership is like, it may be relatively easy to find such a position. At the same time, the diverse membership of the community may frustrate you and complicate this process.

Authority structures in communities are also more complex than those of family or friends. While you are generally privileged to speak because of your membership in the community, in any particular situation you will have to reestablish a certain, specific authority. For example, in an evening conversation at the park with other people your age, friends you went to school with and have known for years, your authority has evolved over time. You are on equal par with the others—even if you have a customary role to play. But when you find yourself talking to your friends' parents at a neighborhood barbecue, there may be a shift. Your reason for speaking and the way in which you will be heard are quite different from what went on in the park among friends. Consequently, so is your word choice, your tone of voice, even your body posture.

Writing Log Entry 7

Recreating a Recollected Conversation

Recall some instances when you have run into members of your community with whom you are comfortable having conversation and other instances when you have run into people you recognize but with whom you speak only because you find yourself in a public setting next to them. Imagine yourself in both situations, and recreate a conversation that you had in each. Identify the setting, include the names of the speakers (if possible), and give as much dialogue as you can recreate—at least a page for each conversation. Because these conversations are recollected from memory, you are not expected to be recalling them word for word. Rather, recall what the gist or general sense of each conversation was and the character of the various members of the conversation; then let your own creativity combine with your memories to write the conversations.

✹ *Language Conventions in Careers and Hobbies*

Before completing our discussion of familiar language, we would like to consider one additional communication circle, language circles formed by individuals who share an intense hobby or a career. One establishes one's membership in the kinds of language circles we have been describing by being born into, physically moving into, or making some other kind of deep commitment to that group. These circles are more stable and probably more deeply part of one's internal language history than language circles formed on the basis of careers and hobbies. Those language circles with which one is most familiar do not depend upon outside learning or training to establish one's membership. One moves into a particular neighborhood, or is born or adopted into a certain family, or is part of a particular ethnic group. And yet, when groups of people share particular, learned interests, they also form a kind of community and develop certain coded ways of communicating. These kinds of circles fall between the familiar community language groups we have been describing and the more generic language of wider communication that we will introduce in the next chapter. Most jobs or intense hobbies require individuals to use at least some language that sounds unfamiliar to "outsiders." This could be the engineering talk of a garage mechanic or an aerospace designer, the horticultural talk of a weekend gardener or landscape architect, the "shop talk" of musicians and dedicated fans, computer specialists and amateur computer experts, or teachers of writing and first-year college students.

Writing Log Entry 8

Identifying Career and Hobby Language Conventions

Talk to someone about the conventional language of his or her career or hobby. Ask him or her to share with you some of the language and the way in which it is most likely to be used. Take notes on what you learn.

C H A P T E R

10

THE LANGUAGE OF WIDER COMMUNICATION

❋ *What Happens to Language When You Leave Familiar Surroundings*

Although the familiar languages of home and community seem to be defined by where they occur, they are sustained over time because of the relationships and shared experiences among the individuals who use them. For example, no matter where you meet your siblings or parents or spouse, you converse with people who are in your close communication circles in certain predictable ways using familiar kinds of slang, phrases, and intonations. Change of location is not likely to change these qualities in your speech patterns. Similarly, if you run into a neighbor or someone you know from a community connection when you are on an out-of-state vacation, you quickly fall into a familiar style of conversation. In fact, odds are good that you will even talk about events in the neighborhood or your community group as much as, or more than, you will talk about the place you are visiting.

Writing Log Entry 9

Taking Familiar Conversations Out of Familiar Locations

As a way of considering how powerful language relations are, write about one of the following.

Recall a time when you found yourself in conversation with a family member or close friend away from home or outside of your

(continued)

Writing Log Entry 9

(Continued)

usual surroundings. You may have been traveling or attending some event together or you may have coincidentally run into one another. For this **Writing Log** entry, recreate a portion of the conversation you had. As you write, especially if a lot of time has passed since the incident you are recalling, feel free to use your imagination to "create" the actual event based on your own familiarity with such conversations.

OR

If you have been to a reunion or have run into someone from your old neighborhood after having moved away, you may have experienced the discomfort of trying to engage in conversations about topics and in ways that are no longer familiar to you (the "What do you say?" syndrome). In your **Writing Log** entry, recollect one such conversation and recreate a portion of it in dialogue form.

❧ *Language of Wider Communication*

Naturally, each of us converses daily for purposes of business, information, education, even casual exchange with many people who are from neither our family nor our neighborhood, who are not part of any of our close communication circles. In these situations the most immediate concern is that communication is effective and efficient. When you find yourself at a stop light needing directions, and you roll down your window to ask the female passenger in the car next to you if she can help, you don't care or expect to hear where she went to high school or that she has twin brothers who play soccer. You want to know how to get to your destination, and you are hoping to get the information before the light changes. When you call the Electric Company because the power shut down as you were printing out an essay, you will be impatient if the person who answers your call speaks in unfamiliar phrases ("We are experiencing a temporary circuit breaker malfunction"). You just want to know how long it will be before you can finish printing out your essay and if you can do so before class starts.

In situations such as these, and the hundreds of others like them, you use and expect to hear what has been called the language of wider communication, a language that is general enough to allow individuals from an enormous variety of family situations, neighborhoods, and communities to speak intelligibly with one another. What is most distinctive about the language of wider communication, in fact, is that it is a dialect that attempts to sound not distinctive at all. That is to say, when people converse in situations requiring this kind of communication, most of the unique or distinguishing language features from home and community are set aside. Washed away from the language are qualities that, because of the necessity for shared experience or historical knowledge, could not be understood by a broad range of individuals, by people who do not know each other or share similar backgrounds.

❊ *Conventions of the Language of Wider Communication*

Along with the expectation that the language of wider communication will be somewhat less personal, more efficient, and more direct than are close-to-home languages, there is also the expectation that the words and phrases used will be in "standard" English. Indeed, the language of wider communication is sometimes referred to as "standard English" because it uses the standard, most widely accepted, conventions of English word usage, verb tense, pronoun reference, and agreement. Although slang words–the code words used with family and community–work their way into standard English, essentially, there is expected to be less use of slang and code words the farther one moves from close communication circles.

As a common language with standard conventions, the language of wider communication may appear to be neutral. In contrast, the use of anything else will seem to be non-neutral in that it will identify the speaker as a member of a particular ethnic, social, regional, or economic group. The use of the term "standard" to describe the language of wider communication, seems to imply that other ways of speaking, other dialects, are non-standard, that is, are a deviation from the origin or norm.

But contrary to what the term standard may imply, the language of wider communication in America is not the original language of the European settlers, and it is certainly not the language of the original inhabitants of America. English, itself, only became the dominant language because its speakers were more numerous than speakers of other languages coming into America and claiming the country as their own. The evolution of the language of wider communication is historically grounded in the social, political, and economic history of the United States.

Standard English conventions, rather than the conventions of other dialects of English, are used in the language of wider communication primarily because the standard conventions have traditionally been used by the middle and upper classes in America. These conventions have become dominant because of their use by those speakers who have had the greatest political impact on American life by virtue of education and economic position. Linguists explain that while American dialects may differ in the ways that verbs are formed, for example, they share the same capacity to allow speakers to express complex thought, discuss philosophy, conduct business, or convey emotion. Working class dialects and dialects of any one ethnic minority group did not become the standard dialect in America because they have not been connected positively to professional standing or economic power in this country, not because they could not achieve the same degree of commonality if any one of these dialects were to have become the "standard."

The language of wider communication, which like all dialects is always undergoing change, taking in new words and sometimes, though more rarely, modifying accepted usage, is considered the preferred dialect and has been selected as the common language of America, the one dialect in which all speakers who wish to obtain college degrees are expected to be fluent.

Writing Log Entry 10

Recreating the Language of Wider Communication

Listen carefully the next time you are somewhere where you are likely to hear the language of wider communication—at the library, the financial aid office, in a bank, in the writing center—any place where you can hear a conversation (in both an unobtrusive and appropriate manner) in which communication seems to require that both parties use what we have been calling the language of wider communication. In this entry, recreate that conversation in as much detail as you can.

✹ Code Switching: Related Risks and Biases

Speakers of various dialects learn to "code switch" as they move from one circle of communication to another. Code switching from the familiar language of family or community to the language of wider communication can be illustrated by thinking of the way a clerk in a small store in an isolated town might speak while handling a transaction and the way the bank manager of a large city's main office might speak. The clerk knows most of the people who come into the store; she speaks the particular dialect of that community and has many shared experiences with her customers. The language she uses reflects this shared history; she addresses people by name or with some familiar greeting appropriate in that community. You expect to "visit" with the clerk while you are completing your business and the language of your visit would include code words that people from outside the community might not understand.

Think now of the bank manager: Let us say she is the sister of the clerk we just described; she speaks fluently the language of the small town where she grew up yet also speaks in the language of wider communication while conducting business in her capacity as bank manager of the large city's main office. Here, "visiting" would be not only inappropriate but impossible given the lack of shared history of the people who frequent the bank. The manager's language sounds more neutral, probably less colorful than her sister's; it is language that anyone, from any part of the large city, could be expected to understand. And it is also the language they expect to hear.

Expecting to hear the language of wider communication in the bank main branch, customers would by surprised if the bank manager we imagined addressed them with: "Hiya sweetheart" or "Yo!" or if she asked them about their love life or told them about the feud between her sister and the owner of the bakery in her home town. The customers might find this conversation unusual or eccentric. They might draw some conclusions about the bank manager's personality, and they might consider her "gossip" to be distracting to the transactions they came in the bank to make. At the same time, it is likely there would be some customers who would enjoy the unusual conversations of the bank manager.

Interestingly, however, it is only if the bank manager's language lacked the conventions of standard English that conclusions might be drawn by some customers or co-workers about the manager's level of education. The lack of standard English conventions would be more likely to reflect negatively on the bank manager than her unexpected and possibly distracting conversation. Expectations about how language is structured in the course of wider communication are more powerful than expectations about its distinctive, regional, or historical qualities. A change in word order ("Please here sign.") or subject-verb agreement

("The money are now transferred.") may not prevent communication, but it will call negative attention to the speaker.

❧ *Expectations About Correctness*

If the most significant purpose of the language of wider communication is, indeed, to communicate, and if this purpose is not hindered by the way verbs are formed, then why do some people still hold such expectations? And, moreover, why are these expectations so powerful? One answer to these questions has to do with the way all languages evolve. As English, Spanish, Cambodian, Mandarin, and other languages evolved through centuries of use, they not only developed a vocabulary that has changed and expanded, they also developed a characteristic set of relationships among words, a syntax. Among English speakers, sentences are expected to have nouns and verbs; verbs are "declined" or changed according to when the action in the sentence occurred. But this is not the case in all languages. Some indicate tense by the context of the situation, leaving the verb itself unchanged. Some do not require separate verbs at all, since the nouns carry with them an implied action.

The fact that languages vary in their structure suggests that while the structures themselves may be arbitrary yet generally agreed-upon characteristics of a language, they are also highly distinctive and, consequently, become expected by users of that language. Over time, as we have mentioned, the most widely accepted language structures, those of wider communication, most often emerge from the language used by those groups that have the highest professional standing or the most economic influence.

Expecting the standard dialectal convention, a listener may respond to the use of another dialect with curiosity about the source of the varied structure, or he or she may react neutrally not even hearing the dialectal difference. Or reaction can also be more negative.

One may also react neutrally as one learns more about the nature of dialectal differences. As you are becoming aware during the course of reading this text, the language of wider communication is an historical and political reality, but it is not the only "correct" English. Each dialect is correct in terms of its own rules of grammar and usage. Because conventions are so tightly bound to the history of a language and, even more so, to the dominant group of users of a language, listeners expecting the language of wider communication may be offended by a "misuse" of these conventions, by hearing an overly familiar language expression or a usage that is correct in Black or Chicano dialects, for example, but that sounds like an "error" appearing in the language of wider communication. Such an "error" marks the user as an individual who has seemingly not accepted or assimilated the conventions set by the dominant group, that is, who has not switched codes in the expected way.

Doing this intentionally, the speaker may be purposely setting himself against the dominant group, dressing in a culturally identifying way and speaking in a manner most familiar to his or her community group. The individual then accentuates the difference and distance between him or herself and the listener. This could be done to demonstrate or recreate, for the listener, the alienation the speaker feels or to isolate and celebrate the speaker's identity. On the other hand, making such conventional "errors" unintentionally, the speaker may have unwittingly created bias against him or herself, as the listener makes this into an opportunity to assert authority.

Writing Log Entry 11

Sharing Memories About "Misused" Conventions

Make a list of some of the times in your life when you either intentionally or accidently misused the expected set of conventions when you were speaking. These could have been in formal settings with large audiences or intimate settings with small audiences.

For this **Writing Log** entry, share one of the stories you have listed with a classmate and take notes on your classmate's story. Encourage your classmate to give you as many details as he or she can about where this happened and the result of its occurrence for him or her or other people who were involved. Take notes on each other's stories.

❧ *Social Implications*

In writing the previous section of this chapter we have touched on some complex social issues connected to the use of the language of wider communication in America. As professors of Composition who have studied writing development and language use, we can see no particular advantage to having selected standard English conventions as those most appropriate for college writing. As we mentioned earlier, linguists have found no one dialect that more effectively allows for the full range of language expression than any other dialect. But we also see little indication that the conventions of other dialects are soon to be considered appropriate for most college writing.

In our experience, however, we have found that college students who are speakers of various dialects become proficient code switchers by giving attention to a relatively few conventions–those that we have been identifying in the editing chapters of each section of the text. This switching does require conscious attention and may make the process of preparing a final version of an essay more time-consuming than it might otherwise be, although our own experience as writers leads us to believe that editing is always time-consuming. Writers, unlike speakers, can take time to adjust the way they present their material. In order to focus readers' attention more closely on the content of the writing, we recommend that students work to standardize their editing conventions in the final versions of papers.

CHAPTER

11

DISCOVERING AND CREATING YOUR DRAFT

Essay 3

Select some issue or concern about language that you would like to reflect on more extensively from your **Writing Log** notes on conversations with and observations of other people. Once you have made your selection, use the **Perspectives and Focusing** activities to analyze and interpret the notes and to determine the explicit purpose for your essay.

The notes in your **Logs** cover a variety of concerns: how individuals have been affected by language or have changed their language for different people and settings; how others have or have not been successful establishing authority in various language settings; the impact of conflicting expectations about the way words and conventions are used when individuals move from their close to home communication circles to school or business or a profession; the "code words" or conventions that are used in different situations and what their effect is on different speakers, and so forth. Ultimately, in your essay, the details of what you have heard and observed will provide you with a means of supporting and developing a particular point or points about the way one or more individuals use and/or are affected by language.

WRITING ESSAY 3

Think of the conversations and observations from which this essay (and the next) will emerge as *field research,* information you gather, as a writer/researcher, from direct interaction and contact with other people. It is by closely observing individuals or systematically interviewing them that many anthropologists, psychologists, sociologists, and other social scientists begin their own research. Carefully analyzing their notes, interpreting patterns of response or behavior, these researchers develop theories about particular individuals or about human behavior in general. Frequently, they will return to the field to add to their existing bank of information, seeking additional support for their theory. Similarly, though you have already conducted a great deal of field research in the course of completing the **Writing Log** entries, you will likely want to go out and collect more information once you have determined the explicit purpose for your essay and have begun to develop your essay.

Indeed, there is another kind of conversation that we did not include in the **Writing Log** entries that you may want to take advantage of–conversation that occurs through the Internet. Although most college students have access to a computer or word processor at school or at home, we could not presume that everyone using *Shoptalk* would have access to on-line capabilities. If you do have access to the Internet you can talk to other people on-line by sending and receiving e-mail messages, by logging on to a chatroom conversation, by subscribing to various newsgroups, listservers, and so on. Some of this conversation can be a rich source of information for your field research.

DISCOVERING AND CREATING YOUR ESSAY

In the course of writing and gathering information so far and of reading, discussing, and thinking, you may have already come across questions and observations that you would like to analyze and interpret more closely. In order to help you draft Essay 3, once again we ask you to complete two kinds of activities for generating and focusing your ideas: **Taking on Different Perspectives** and **Focusing Your Direction.** Using freewriting, focused freewriting, and rereading, you can reconsider what you have already written, looking for connections, surprising perspectives, sets of belief or opinion, or other points from which the subject and purpose of your essay might emerge. Reviewing your **Writing Log** entries, listening carefully to what they say to you, and identifying how they may connect with one another should help you find your own emerging essay. Just as your first two essays were based on your recollections of experience but were not simply a retelling of those experiences, the essays in this section of the book are based on what other people have said, but are not simply a recording of those words. Your challenge is to draw some conclusions from the information you gather, to locate in your data what it is you have to say about the information, and what this material seems to mean or suggest.

We have included **Professional Demonstration** essays at the end of this chapter to illustrate the wide variety of ways that writers' ideas and purposes can emerge from the observations they make and the conversations they hear related to language use. We have also included **Student Demonstrations** throughout the next part of this chapter. These demonstrations are not models whose structure you will follow, but examples of ways to find solutions to writing problems, examples of how some writers dealt with the same kinds of choices you face now in beginning Essay 3.

As you work your way through to the end of this chapter you will be generating a first exploratory draft and then a second draft that is more focused, that uses observation and conversation as a way of expressing an explicit purpose. Once the second draft is completed and your purpose is clear, we then ask you to reevaluate your material and to collect more information if it is needed. Although you may find additional support for the points you wish to make in your own experience or in information from written texts, information gathered from conversation and observation will be the primary source for this essay.

TAKING ON DIFFERENT PERSPECTIVES
PERSPECTIVES: *Questions and Connections*

Reread the **Writing Log** entries you have done for this part of the book. Jot down some ways you can make connections among the various entries. For example, you might consider the following kinds of questions: What do your log entries seem to illustrate about how individuals acquire the "privilege" or authority to speak in different situations? What do they suggest about how the conventions of language seem to shift across situations? Do any of the ways in which language is used or authority is awarded seem to compete with one another? Looking at those **Writing Log** entries in which you exchanged stories or information with a peer, did you find that your experiences were similar or not? What conclusions can you draw from these observations? What is there in any of the individual entries that seems particularly intriguing to you? Are there some entries about which you have more to say? You may be able to make many other connections that are not referred to in these questions.

Student Demonstration

PERSPECTIVES: *Questions and Connections*

Example 1

1. When speaking to older people Christie tends to speak formally, cut down on use of slang or code words.

2. When speaking to friends, my own friends tend to use slang and short unelaborated sentences.

3. When I listened to people who knew more about a particular subject than I, they would dominate the conversation.

4. In exchanging stories with classmates, I found that their stories were similar to mine. For example, the authority in their household was their father/older siblings. This shows how people can only reach an authoritative status because of gained knowledge over periods of time and because of their age. Older people seem to always dominate conversations.

5. In **Writing Log 11,** I wrote about different language/dialects among different races and cultures and how they are sometimes not easily comprehended by other different groups. These differences interest me.

Example 2

At Longs Drugs, a particular speech is required when talking to customers and fellow employees. I always expect to hear formal speech that is respectful, polite, and caring. The idea is to make it so the customers want to come back. We use "Sir" and "Ma'am" and always start with "How are you doing today" and end with "Thank you for shopping with us." The speech is always courteous. Management always has the most authority to speak amongst employees, and we try to allow the customers more authority in shopping situations because they pay our paychecks! You would never expect four-letter words when an employee addresses anyone. Any type of speech that is really not job-related or a pleasant conversation is considered inappropriate. Pretty much everyone can be included in the conversations that are carried on at work.

PERSPECTIVES: *Conflicting Points of View*

One way to find the observation or question you are interested in developing for your essay is to see the abstract "topic" of language in very real, concrete examples and to use these examples as a means of finding unexpected angles, contradictions, and controversies. Included in the **Writing Log** entries you have just completed in Part Two are some specific comments about changes that occur as one moves from the language of home and family to that of the neighborhood and, finally, to that of wider communication. Each of these communication circles has its own vocabulary and set of formal, structural features. For this freewriting exploration, imagine how this concept might look in real life experience. For example, what might happen when someone who is familiar and comfortable with some disciplinary conventions within the university, travels to his high school reunion–when the famous biology or economics professor goes back to his small, rural home town? Or what conversation would you expect to hear when the elderly woman who has lived in a city neighborhood for twenty-five years meets her new neighbors–19 year-old college students who are renting the house next door for the summer? How might an individual respond to a social or business situation in which the traditional structures of power and authority that apply to his or her family are turned upside down–for example, when the young, female office manager supervises an older male employee? Write a dialogue (of at least one page) that plays out one of these three scenarios or another one that you create yourself. In creating your own scenario, remember that the idea is to dramatize a particular conflict arising because of the way language works in various settings.

PERSPECTIVES: *Metaphoric Thinking*

One way to explore an object or concept is by making a comparison between it and something else that is equally or more familiar to you. Reread the freewriting you have done so far and identify a concept or object that appears in or is suggested by the writing. Make three comparisons between the original concept or object and something else that, somehow, it reminds you of (talking to my boss is like . . . ; my friend's story about her family is like . . . ; the language of politics is like . . . , etc.). Then, explain each comparison, freewriting for a few minutes about how the comparison works, looking for what the comparison shows you about the concept or object that you might not have otherwise noticed.

Student Demonstration
PERSPECTIVES: *Metaphoric Thinking*
Example 1

Correcting a student's work for them is like giving a brand new driver an expensive sports car.

When teachers or tutors correct a student's work, obviously it's going to make the paper get better. It's much the same as having a new driver drive a sports car. The driver knows how to drive the car as much as the writer knows how to put the changes down on the paper. However, a new driver will not know how to really use a sports car to its true ability just as the writing will not be able to show the reasoning behind the corrections.

FOCUSING YOUR DIRECTION
FOCUSING: *Questions and Connections*

What connections can you make, what ideas do you see emerging from the **Perspectives** activities? Write three or four sentences about the connections that you see for yourself among the **Perspectives** activities. At this point, what can you say about your subject? What would you like to know more about? You might also put these thoughts into the form of a question to which you would like to find an answer.

Student Demonstration
FOCUSING: *Questions and Connections*
Example 1

Many people have speech impediments. What does that mean, though? Does an impediment reflect something about a person? Since it isn't the conventional way to speak, does that make it wrong? What gives somebody the right to decide if another person has an impediment? Why do people want to "fix" these impediments? Can a person with a speech impediment live a life and be just as happy and successful as a person who does not?

FOCUSING: *Writing More*

Use the statement or question that you wrote above as a focus from which to begin this freewriting. Push yourself to write two or three pages. The only parameters are those set by the sentences you have already written.

FOCUSING: *Rereading and Writing Again*

Reread the pages you have written; while doing so, underline all of the sentences or sections of your writing that jump out at you, the ones that catch your eye and stay with you. Find a sentence or two that raise some questions for you or that you might want to reflect on further, or something that you feel is worth telling others. Take three or four of these as a place to begin your focus, and freewrite further.

FOCUSING: *Rereading, Reseeing, and Rewriting*

Together, all of the writing you have done so far makes-up the exploratory draft for Essay 3. Like the exploratory writing you did for the first two essays, this draft was initially somewhat random and disconnected. But the more you wrote, crossed out ideas, added and developed ideas, the more focused and full of direction it became.

Reread all of the pages you have written in these activities, paying particular attention to the focused freewriting at the end. Ask yourself what explicit purpose for writing emerges from this first draft. What is it that you are writing about and to what end?

With this subject and purpose in mind, and with all of the writing you have done so far at hand, write a second draft.

EVALUATING YOUR INFORMATION AND GATHERING MORE

At this point, in order to provide adequate and convincing support for your purpose, take time to evaluate the information you have included in your second draft and decide whether you need to collect additional or more persuasive references and illustrations.

Once you have determined and focused the purpose for your essay, you may see that not all conversations and observations are of equal value or allow you to write with the same authority. For example, an argument about the connection between junior high slang and contemporary rap music will be more convincing to the reader if it includes actual examples of slang you overheard on a junior high playground than it would if you were merely to ask your 12 year-old sister what slang she uses. Or if you intend to explain the use of coded language in a particular profession, you would not be able to write a very convincing illustration had you never spoken with anyone who actually practiced this profession.

Another consideration when you evaluate your information is the authority of any individual source. If, for instance, you enter a general chatroom on the Internet to ask what the other participants think of bilingual education, the information you gather from the resulting conversations would be extremely limited in value by the fact that the "speakers" have no verifiable knowledge or experience with the subject. Furthermore, the speakers are anonymous and aren't in any way accountable for what they say. However, were you to join a newsgroup or listserve designed for elementary school teachers, the views of the "speakers," who identify themselves by name and school affiliation, would carry considerable authority.

Once you have evaluated the information included in your draft and determined what more you need, ask yourself what additional field research you could do. How might you collect this information and from whom? Are there questions that occur to you now that you didn't think of when you were first gathering information? Is there a place you need to visit again? Are there additional people you need to speak with? Keep in mind that as you draft and revise you may have to pause at other points, as well, to collect whatever seems to be missing.

Student Demonstration

REFLECTIVE ANALYSIS OF INFORMATION GATHERED FROM OTHERS

Example 1

> Together, both of these concerns raise two more, should Ebonics be treated like a separate or foreign language and should teachers be "trained" in the use of Ebonics? Recently, I spoke with Susanna Briggs, a former English teacher at California High School, part of the Los Angeles School District. Because of her background, I wanted to know her professional views on whether Ebonics should be taught as a separate language and whether this required that we train educators who teach a substantial number of African-American students to become familiar with Ebonics.
>
> Ms. Briggs explained that she does not consider Ebonics as being a separate language. She sees it as a variation of what is called English within English. African-Americans have put their mark on the language, but the language

is essentially English and should not be viewed as a separate language.

While it would seem that her argument might suggest that teachers don't need any special training, Ms. Briggs does see that Ebonics is different enough from standard English and important enough to students to mean that teachers need special training. She believes that teachers should be aware of Ebonics if they want to successfully reach their students. It is crucial in a multi-ethnic, complex environment that teachers know as much as they can about the backgrounds of their students, which includes aspects of what they call their "language."

Example 2

Dean, who is also an English major at CU, does not use the language of wider communication. His language consists of personalized phrases and words that are not clearly comprehensible by people outside of his primary relationships. He does not have as much success communicating as Sean does. Knowing that Dean had seen a new movie, his friend asked, "How was the movie last night?"

Dean replied, "It was cool. I mean, the movie was O.K. but my date was actin' like a buster.

"What do you mean she was actin like a buster?" Dean's friend inquired.

"Well, basically, I mean she was whack," explained Dean.

"What do you man by she was whack?" his friend probed.

"What I mean is that my date was conceited and expected me to pay for everything," said Dean.

What Dean had originally said to his acquaintance was not clearly communicated since Dean used slang rather than the language of wider communication. It made it difficult for his friend to understand him. By choosing not to use the language of wider communication, Dean demonstrated his lack of interest in his friend's understanding and his unwillingness to expand or adjust his language for different people and situations.

❧ *Professional Demonstration Essays*
SOME QUESTIONS FOR CONSIDERATION

The following essays demonstrate several ways that writers have used information they gathered about words, conventions, and language use from talking with others, listening to TV and radio, and general observations. The purpose of each essay is different–to make arguments, offer personal analysis, reveal and explain patterns. But what these essays share is that each one relies on stories, conversations, and observations that the writer has collected over time and from a variety of individuals. While several of the essays also include the writers' own personal experiences, these are not their primary sources of support for what they are saying.

As you explore the ideas you have already written about and brainstorm some new ones, you might refer to these essays to see the range of options available to you when you write from gathered information and to examine how writers integrate this information into their essays, using it to illustrate and support the purpose for which they are writing.

Use the following questions to help you study each demonstration essay in more detail:

1. In a sentence or two, how would you summarize the explicit purpose of each essay? Imagine you were to ask the writer what the essay was about and then ask, "So what?" How might he or she answer?

2. How do the writers make their points explicit? What are the sentences or parts of the essay that make these points available to the reader?

3. How do the writers use observations and conversations to support or illustrate the purpose of their essays? How is this information integrated into the text and used as a source of authority?

SHE'S YOUR BASIC L.O.L. IN N.A.D.*

Perri Klass

1   "Mrs. Tolstoy is your basic L.O.L. in N.A.D., admitted for a soft rule-out M.I.," the intern announces. I scribble that on my patient list. In other words Mrs. Tolstoy is a Little Old Lady in No Apparent Distress who is in the hospital to make sure she hasn't had a heart attack (rule out a myocardial infraction). And we think it's unlikely that she has had a heart attack (a *soft* rule-out).

2   If I learned nothing else during my first three months of working in the hospital as a medical student, I learned endless jargon and abbreviations. I started out in a state of primeval innocence, in which I didn't even know that "s̄ C.P., S.O.B., N/V" meant "without chest pain, shortness of breath, or nausea and vomiting." By the end I took the abbreviations so for granted that I would complain to my mother the English Professor, "And can you believe I had to put down *three* NG tubes last night?"

3   "You'll have to tell me what an NG tube is if you want me to sympathize properly," my mother said. NG, nasogastric–isn't it obvious?

4   I picked up not only the specific expressions but also the patterns of speech and the grammatical conventions; for example, you never say that a patient's blood pressure fell or that his cardiac enzymes rose. Instead, the patient is always the subject of the verb: "He dropped his pressure." "He bumped his enzymes." This sort of construction probably reflects that profound irritation of the intern when the nurses come in the middle of the night to say that Mr. Dickinson has disturbingly low pressure. "Oh, he's gonna hurt me bad tonight," the intern may say, inevitably angry at Mr. Dickinson for dropping his pressure and creating a problem.

5   When chemotherapy fails to cure Mrs. Bacon's cancer, what we say is, "Mrs. Bacon failed chemotherapy."

6   "Well, we've already had one hit today, and we're up next, but at least we've got mostly stable players on our team." This means that our team (group of doctors and medical students) has already gotten one

---

*Klass, Perri. "She's Your Basic L.O.L. in N.A.D." Reprinted by permission of The Putnam Publishing Group from *A Not Entirely Benign Procedure* by Perri Klass. Copyright © 1987 by Perri Klass.

new admission today, and it is our turn again, so we'll get whoever is next admitted in emergency, but at least most of the patients we already have are fairly stable, that is, unlikely to drop their pressures or in any other way get suddenly sicker and hurt us bad. Baseball metaphor is pervasive: A no-hitter is a night without any new admissions. A player is always a patient—a nitrate player is a patient on nitrates, a unit player is a patient in the intensive-care unit and so on, until you reach the terminal player.

7   It is interesting to consider what it means to be winning, or doing well, in this perennial baseball game. When the intern hangs up the phone and announces, "I got a hit," that is not cause for congratulations. The team is not scoring points; rather, it is getting hit, being bombarded with new patients. The object of the game from the point of view of the doctors, considering the players for whom they are already responsible, is to get as few new hits as possible.

8   These special languages contribute to a sense of closeness and professional spirit among people who are under a great deal of stress. As a medical student, it was exciting for me to discover that I'd finally cracked the code, that I could understand what doctors said and wrote and could use the same formulations myself. Some people seem to become enamored of the jargon for its own sake, perhaps because they are so deeply thrilled with the idea of medicine, with the idea of themselves as doctors.

9   I knew a medical student who was referred to by the interns on the team as Mr. Eponym because he was so infatuated with eponymous terminology, the more obscure the better. He never said "capillary pulsations" if he could say "Quincke's pulses." He would lovingly tell over the multinamed syndromes—Wolff-Parkinson-White, Lown-Ganong-Levine, Henoch-Schonlein—until the temptation to suggest Schleswig-Holstein or Stevenson-Kefauver or Baskin-Robbins became irresistible to his less reverent colleagues.

10   And there is the jargon that you don't ever want to hear yourself using. You know that your training is changing you, but there are certain changes you think would be going a little too far.

11   The resident was describing a man with devastating terminal pancreatic cancer. "Basically he's C.T.D.," the resident concluded. I reminded myself that I had resolved not to be shy about asking when I didn't understand things. "C.D.T.?" I asked timidly.

12   The resident smirked at me. "Circling The Drain."

13   The images are vivid and terrible. "What happened to Mrs. Melville?"

14   "Oh, she boxed last night." To box is to die, of course.

15   Then there are the more pompous locations that can make the beginning medical student nervous about the effects of medical training. A friend of mine was told by his resident, "A pregnant woman with sickle-cell represents a failure of genetic counseling."

16   Mr. Eponym, who tried hard to talk like the doctors, once explained to me, "An infant is basically a brainstem preparation." A brainstem preparation, as used in neurological research, is an animal whose higher brain functions have been destroyed so that only the most primitive reflexes remain, like the sucking reflex, the startle reflex, and the rooting reflex.

17   The more extreme forms aside, one most important function of medical jargon is to help doctors maintain some distance from their patients. By reformulating a patient's pain and problems into a language that the patient doesn't even speak, I suppose we are in some sense taking those pains and problems under our jurisdiction and also reducing their emotional impact. This linguistic separation between doctors and patients allow conversations to go on at the bedside that are unintelligible to the patient. "Naturally, we're worried about adeno-C.A.," the intern can say to the medical student, and lung cancer need never be mentioned.

18   I learned a new language this past summer. At times it thrills me to hear myself using it. It enables me to understand my colleagues, to communicate effectively in the hospital. Yet I am uncomfortably aware that I will never again notice the peculiarities and even atrocities of medical language as keenly as I did this summer. There may be specific expressions I manage to avoid, but even as I remark them, promising myself I will never use them, I find that this language is becoming my professional speech. It no longer sounds strange in my ears—or coming from my mouth. And I am afraid that as with any new language, to use it properly you must absorb not only the vocabulary but also the structure, the logic, the attitudes. At first you may notice these new alien assumptions every time you put together a sentence, but with time and increased fluency you stop being aware of them at all. And as you lose that awareness, for better or for worse, you move closer and closer to being a doctor instead of just talking like one.

࿔࿔࿔

LOCKER ROOM TALK*

Stephen Dunn

Having been athletic most of my life, I've spent a fair amount of time in locker rooms and have overhead my share of "locker room talk." For reasons I couldn't understand for many years, I rarely participated in it and certainly never felt smug or superior about my lack of participation. In fact, I felt quite the opposite; I thought something was wrong with me. As a teenager and well into my twenties I'd hear someone recount his latest real or wishful conquest, there'd be a kind of general congratulatory laughter, tacit envy, but what I remember feeling most was wonderment and then embarrassment.

There was of course little or no public information about sex when I was growing up in the forties and fifties. The first time I heard someone talk about having sex was in the school yard (the locker room without walls) when I was twelve or thirteen. Frankie Salvo, a big boy of sixteen. Frankie made it sound dirty, something great you do with a bad girl. It was my first real experience with pornography and it was thrilling, a little terrifying too. My mind conjured its pictures. Wonderment. Not wonderful.

Some years later, after experience, wonderment gave way to embarrassment. I wasn't sure for whom I was embarrassed, the girl spoken about, the story teller, or myself. Nevertheless, I understood the need to tell. I, too, wanted to tell my good friend, Alan, but for some reason I never told him very much. In retrospect, it was my first test with what Robert Frost calls knowing "the delicacy of when to stop short," a delicacy I took no pride in. I felt excessively private, cut off.

I began thinking about all of this recently because in the locker room at college a young man was telling his friend—loud enough for all of us to hear—what he did to this particular young woman the night before, and what she did to him. It was clear how important it was for him to impress his friend, far more important than the intimacy itself, as if the sexual act weren't complete until he had completed it among other men.

---

*Dunn, Stephen. "Locker Room Talk." From *In Short: A Collection of Brief Creative Nonfiction* eds. Judith Kitchen and Mary Jones. Copyright Stephen Dunn. Reprinted with author's permission.

This time I knew something about the nature of my embarrassment. It wasn't just that he had cheapened himself in the telling, but like all things which embarrass us it had struck some part of me that was complicitous, to a degree guilty, the kind of guilt you feel every time there's a discrepancy between what you know you're supposed to feel (correct feelings) and what in fact you've thought of, if not done. But more than that, I was embarrassed by the young man's assumption–culturally correct for the most part–that we other men in the locker room were his natural audience. There were five or six of us, and we certainly didn't boo or hiss. Those of us who were silent (all of us except his friend) had given our quiet sanctions.

What did it all mean? That men, more often than not, in a very fundamental way prefer other men? Or was it all about power, an old story, success with women as a kind of badge, an accoutrement of power? Was the young man saying to the rest of us, "I'm powerful"? I thought so for a while, but then I thought that he seemed to be saying something different. He was saying out loud to himself and to the rest of us that he hadn't succumbed to the greatest loss of power, yielding to the attractiveness and power of women, which could mean admitting he felt something or, at the furthest extreme, had fallen in love.

Some Samson, to the knight in Keats' poem "La Belle Dame Sans Merci," to countless examples in world literature, the warning is clear: women take away your power. To fall in love with one is to be distracted from the world of accomplishment and acquisitiveness. But to have sex and then to talk about it publicly is a kind of final protection, the ultimate prophylactic against the dangers of feeling.

"Love means always having to say you're sorry," a friend once said to me. The job had its truth, and it implied–among other things–a mature love, a presumption of mutual respect and equality. On some level the young man in the locker room sensed and feared such a relationship. He had ventured into the dark and strange world of women and had come out unscathed, literally untouched. He was back with us, in the locker room which was the country he understood and lived in, with immunity. He thought we'd be happy for him.

Literary Metaphors and Other Linguistic Innovations in Computer Language*

Kelvin Don Nilsen and Alleen Pace Nilsen

An important linguistic principle is that when speakers meet new concepts that they don't have words for, they are not likely to create new sets of sounds to arbitrarily attach to the new ideas; instead they will adapt old words to new concepts. Over the last three decades, we've seen this principle illustrated by people working with computers.

These people form a distinctive sub-culture which has developed its own language. We don't mean the language or "codes" that computer programmers use to communicate with their machines but instead the very human kind of language that people use to talk with each other about computers. While this language is based on English sound patterns and grammar and is built from English words (often with adapted spelling, capitalization, and spacing), the end result is nevertheless quite different from mainstream English. As an exploration of how a sub-culture goes about developing its own language, we have gathered examples of names, concepts, and allusions that have been adapted from literature and given new meanings in relation to computers.

Just as speakers who study a foreign language sometimes gain insights about their own language, an examination of aspects of language change brought about by computers will also provide insights. First, both teachers and students will increase their understanding of "computer language," and second, they will come to a greater understanding of how languages change in relation to changing needs.

WHO CREATES "COMPUTER TALK"?

The creators of "computer talk" come from two different camps. On one end are the *hackers* (see **Notes**), those individuals who spend inordinate amounts of time at computer terminals as they devise software, create challenges for themselves and their machines, and communicate with

---

each other via electronic or *e-mail*. In the other camp are those the hackers call the *suits* or *marketroids*. These are the company managers and the sales people who create product names and manage the advertising campaigns. In between is a much larger group of people who use computers as a tool for their daily work but whose primary interest is not in the computer itself as much as in how it can help them accomplish their other goals. Hackers call the most computer-knowledgeable of these people *techies*, while they refer to those who barely get by as *lusers*–a pun on user and loser. Although some interesting product names have been created for both hardware and software, we are looking here at the more creative language bubbling up from computer hackers, some of which makes its way into techie language or even into mainstream English.

While hackers are connected electronically so that they exchange written messages almost instantaneously–either between individuals or with all members of a like-minded group–they are basically strangers to each other in that their messages lack the benefits of eye contact and voice intonation. This means that when a hacker relies on a literary reference, the communication will fail unless the receivers of the message are already familiar with the piece being cited and unless the image being invoked is clearly memorable.

LITERARY ORIGINS AND REFERENCES

For English teachers, an important point of interest is which literature satisfies these requirements for this cultural subset. Although hackers say that women are welcome and respected members of the community (in faceless and sometimes nameless communication, who's to know?), the literature that has become part of their vocabulary is what used to be labeled as "boys' books." We found no references to Shakespeare or to romances, but lots of references to science fiction and fantasy. *Heavy wizardry* is a term used to talk about the integration and maintenance of components within large, complicated, poorly documented software systems; while *deep magic*, a term borrowed from C. S. Lewis' Narnia books, refers to the implementation of software that is based on difficult-to-understand mathematical principles.

Lovecraft, Orwell, Tolkien

The Internet is respectfully, or fearfully, spoken of as the *Shub-Internet* a reference to H. P. Lovecraft's horror fiction and his evil *Shub-Niggurath*, the Black Goat with a Thousand Young. The definition in *The Jargon File* (see **Notes**) clarifies this harsh personification as:

Beast of a Thousand Processes, Eater of Characters, Avatar of Line Noise, and Imp of Call Waiting; the hideous multi-tendriled entity formed of all the manifold connections of the net . . . its purpose is malign and evil, and is the cause of all networks slowdown.

A slightly less malevolent reference is to *code police* as a comparison to the *thought police* in George Orwell's *1984*. Code police take upon themselves the responsibility of enforcing idealized styles and standards for programming language codes. The term is generally used pejoratively, and the feeling among the hacker community is that those who are most likely to assume this role are outsiders (management, ivy-tower academics) who rarely participate in the practice of software development. A closely related term is *net police*, which describes members of the network community who assume the role of enforcing protocol and etiquette standards. In public e-mail and electronic bulletin board forums, the net police shame anyone who violates the established rules.

Archaic operating systems that print only uppercase letters are called *Great Runes*, a usage probably influenced by the writings of J. R. R. Tolkien, who has contributed more words to hacker language than has any other author. Hackers talk of the pre-1980s as their *elder days*, while they use *Hobbit* to describe the high-order bit of a byte (see **Notes**). An infamous 1988 bugging of the Internet was called *The Great Worm*, named after Scatha and Glaurung, Tolkien's powerful and highly feared Middle Earth dragons. Printers, and especially the people who use printers to provide unnecessary paper copies, are called *Tree-killers* based on what Treebeard the Ent called the Orcs. *Elvish*, the name of the fictional language that Tolkien created in *The Lord of the Rings*, was first used to refer to a particularly elegant style of printing, but is now used more generally for any odd or unreadable typeface produced through graphics.

Science Fiction

Terms coming from various sources in the genre of science fiction include *hyperspace,* which describes an errant memory access (Valid memory regions include *code* or *test space, static space, stack space,* and *heap space.* Anything else is considered *hyperspace*); *cyberpunk,* which refers to an imagined world in which anthropomorphized computers participate in human interactions as if they were human; and *cyberspace,* which characterizes future human-computer systems in which humans communicate with the computer as if by mental telepathy. In cyberspace, computers display images directly within the user's mind, similar to prophetic visions as described in biblical writings. Similarly, the science fiction term *martian* is used to describe a network packet received from an unidentifiable network node.

Droid, from *android*, a science fiction term since the 1920s, was popularized in the *Star Trek* television series. Computer hackers frequently use droid or the suffix *-oid* in a derogatory way to imply that a person is acting mindlessly, as though programmed. Thus, *marketroids* and *sales droids* promise customers things which can't be delivered, while a *trendoid* is concerned only with being up-to-date with the latest fads.

The term *Vulcan nerve pinch* also comes from the original *Star Trek* television series. It describes the keyboard action of simultaneously pressing on three keys as when rebooting with the control, alternate, and delete keys.

When there is a need for a random number that people will recognize as such, *42* is often used because in *The Hitchhiker's Guide to the Galaxy* (1980, New York: Harmony) that's what Douglas Adams had his computer give as "The Answer to the Ultimate Question of Life, the Universe, and Everything."

Another interesting term is *Twonkie*, a software addition that is essentially useless but nevertheless appealing in some way, perhaps for marketing purposes. Its meaning is made clear by its resemblance to *Twinkie*, which has become almost a generic term for junk food. However, its source is thought to be the title of Lewis Padgett's 1942 short story "The Twonky," which has been frequently anthologized since its original publication in *Astounding Science Fiction*.

Grok, from Robert Heinlein's *Stranger in a Strange Land* (1961, New York: Putnam), is used to mean that a computer program understands or is "one with" a particular idea or capability. Often, older versions of commercial software products can't grok data files produced by newer releases of the same product. In a more playful usage from Heinlein's *The Moon Is a Harsh Mistress* (1966, New York: Putnam), the acronym *TANSTAAFL* has become a quick and socially acceptable way to tell someone "There Ain't No Such Thing As A Free Lunch." Another Heinlein usage is *Waldo*, taken from the title of his 1942 story in which he invented mechanical devices working under the control of a human hand or foot. Computer hackers prefer the term Waldo, but NASA, which hopes to use such devices to manipulate robot arms in space, has chosen the more technological sounding name *telepresence* (see **Notes**).

Star Wars

Two of the cleverest science fiction references are based on the *Star Wars* movies. *UTSL* is a shorthand way to send someone the message that they should do some research before they send out a network call for help. It is an acronym for "Use The Source, Luke!," a play on the line, "Use the Force, Luke!," (see **Notes**). An *Obi-Wan error*, a pun on the name of Obi-Wan Kenobi, refers to any computation that is off-by-one, as when a programer started counting a particular quantity at 1 instead of 0. By analogy, an Obi-Wan code would give the name *HAL* (from the movie *2001*, each letter is one away from the corresponding letter in the original acronym) for IBM. In another *Star Wars* allusion, someone who uses computer skills for devious purposes is called a *dark-side hacker* (as opposed to a *Samurai*), meaning the person is like Darth Vader in having been seduced by the "dark side of the Force."

Children's Literature

There are relatively few references to traditional children's literature. However, in the 1960s people spoke of *IBM and the Seven Dwarves* with the dwarves being Burroughs, Control Data, General Electric, Honeywell, NCR, RCA, and Univac. Lewis Carroll's *Snark* is an appropriate name for any unexplained foul-up that programmers have to go hunting for. In a classic computer hacker story about a conflict between Motorola and Xerox, two hackers at Motorola wrote a pair of "bandit" background processes they affectionately named *Robin Hood* and *Friar Tuck*. These two processes took over the Xerox developer's main computer system. The point of this activity was to get the attention of the Xerox team in order to deliver an important message that had been repeatedly ignored during the several months prior to the attack. The *Trojan Horse* legend provides the name for a program that is designed to get around security measures by sneaking into a system while disguised, perhaps as a game or a useful utility. When the program is invoked, it does unexpected and unwanted harm to a computer system, in addition to providing the advertised functionality.

Moby Dick

One of the most common references to a piece of traditional literature is *moby*, meaning something immense or huge. Although this comes from Herman Melville's *Moby Dick*, its use was popularized in pre-computer days by model train fans and such usages as *Moby Pickle*. Hackers use it in such sentences as "The disk crash resulted in moby data loss," and "Writing a new back-end for the compiler would be a moby undertaking!" Several years ago when the University of California Library System named its library access program *Melvyl* after *Melvyl Dewey*, developer of the Dewey Decimal System, some users assumed a connection to Herman Melville because it was such a moby of a data base.

OTHER REFERENCES FROM LITERATURE, FILM, AND TV

There's always a lag between the popularization of a term and its being adapted to a new use. However, today's instant communication shortens the lag as shown by two fairly recent references. *Feature Shock* is a play on the title of Alvin Toffler's *Future Shock* (1970, New York: Random House). It describes a user's reaction to a program heavy on features, but light on explanations. The other recent usage is *Sagan* from the name of Carl Sagan, star of the TV series Cosmos, who is often heard repeating the phrase "billions and billions." His name is used as shorthand for any large number as in "There's a sagan different ways to tweak EMACS."

One thing this discussion shows is the importance of television and movies in contributing to the store of literary images from which hackers take their references. A *Godzillagram,* based on the hero of Japanese monster movies, is a network packet of maximum size or one broadcast to every conceivable receiver. *Dr. Mbogo,* the witch doctor from the old Addams Family television show, has his name memorialized in *Dr. Fred Mbogo* (hackers often use *Fred* as a random name because it's so easy to type) as a humorous identifier for someone with "bogus" skills.

Computer hackers are relatively young (ranging from teenagers to their mid-forties) and they grew up watching *Sesame Street,* hence the name *Cookie Monster* for a hacker who manages to deny computer access to other uses of a system, thereby obtaining exclusive access for selfish purposes. *Double Bucky* is a play on the *Sesame Street* "Rubber Duckie" song. It originated as a joke when human-computer interface designers were trying to figure out how to get more characters from the same keyboard. One suggestion was that foot pedals be added to serve as extra shift keys which would allow typists to make more changes without moving their fingers from their home keys.

Real programmers (a reference to the book *Real Men Don't Eat Quiche*) refer to aspiring teenaged programmers as *Munchkins* in memory of the little people in *The Wizard of Oz.* Depending on their behavior, such hackers might also be called *Wabbits,* from cartoon character Elmer Fudd's famous "You wascawwy wabbit!" The specific meaning of the latter term is a trouble-making hacker who programs something so that it will keep repeating itself. In contrast, a protocol that accidentally includes a bug resulting in multiple messages being sent or multiple instances of a particular abstract object being created is described as being in *Sorcerer's Apprentice mode,* a reference to the Walt Disney movie *Fantasia.*

USING COMPUTER TALK IN THE CLASSROOM

One of the advantages of looking at these literary references from the perspective of a computer person is that we see the literature with fresh eyes. Something similar can happen in the classroom when we look at other metaphors and kinds of language change brought about by computers. While English teachers know more about processes of language development than do students, many students know more computer language than do their teachers. Because of this, bringing computer language into the English classroom sets up a good teacher/student partnership with information and insights coming from both sides of the table.

The following class activities can be done as a discussion with a whole class or assigned to small groups who will do their research and then present it to their classmates. Oral presentations can be supplemented with display posters, handouts, or mini-dictionaries. A bibliography of resources is attached, but the main resource should be students' own experiences and what they can find out from interviewing other students and adults who work with computers.

This is a unit designed to provide computer whiz kids their day of glory in the English classroom. And because computers are such a new part of American culture, students can have the experience of doing original field work.

Collect Semantically Related Metaphors

Using a broad definition of metaphor to mean any computer term that is based on a similarity between what is being named and what the base word refers to in standard English, search for terms taken from specific semantic areas. Help students compare the standard English meaning to the specialized computer meaning. Just as we collected computer metaphors related to literature above, different groups of students can collect metaphors related to transportation *(driver, bus, channel, map, information highway, hard drive crash, cruising the Internet),* food and kitchen *(menu, byte, nybble, cooked, raw, fork, filter, fold, stack),* human activities *(handshaking, bootstrapping or booting, memory, massage, motherboard, daughtercard, "smart" and "dumb" terminals, "second" and "third" generations),* architecture *(back door, port, window, screen, pane, desk top, trap door,* and *pipe* or *pipeline),* and pre-computer kinds of writing and printing *(envelope, mail, file, address, clipboard, format, scroll,* and *bulletin board*). This latter set is a good illustration of how new inventions are described with the language of their predecessors– as when cars were called horseless carriages and vans were named after the kinds of caravans that depended on camels and oxens instead of machines.

Collect Alternate Spellings

Computer users purposely "misspell" some of their words to identify them as computer words and to keep them from being confused with similar words. For example, *byte* is spelled with a *y* because it was important to distinguish it from *bit.* The *y* spelling caught on as "computer talk" and is also seen in *nybble. Luser,* as a pun on loser and user, influenced the spelling of *turist* as someone who out of curiosity temporarily joins various groups; *c.f.* TV channel surfing. Have students list standard spelling alongside "computer" spelling and see if they can figure out whether the change was simply to communicate a specialized use of the word or was commercially motivated as when a company creates a trademark that it wants to protect legally.

Look at Capitalization Patterns

In the dinosaur days of computers, some machines printed only capital letters. Ever since, computer users have had a unique attitude toward upper and lower case letters. Bicapitalization describes the practice of inserting caps inside words as with these trademarks: *WordPerfect, NeXt, GEnie, TeX, VistiCalc, dBASE, FrameMaker,* and *CompuServe* (often spelled playfully by hackers as *Compu$erve* because this public network access provider costs so much in comparison with university and employer facilities). Students could clip product names from old catalogs and make a poster to use as part of a discussion of whether the deviant capitalization helps the names to be memorable. (Another reason for the practice is so companies can register them as original trademarks.)

Collect Acronyms

Computer hackers even have acronyms for acronyms. *TLA* stands for Three Letter Acronym while *YABA* stands for Yet Another Bloody Acronym. When new names are chosen, creators check to make sure they are "YABA compatible," meaning the initials can be pronounced easily and won't make a suggestive or unpleasant word. But no matter how carefully acronyms are chosen, hackers will still try to create new meanings as when they say that the true meaning of *LISP* (LISt Processing Language) is "Lots of Irritating Superfluous Parentheses." In discussing acronyms, students can talk about their space saving features as compared to their potential for confusion. What's the difference between the ones that run together in people's minds and the ones like *GIGO* (Garbage In, Garbage Out) that are becoming part of mainstream English?

Trace the Influence of Computer Language on Mainstream Language

The name of the television news program *Hard Copy*, which suggests both "hard line" and "hard core," was undoubtedly influenced by the computer *hard copy* for something printed on paper (i.e., "documented") compared to soft copy for something in the machine. As a comparison to e-mail and Internet, people refer to the U.S. Postal Service as *USnail, snail mail,* or *papernet.* The widespread use of computers has also increased the general use of such words as *glitch, bug* and *debug, user-friendly, protocol, input, zap,* and *de-programming* people or things other than computers. Students can collect headlines and news clippings for a display of such new usages. They can then compare their specialized computer meanings with their original and now their new meanings in mainstream English.

Computer Brand Names

Steve Jobs was "into" health foods, and when it came time to choose a name for the new computer he had designed for ordinary people rather than professional computer whizzes, he settled on *Apple* to stand out from other companies' high tech names. Apple included such positive connotations as "an apple for the teacher" and "an apple a day keeps the doctor away." It also provided for a "family tree" with such later names as *Macintosh* and *Newton. Lotus* software has an equally inspired name based on the comparison of a lotus blossom opening out and the creation of a spread sheet. And what could be more persuasive in getting customers to buy a product than the name *WordPerfect?* Another tricky bit of persuasion is that when users want to get into their *Windows* program, they have to type *WIN?*

   Once students have gathered a list of product names, both for hard- and software, they can pull out specialized lists; for example, names based on metaphors, names that include unorthodox spelling or capitalization, names made from morphemes (small units of words that carry meaning), and "families" of names that are designed to show relationships between one product and another. They might divide their list into names designed to appeal to the general public as contrasted with those for computer specialists. What differences will they find? In which group will they find code numbers and letters? In which group will they find such poetic techniques as rhyme, alliteration, and allusion?

Examples of Pejorative Language Play Used to Relieve Frustrations
It's common for people who feel frustrated or out of control to make jokes that release some of the nervousness or hostility they are feeling. For example, the computer building at Stanford is named the Margaret Jacks Hall, but students refer to it as the *Marginal Hacks Hall.* Computer hackers also refer to the IBM 360 as the *IBM Three-Sickly,* to a Macintosh as a *Macintoy* or *Macintrash,* and to programs coming from the University of California at Berkeley as *Berzerkeley.* And frustrated users of newly released technology often lament that they are living on the *bleeding edge* (a play on *leading edge*). Chances are that students in your school have their own share of pejorative jokes related to computing– some of which will be appropriate for sharing in the English class.

Notes
Hackers: In common usage, hacker has several different connotations. Some readers will be more familiar with the following definition of hacker: "A malicious meddler who tries to discover sensitive information by poking around." R. Raymond's *The New Hacker's Dictionary, Second Edition* (1993, Cambridge, MA: MIT Press), written and maintained by the community of friendly hackers (as defined in the main body of this text), suggests that the malicious meddler is more properly titled a *cracker.*

Bits and *Bytes:* Within a computer, all numbers are represented by strings of bits (a bit is a binary digit, each bit representing either a 0 or 1). A byte is a string of exactly eight bits. The least-significant bit represents the 1s, the next bit represents 2s, and the third represents 4s. The most-significant (high-order) bit within a byte represents 128s. Compare this with our base-ten numbering system in which the least-significant digit represents 1s, the next digit represents 10s and so on.

Telepresence: Allows a human user on earth, for example, to manipulate a mechanical arm belonging to a robot walking on the surface of the moon. Visual and sensual feedback are provided to human operators in order to portray the illusion that they are actually present on the moon.

Sources and *Object Codes:* Modern computer software is written in high-level programming languages designed to simplify programming effort. Compilers are programs that translate the high-level programming languages to the machine language required for execution of the program in a particular environment. The high-level program written by the user is called the source code, whereas the program's machine-language translation is called the object code. Most commercial applications are supplied only in object-code form, as the object code hides many of the developer's trade secrets. However, members of the hacker sub-culture regularly share source codes with one another. When user-level documentation is missing or unintelligible, hackers are encouraged to refer directly to the source code to better understand the program's features and capabilities.

The Jargon File: We could not have written this article without the help of innumerable hackers who over the past 15 years have contributed definitions and examples to *The Jargon File,* most recently edited by Eric Raymond (eric@snark.thyrsus.com). *The Jardon File* can be downloaded by anonymous ftp from prep.ai.mit.edu as pub/gnu/jarg300.txt.gz. The contents of this file were recently published as *The New Hacker's Dictionary, Second Edition.* Many of the examples presented in this paper were prompted by this resource.

Suggested Reference Material for Classroom Teachers

Microsoft Press Computer Dictionary, Second Edition. 1994. Redmond, WA: Microsoft Press.

Raymond, R. ed. 1993. *The New Hacker's Dictionary, Second Edition.* Cambridge, MA: MIT Press.

Spencer, D. ed. 1992. *Webster's New World Dictionary of Computer Terms, Fourth Edition.* Englewood Cliffs, NJ: Prentice Hall, Inc.

Tidrow, R. and J. Boyce. 1993. *Windows for Non-Nerds.* Carmel, IN: New Riders Publishing. (The concluding chapter is a dictionary of computer terms.)

18-Section Insert on Computer Technology, *The Wall Street Journal,* June 27, 1994. (Reprints available for $2.00 from Technology/Dow Jones and Company, Inc., 200 Burnett Road, Chicopee, MA 01020.)

12

RESPONSE AND COLLABORATION

❧ *Four Ways of Responding*

We have listed below the four forms of **Response** that are useful for all essay drafts. We have also included an additional response question that directs the reader's attention to how effectively the writer has used information gathered from field research.

Consider, again, the different individuals from whom you might receive responses to your draft. If, for the first two essays, you have been relying mainly on one particular source of **Response** (a certain classmate, group of classmates, or tutor), broaden the **Response** you receive by working with someone different. This will provide you with a new perspective on your writing and help to keep the response you receive from becoming too predictable.

LISTENING

The first kind of **Response** most writers need is simply to be heard, to know that someone is really listening and taking in what they have written. This form of **Response** is critical to all the other forms; it is the foundation for your ability to be a helpful responder.

LISTENING 1: RECEIVING

Listen carefully to the essay as it is read. Respond without words. Your job is to receive the writing, to take it in, to have any reactions you naturally have. That is, you might find yourself nodding in agreement or smiling or feeling sad but you will not, at this time, articulate your response in words. Simply say "thank you" to the writer for reading, or clap for the writing if you are in a larger group. The writer has had an attentive audience hear what she or he has to say.

LISTENING 2: ECHOING

Use the writer's own words as your response. As you hear the piece of writing again or read it to yourself, jot down or underline words and phrases that stand out for you, that strike you in some way. Without using any other words, repeat the writer's words you have noted. By echoing back the writer's own words, you are letting the writer know what especially got through to you.

REPORTING

Next, the writer can benefit from knowing how different readers understand his or her writing. Your job in Reporting is to report on your own reading of the text. You cannot know with certainty exactly what the writer intended, but you are an authority on your own reading. The following are strategies for reporting your reading to the writer.

REPORTING 1: MAIN POINTS

List for the writer what seem to you to be the main points he or she is making in the draft. What seem to be the main ideas that are included so far in what you have read?

REPORTING 2: FOCUS

What do you feel is the focus for the whole essay, so far? Is the writer's purpose or reason for writing explicit and clear? How does the essay accomplish this? You might come up with a title that, for you, represents the heart of what the draft seems to be saying.

REPORTING 3: SUMMARY

Give a summary of what you read. The summary gives more detail than the list of Main Points, but of course it doesn't include everything. You might summarize by writing down a few sentences that elaborate your understanding of each main point or by recording what you remember from the piece without looking at it.

Reporting 4: Story of Your Own Reading

Tell the writer what you thought and what you felt as you read the piece of writing. The idea is to try to tell the story of what happened to you, in you, as you read. The story of your own reading is not a summary or an analysis, it is a narrative of what went through your mind and what feelings you had at specific points as you read or heard the draft.

ELABORATING

In the next kind of **Response,** you move beyond your immediate reaction to the text to make connections between your own experience and knowledge and what you have read. Elaborating helps you provide the writer with a broader understanding of his or her material since different readers will make different connections to and have different commentary on what the writer has said.

Elaborating 1: Connections

What does the writing connect to in your own experience? What have you read that corroborates what has been said? What can you add to the points the writer has made? What further examples can you think of? In what ways do you agree with the piece of writing? What parts of the writing do you particularly agree with or feel particularly connected to?

Elaborating 2: Contradictions

Is there anything in the piece of writing that contradicts your own experience or something you have read? What alternative perspectives can you offer on the points the writer has made? What is there in the piece of writing with which you disagree? Is there something that seems to you to be left out of the piece?

QUESTIONING

Finally, it is valuable to ask the questions you have about a work-in-progress. Don't hold back on any questions that come to you, for it will be useful to the writer to know what questions the piece, in its current version, raises for different readers.

QUESTIONING 1: WHAT I'D LIKE TO HEAR MORE ABOUT

Ask the writer about any aspect of the writing you would like to hear more about. The writer may choose to include some of this material or may choose not to add this information in subsequent versions of the piece depending on his or her purpose and the audience for whom the writing is intended.

QUESTIONING 2: WHAT I DON'T YET UNDERSTAND

Ask the writer for clarification of any points, ideas, words, or phrases that you have questions about. Again, the writer may find that in the next draft she or he wants to make some changes as a result of the questions she or he was asked.

QUESTIONING 3: THE WRITER ASKS YOU QUESTIONS

At this point, the writer can ask for comment about any aspect of the draft she or he wants response to that doesn't seem to have been addressed. Again, the feedback is a non-judgmental form of response.

❧ *Responding to the Writer's Use of Information Gathered from Conversation and Observation: Questions for Response*

Some response that readers can give is specific to the kind of information that is the source for the essay. The following are some questions responding readers might ask to help the writer think about how he or she has used the words of others gathered from conversation and observation, the information source for this essay. Before answering these questions, responders should first remind themselves of what they found to be the essay's explicit purpose or meaning. Keeping that purpose clearly in mind, use these questions to give the writer your sense of how he or she used the information in this draft.

1. How does the writer use information gathered from conversation and observation to support or develop the purpose of the essay? How does the writer limit the extent of the conclusions he or she draws from the information?

2. What claims or observations does the writer make based on his or her understanding or interpretation of the conversations and interviews

he or she has gathered? Tell the writer what makes these claims convincing for you. Tell the writer any claims that feel unconvincing to you. What kind of information or additional interpretation would make these claims more convincing for you?

3. Where in the essay does the writer paraphrase conversations and/or include direct quotations? Tell the writer what seems to you to be the purpose for which each quotation or paraphrase is included. Do you feel the need for any of these passages to be more complete? Do you feel that some of the passages are longer than needed? (Note that the next chapter includes proofreading and editing advice on these issues.)

4. How has the writer interpreted, for the reader, what others have said? How has he or she explained or discussed the words or actions of someone else to illustrate or extend the point being made in his or her essay? If the interpretation or explanation seems inadequate or unclear, point this out to the writer.

5. What does the writer do in the essay to make the information seem credible and authoritative? How does the writer make clear who is the source and why this source would be appropriate and convincing in relation to the purpose of the essay?

13

EDITING, PROOFREADING, AND A FINAL WRITING AND REFLECTION

❧ *Editing and Proofreading Strategies for Essay 3*

As you make your final proofreading decisions, you may need to refer to the descriptions listed below. The descriptions also include information about conventional ways to use and integrate others' words into your text–how to integrate and cite information gathered from conversations and observations.

Keep in mind that when you are proofreading and editing someone else's text, you are not being asked to make any changes on the draft. Your task is to locate any places where you feel there may be distractions for the reader about which the writer must make an editing decision.

SILENT DISTRACTIONS

1. SPELLING

Academic *readers* often make severe judgments about writers' abilities based on the correctness of their spelling. It is common for readers to assume that an inordinate number of misspellings indicates laziness or irresponsibility in the writer. The assumption that writers just don't care is especially strong when they misspell common words (for example, "alot" instead of "a lot;" "there" when it should be "their" or "they're"; "it's" when it should be "its") or make common errors, ones that readers have seen so many times that they become pet peeves or annoyances. *Writers* can correct spelling errors using a spell check on the computer or a good dictionary. In fact, because spell checkers can't identify homonyms (a spell checker will find that "threw" is spelled correctly even if you really mean to use "through") or misplaced words ("She it the one who threw it."), it is important to have a dictionary on hand too.

Some people who have good visual memories are adept at spelling. Others, including many famous writers, need to look up words before letting a piece of writing stand on its own. If spelling is not particularly easy for you, you will need to take time to look up longer or uncommon words in a dictionary.

2. TYPOS

Like spelling errors, typos may be used by *readers* to make a quick determination of your skill and the commitment you have to your writing. *Writers* can locate some typos using a spell checker; others will get by since they may be correctly spelled words, but not the words you intended. One useful strategy for "seeing" typos is to read your essay from the end, moving word by word backwards through the text. This process can help highlight the typos for you. Final versions of essays need to be proofread for typing mistakes. If you notice a mistake just as you are turning in a final version of a paper, it is always better to correct it than to have a perfectly neat paper.

3. CAPITALIZATION

Capitalization has virtually no effect on the *reader's* understanding of a text but a misplaced capital, or a missing one, sends a distress signal to an academic reader that may take his or her attention away from your essay. Because capitalization errors are often the result of a typing mistake, it is important for *writers* to check that words that need capitals, like names of people or places and first words of sentences, are capitalized and that words that don't need capitals are not capitalized. Reading the essay backwards word by word is often a useful strategy for finding missing capitalizations too.

4. FORMATTING

Like spelling, typos, and capitalization, formatting has no effect on meaning. However, academic *readers* expect paragraph indentations and will be disturbed if your whole essay appears in one paragraph. It is a matter of *writer's* choice where to break paragraphs. Two page and single sentence paragraphs are unusual but are not incorrect. The general wisdom about paragraphing is that when you move on, in some way or degree, to a new topic, it is time for a new paragraph. Reread any chapter of this text (or any other academic text) to get a sense of paragraphing.

Other usual formatting issues are that most academic papers are double spaced, typed, have standard one-inch margins, use average size type, and are presented on standard weight, white, 8½ ¥ 11 inch paper. Academic papers are expected to look alike.

5. Possessives

We have listed possessives under silent distractions because the proofreading concern we want to highlight regarding possessives is the apostrophe ('). Whether or not we hear, in speech, the "s" signifying the possessive in "the boy's bike" or the boys' bikes, in college writing, *readers* expect the apostrophe to appear, standing for "belongs to." While checking for possessives, the *writer* should look for missing instances as well as for any apostrophes that appear in the text unnecessarily. Apostrophes are only used in forming contractions (like can't or wouldn't) and for possessives. No apostrophe should appear where a plural is intended except if it is a plural possessive.

6. Sentence Boundaries

When we speak it is often not possible and it is certainly not necessary to identify where one sentence ends and the next begins. Like the first four distractions, sentence boundaries are of concern only to *readers*, not to listeners. Sentence boundaries seem to matter a great deal to academic readers even though, like the other silent distractions, they usually have no effect on one's ability to understand a text. In editing one's own essay, the *writer* should know that there are only two possible inconsistencies in the category of sentence boundaries: 1) fragments, in which you write part of a sentence but punctuate it as if it is a complete sentence and 2) fused or run-on sentences, in which you write two sentences together but punctuate as if you have written one sentence. Under certain circumstances–for emphasis–fragments are acceptable, though usually student writing is expected to be free of fragments; fused and run-on sentences are not acceptable in college writing, although long, correctly punctuated sentences are sometimes valued as part of a particularly "academic" style.

We know of no fully reliable rule for what makes a complete sentence in English. The general formula is that one needs a subject and a predicate, the person or thing the sentence is about and a description of that subject's action or state of being. "He stands" is a complete sentence, but "standing, idly by the streetlight, the sirens blaring, the horns honking" is not a complete sentence because there is no subject; you're left to say, "Who is standing, idly . . . ?" "The quiet, long-haired boy in the front of the line," is also an incomplete sentence because there is no predicate. You're left to say, "What about 'the quiet, long-haired boy'?" Our favorite test for complete sentences is to imagine that the sentence is all someone said when he walked into the room; would the sentence make some kind of complete sense or would you ask the kind of questions the fragments in the example above provoke?

It is difficult to notice fragments because they are usually made complete by attaching them to the previous or preceding sentence. So, when you are writing, you make that connection in your mind. Run-on or fused sentences are a little more difficult to detect, and it is our experience that they occur in student writing less frequently than fragments. If you have two complete sentences you can either divide them up with a period (.) or you can join them together with a semicolon (;) or with a comma and a conjunction such as "and," "or," and "but." You can't join two sentences together with a comma (,). The best technique we know of for checking sentence boundaries is to read a paper, sentence by sentence, backward. If you start with the last sentence of the essay, then read the next to last, and so on, you will be able to focus on sentence completeness without being influenced by the meaning of the text.

AUDIBLE DISTRACTIONS

7. AGREEMENT

The meaning of a sentence is rarely affected by the convention of agreement but non-standard agreement is a particularly powerful distraction for academic *readers*. Agreement means that there is consistency within a sentence. The main parts of the sentence are either both plural or both singular. The form of the verb depends on whether the sentence contains a singular or plural subject. In the same way, singular or plural pronouns match singular or plural antecedents. To meet the expectations of academic readers you will need to check for both subject/verb agreement and pronoun/antecedent agreement.

Using a handbook is often a useful way for *writers* to check for agreement. In general, you will need to review each sentence first to see that the form of the verb matches that of the subject: In the sentence, "Each student has a notebook," the singular subject "student" matches the verb form "has." In the sentence, "Students take tests in chemistry," the plural subject "students" matches the verb form "take." Second, you will need to see that in a sentence the antecedent, which is the word a pronoun refers to, is plural if the pronoun is plural, and singular if the pronoun is singular. In the sentence, "Musicians must practice if they want to become accomplished performers," the plural pronoun, "they" matches the plural antecedents, "musicians" and "performers." In the sentence, "A musician must practice if he or she wants to become an accomplished performer," the singular pronouns "he or she" match the singular antecedents "musician" and "performer." Again, agreement is a convention of standard, college writing that you can give attention to at the point in working on your draft, when you are making the presentation of your essay conform to the expectations of academic readers.

8. Tense

The academic *reader* who encounters a surprising, non-standard tense shift in a college essay will, as with the other audible distractions, still be able to understand what is being said. He or she may pause to reflect on the writer's language history or background, surmising that this is a speaker of other languages besides English or other dialects besides the standard one. Even if the writer's background or history is the subject of the essay, the academic reader will expect the writer's knowledge of other languages and dialects to remain invisible in the finished text. (We believe that, at this time, the academic world is biased in favor of the standard form, although this bias is undergoing debate and change.)

In **Editing and Proofreading,** the *writer* will want to focus, again, on the verbs in the sentences, perhaps using a handbook to help. Are the verbs in their standard form? Is the tense consistent within sentences or paragraphs and, when there is a tense change, does it make sense in the context of the rest of the paragraph or essay?

9. Word Choice

The final audible distraction is word choice or diction. Academic *readers* find acceptable a wide range of language and diction. But they expect words to be used in conventional ways. As a *writer*, you may want to review your draft for the accuracy and appropriateness of the words, something that is not always easy to distinguish. We advise you to choose words from your own vocabulary, which is enormous, rather than use a thesaurus to find unfamiliar words that you may not be able to use conventionally. We also encourage you to ask others if you are unsure of the choice you have made; be sure to ask for their explanation, not just their decision. Word choice options include not only replacing words that are used incorrectly, but finding the most precise words to express your ideas and reach your audience.

ADDITIONAL DISTRACTIONS

10. CITING AND REFERENCING INFORMATION

In writing this essay, you have integrated information you gathered from conversations and observations. As with all college writing, to be honest and to establish the authority of your information, it is necessary that you cite your information and do so conventionally. As you read the examples below, be sure to notice the use of quotation marks and the placement of punctuation. If you are unsure about this, refer to your handbook.

You can include what someone said by using a direct quotation, an exact replication of what was originally said. The person who stated the words can be identified at the beginning, end, or middle of the quote. For example, inserting the speaker's identity into the middle of the quote, you might write:

> "The first time I used my pager," explained my friend Nancy, "I had no idea what some of the codes meant or how to find out their meaning."

And, if appropriate, the source of the reference—where or when it was initially spoken—is also included:

> Speaking at a school town meeting, Mr. Jones argued, "If our children are to become better readers and writers, we need to be willing to pay for smaller class size and better teachers" (October 1997).

You can also convey what someone said less exactly using an indirect quote or paraphrases; these are instances in which the writer rephrases, in his or her own words and in a structure appropriate to the essay he or she is writing, the words of someone else. As in a direct quote, however, the source of the information is included. This can be incorporated into the body of the essay. For example, an essay might include an indirect quote to Mr. Jones' comment about schools:

> Improving children's reading and writing skills is not something that can be done without expense to taxpayers. Mr. Jones, the local school principal, has argued to parents at the October school board meeting that the single best way to improve reading scores and help children write better is to reduce the number of students in each class. This, of

course, would mean that more teachers would have to be hired and paid for their work.

❋ *A Final Rewrite*

Rewrite your essay one last time including all the editorial and proofing changes. You may find that some editorial changes lead you to further revision.

Writing Log Entry 12

On Writing Essay 3

Write a page about what it was like to have written your third essay. What were the most freely flowing parts of the writing for you? Where did you get bogged down? What do you hope a reader will take from your essay? What did you learn that you might take with you to your next essay assignment?

CHAPTER

14

WRITING TO LEARN

Writing a Second Essay from Conversation and Observation

Reconsidering the Writing Process

In the course of writing Essay 3, you had the challenge of selecting an issue about language that interested you enough to warrant your further reflection and, at the same time, you had the challenge of writing an essay based on information you collected from other people. Whatever you decided to write about and whatever purpose you chose for the focus of your essay, you were limited by the field research you conducted–the information you were able to collect, analyze, and interpret and the people you were able to collect it from. You had to ask yourself what kinds of claims you could make about your subject given the information you had, what parameters would be set by this material and, in the course of drafting, what additional information you might need to collect. Also, as you wrote the essay, you were faced with choices about how to present the information–direct or indirect quotes, dialogue or summary–how to identify the speakers, and how to present your connection to each of them.

WRITING ESSAY 4

In this assignment you will be using the writing activities you are already familiar with from the first three assignments to write a fourth essay that is informed by the words, recollections, shared stories, observations, and commentary that you collect from other people. Though you may include yourself among those from whom you gather information, you will not be the primary source. However, you will play a major role in the essay as the interpreter of the information you collect. Just as someone who reads many books and articles for a research paper must pull together and interpret what she or he reads, writers of this kind of essay must pull together and interpret what they hear and are told. This material then allows the writer to support and explain his or her explicit purpose in the essay.

Because the way you write your essay will depend on what you want to say about your subject and what information you have gathered, there are numerous ways that your essay might evolve. The **Perspectives** and **Focusing** activities are designed to help you find your topic and your way into it; the **Response** activities to help you revise, and the **Editing and Proofreading** to ensure that the essay is ready to stand without you.

We have included several **Professional Demonstration** essays at the end of this chapter. You may want to refer to these now or once you have begun moving through the **Perspectives** and **Focusing** activities. We have also included **Student Demonstrations** throughout the next section of the chapter.

Essay 4

Select any topic on which you would like to reflect more extensively. Use the Perspectives and Focusing activities to help you find a topic and to find a question, issue, or concern that will become the explicit purpose or focus of your essay. Then, you will need to conduct the field research through which you will develop this purpose. Ultimately, your interpretation of your research, the information you gather from observation and from conversations with others, will provide you with the means for establishing and supporting the purpose of your essay.

DISCOVERING AND CREATING YOUR ESSAY
TAKING ON DIFFERENT PERSPECTIVES
PERSPECTIVES: *Tapping into Your Thinking*

As a way to begin, quickly list what is on your mind right now. This list may be similar to the one you wrote in preparation for Essay 2, but given the time that has passed since then, there will most likely be new ideas that occur to you. As before, you might ask yourself what questions and issues you are currently thinking about or struggling with. You might reflect on situations at home, at school, or in the community; movies or plays you have recently seen; places you have visited; people in your life; events currently in the news; articles or books you have recently read–don't feel that the list must be remarkable in any way other than that it provides a quick snap shot of some of what is going on in your mind at this time.

PERSPECTIVES: *Your State of Mind*

Underline two items from your list that currently look most inviting. You can make your decisions on any basis you choose, narrowing down to the two items on the list that seem to be the most compelling thoughts or subjects, ones you would not mind giving a few minutes of your attention to today.

Write briefly–5–10 minutes–about each one. This writing is expected to be unfocused and is intended to explore your knowledge, feelings, and state-of-mind about each item.

Reread your two brief writings and select the one about which you have the most to say, the most curiosity, the greatest feeling, or even the greatest confusion.

Student Demonstration

PERSPECTIVES: *Your State of Mind*

Example 1

> Picking a major: I'm running out of time. I technically have nine days to figure out what I'm going to do for the rest of my life. I've been thinking about Speech Pathology, but I'm somewhat apprehensive because some of the classes seem pretty hard. Neurology, Anatomy, and Physiology. They do not sound too inviting to me. I'm not sure if my brain is equipped for such topics. I'm sure if I study hard, I can do anything. It's very tempting to take the easy way out and become a kinesiology major but what kind of life do I want for myself?

Example 2

> Raising two baby blue jays: While I was getting dressed for school Tuesday morning, my mother called me to come look outside of our kitchen window. To my amazement, there were two small, young baby blue jays on the ground, and

they were still breathing. My mother and I quickly grabbed
an old shoe box, went outside, and placed the blue jay
chicks in the box. Now I'm wondering how to take care of
these chicks. What should we do to keep them alive and
well? I will call Petco when I get home today, and maybe
Dr. Chong could give me some advice. I wonder how long it
will be before the chicks can fly—and what we have to feed
them in the meantime!

PERSPECTIVES: *What You Know, Need to Know, Could Never Know*

Thinking about the topic you have chosen, freewrite a page or so in response to each of the following questions:

1. What do you already know about the topic, issue, or concern that you have selected? Describe it in detail. Tell about your current feelings and understanding of the topic.

2. What do you feel you need to know about the topic? What are the most pressing questions and concerns you have? Why do you need to know these things–to what end?

3. What can you find out about your topic from other people? How could they help you learn about it, find answers to your questions, show you perspectives or angles that you could never see on your own?

4. What are the kinds of things that you could never understand about the topic and what would prevent that understanding?

PERSPECTIVES: *Gathering Information*

Reread the four **Perspectives** writings that you have just completed. Then, looking particularly at the last one, brainstorm some ideas about how you will collect this information and from whom. First, don't limit yourself by "reality"–if anything were possible, to whom would you speak and what conversations would you want to overhear? Once you have given yourself a chance to do some freewriting, reread what you have written and brainstorm some more this time considering what you might actually be able to do and whom you could actually contact within the time limits of the assignment.

In order to make the process of gathering information most useful and productive, plan carefully the questions you will ask, the conversations you need to hear, which stories and recollections you need to be retold. Now use the next few days–or however long the assignment allows–to conduct your research, being sure to take complete and specific notes about what you hear or are told and the identity of the speakers.

Student Demonstration

PERSPECTIVES: *Gathering Information*

Example 1

> The first person I would speak to about my surgery would
>   be a surgeon—either Dr. H. or Dr. M.
> I would want to overhear their former patients talking
>   about this same procedure as I am about to have.
> I can speak with Dr. S., my own doctor.
> I can speak with Dr. S.'s secretary about her husband's
>   procedure.

Example 2

> I can ask every one in my immediate family.
> I can ask my friends who ski: Jake, Luis, and Yvette,
>   especially.
> Then I can ask some people who snowboard.
> I could go skiing and ask people riding on the lifts!

Example 3

> I could interview people that I regularly e-mail or who
> I know regularly use e-mail for business or personal uses. I
> could interview: Karen, Alisa, Prof. Steinberg, Mom, Victor,
> people in the computer lab . . .
>   Questions:
> Why do you use e-mail?
> Who do you e-mail?
> Do you use e-mail instead of writing a letter?
> Do you have e-mail at home or at work?
> Do you use it instead of talking on the phone?
> Have you ever had misunderstandings develop because of e-
>   mail?

PERSPECTIVES: *Finding New Answers and New Questions*

Reread all of the information you have collected. Jot down a page of notes reflecting on how this information begins to answer the particular questions you had about the subject and how it begins to provide you with larger observations, claims, arguments, that you might make about the topic. Also, make note of any ways in which the information you have gathered raises additional questions, ones you had not expected.

PERSPECTIVES: *Conflicting Points of View*

Most likely, the information you have gathered came from various people or even from one person whose thinking is not always entirely consistent. Within the interviews, discussions, observations, and overheard comments that you recorded, there are probably two or more conflicting perspectives on the topic. Identify several perspectives that emerge from what you have heard so far, and then listen to them as if they are distinct voices, "individuals" who maintain singular perspectives. Write out a conversation among these voices.

Focusing Your Direction

FOCUSING: *Questions and Connections*

What can you say about the subject and your understanding of the questions you had about it? What can you say about it now based on what you have learned from others that you couldn't have said before? Write three or four sentences about the connections that you see emerging.

FOCUSING: *Writing More*

Use the sentences that you wrote above as a focus from which to begin freewriting. Push yourself to write two pages. The only parameters are those set by the sentences you have already written.

FOCUSING: *Rereading and Writing Again*

Reread the pages you have written, including the information you gathered from others. While doing so, underline all of the sentences or sections of your writing that jump out at you, the ones that catch your eye and stay with you. Find a sentence or two that raises some questions for you or that you might want to reflect on further, or something you feel is worth telling others. Take 3 or 4 of these as your focus and freewrite further.

FOCUSING: *Rereading, Reseeing, and Rewriting*

By completing the **Perspectives** and **Focusing** writing, you have also completed an exploratory draft. This draft has become increasingly focused as you have continued to write.

Reread all the pages you have written in these activities. Look particularly at the **Focusing** writings. Ask yourself what *explicit* purpose for writing emerges from this first draft. What is it that you are writing about and to what end?

With this subject and purpose in mind, and with all of the writing you have done so far at hand, write a second draft. Unlike writing your exploratory draft, you begin this second one with a sense of purpose and some idea about how the observations and conversations you recorded and reflected on can help you to accomplish that purpose.

EVALUATING YOUR INFORMATION AND GATHERING MORE

At this point, in order to provide adequate and convincing support for your purpose, take time to evaluate the information you have included in your second draft and decide whether you need to collect additional or more persuasive references and illustrations. As you did in writing Essay 3, consider how authoritative your sources are, whether some information, because of its source, will not be as convincing to academic readers as other information you have gathered. If some of your information has come from the Internet, are you able to cite who the speakers were? What is their authority and the authority of your other sources to speak on your subject?

Once you have evaluated the information you have included in your draft and determined what more you need, or what might need to be revised or deleted, ask yourself what additional field research you should do. How might you collect this information and from whom? Are there questions that occur to you now that didn't when you were first speaking with others? Is there a place you need to visit again? Are there additional individuals you need to speak with?

Student Demonstration

REFLECTIVE ANALYSIS OF INFORMATION GATHERED FROM OTHERS

Example 1

Having any type of surgery is a very big step because there are all kinds of risks and complications. It is normal to be nervous about having surgery, but it is especially normal to be nervous about an experience that will be totally new and unexpected. I have learned that discussing my own concerns with someone who can understand what I am about to go through can be very helpful for dealing with my anxiety, fear, and distrust. It was very useful for me to gather new information from a variety of people. I learned that I needed to make myself ask more questions than those I asked during one consultation, even if they make me seem naive. Now I definitely feel as though my emotions, fear, and anxiety are under control, and I have a better idea of what to expect. I am now prepared to "go under the knife!"

Example 2

Where do immigrants get their strength? Is it the financial despair? Is it a desire to prove to the family that they can take care of its members? I believe the source of all their strength is the family. The Mexican immigrants I spoke with know this and are proud of it. They have tremendous power in their relationships with one another. They care for each other. The family is the highest institution, together in good and bad. Being in the United States, alone, separated from the family makes them suffer, and they work even harder. Most of them miss their family so much that they are not afraid to risk going home and returning back here.

One girl I interviewed went to see her family last Christmas. She went to Tijuana and then flew to Mexico City. On the way back, she had to pay $1,000.00 to cross the U.S. border and get back to the country where she had left her job and her "legal" husband. She took the risk, and she was lucky to get in for the second time. "It was worth the money and the risk," she said, remembering the great Christmas time she had with her family.

Example 3

In only a couple of short weeks, I will be moving into my first apartment. Being inexperienced with my new independence and having a small income make this "event" more than just simply relocating. I have already found an apartment with affordable rent and roommates that I am comfortable with. I need to think about furnishing, starting accounts for utilities, and budgeting money for rent and other expenses. I can easily put myself in debt if I become careless and frivolous. Of course I will not be living in the lap of luxury, but there must be ways to live a comfortable life without struggling too much.

I talked to my father about his first apartment. He told me stories of living off of "bread and soup" and furnishing with "bricks and boards." He had many responsibilities at the time with wife, child, and being drafted into the army. "That was a different time," according to a close friend, Carly. Carly had her first apartment at age eighteen, and she said, "It was beautiful!" Carly purchased most of her furniture second hand through ads in the paper. She spent months and months looking in the newspaper and visiting garage sales in order to find what she wanted. It was a long process, but she said, "It was worth it to have a beautiful home and to know that I did it all by myself."

Carly's experience should be very helpful. She developed a weekly budget for herself that allowed her to afford rent and utilities each month. According to a leasing agent that is affiliated with the "Canyon Apartments," "Utilities cost approximately one hundred dollars per month for three people in a two to three bedroom apartment." Carly calculated her approximate share of the utilities and rent for a month and divided that number by four. This gave her a weekly salary that had to be earned. She added that it was necessary to make sure this amount was surpassed in order to eat, be social, and buy some furniture.

✻ *Getting Response to Essay 4*

Once again, we describe the four ways of responding to drafts of college essays and remind you of concerns that are particular to the source of information you used in creating this essay.

LISTENING

The first kind of response most writers need is simply to be heard, to know that someone is really listening and taking in what they have written. This form of response is critical to all the other forms; it is the foundation for your ability to be a helpful responder.

LISTENING 1: RECEIVING

Listen carefully to the essay as it is read. Respond without words. Your job is to receive the writing, to take it in, to have any reactions you naturally have. That is, you might find yourself nodding in agreement or smiling or feeling sad but you will not, at this time, articulate your response in words. Simply say "thank you" to the writer for reading, or clap for the writing if you are in a larger group. The writer has had an attentive audience hear what she or he has to say.

LISTENING 2: ECHOING

Use the writer's own words as your response. As you hear the piece of writing again or read it to yourself, jot down or underline words and phrases that stand out for you, that strike you in some way. Without using any other words, repeat the writer's words you have noted. By echoing back the writer's own words, you are letting the writer know what especially got through to you.

REPORTING

Next, the writer can benefit from knowing how different readers understand his or her writing. Your job in reporting is to report on your own reading of the text. You cannot know with certainty exactly what the writer intended, but you are an authority on your own reading. The following are strategies for reporting your reading to the writer.

REPORTING 1: MAIN POINTS

List for the writer what seem to you to be the main points he or she is making in the draft. What seem to be the main ideas that are included so far in what you have read?

REPORTING 2: FOCUS

What do you feel is the focus for the whole essay, so far? Is the writer's purpose or reason for writing explicit and clear? How does the essay accomplish this? You might come up with a title that, for you, represents the heart of what the draft seems to be saying.

REPORTING 3: SUMMARY

Give a summary of what you read. The summary gives more detail than the list of Main Points, but of course it doesn't include everything. You might summarize by writing down a few sentences that elaborate your understanding of each main point or by recording what you remember from the piece without looking at it.

REPORTING 4: STORY OF YOUR OWN READING

Tell the writer what you thought and what you felt as you read the piece of writing. The idea is to try to tell the story of what happened to you, in you, as you read. The story of your own reading is not a summary or an analysis, it is a narrative of what went through your mind and what feelings you had at specific points as you read or heard the draft.

ELABORATING

In the next kind of response, you move beyond your immediate reaction to the text to make connections between your own experience and knowledge and what you have read. Elaborating helps you provide the writer with a broader understanding of his or her material since different readers will make different connections to and have different commentary on what the writer has said.

ELABORATING 1: CONNECTIONS

What does the writing connect to in your own experience? What have you read that corroborates what has been said? What can you add to the points the writer has made? What further examples can you think of? In what ways do you agree with the piece of writing? What parts of the writing do you particularly agree with or feel particularly connected to?

ELABORATING 2: CONTRADICTIONS

Is there anything in the piece of writing that contradicts your own experience or something you have read? What alternative perspectives can you offer on the points the writer has made? What is there in the piece of writing with which you disagree? Is there something that seems to you to be left out of the piece?

QUESTIONING

Finally, it is valuable to ask the questions you have about a work-in-progress. Don't hold back on any questions that come to you, for it will be useful to the writer to know what questions the piece, in its current version, raises for different readers.

QUESTIONING 1: WHAT I'D LIKE TO HEAR MORE ABOUT

Ask the writer about any aspect of the writing you would like to hear more about. The writer may choose to include some of this material or may choose not to add this information in subsequent versions of the piece depending on his or her purpose and the audience for whom the writing is intended.

Questioning 2: What I Don't Yet Understand

Ask the writer for clarification of any points, ideas, words or phrases that you have questions about. Again, the writer may find that in the next draft she or he wants to make some changes as a result of the questions she or he was asked.

Questioning 3: The Writer Asks You Questions

At this point, the writer can ask for comments about any aspect of the draft she or he wants response to that doesn't seem to have been addressed. Again, the feedback is a non-judgmental form of response.

Responding to the Writer's Use of Information Gathered from Conversation and Observation: Questions for Response

It is also helpful to respond to the way a writer has made use of the specific information source for the essay. Responding readers can ask the following questions to help the writer think about how he or she has used the words of others gathered from conversation and observation, the information source for Essay 4. Before answering these questions, responders should remind themselves of what they found to be the essay's explicit purpose or meaning. Keeping that purpose clearly in mind, answer these questions to give the writer your sense of how he or she used the information in this draft.

QUESTIONS FOR RESPONSE

1. How does the writer use information gathered from conversation and observation to support or develop the purpose of the essay? How does the writer limit the extent of the conclusions he or she draws from the information?
2. What claims or observations does the writer make based on his or her understanding or interpretation of the conversations and interviews recorded? Tell the writer what makes these claims convincing for you. Tell the writer any claims that feel unconvincing. What would make these claims more convincing for you? What additional interpretation or support would be effective?
3. Where in the essay does the writer paraphrase conversations and/or include direct quotations? Tell the writer what seems to you to be the purpose for which each quotation or paraphrase is included. Do you

feel the need for any of these passages to be more complete? Do you feel that some of the passages are longer than needed? (Note that the next chapter includes proofreading and editing advice on these issues.)

4. How has the writer interpreted, for the reader, what others have said? How has he or she explained or discussed the words or actions of someone else to illustrate or extend the point being made in the essay?

5. What does the writer do in the essay to make the information seem credible and authoritative? How does the writer make clear who is the source and why this source would be appropriate and convincing in relation to the purpose of the essay?

❧ *Editing and Proofreading the Penultimate Draft of Essay 4*

As you edit and proofread your own or a classmate's penultimate draft, refer to the descriptions of the silent and audible distractions for academic readers that are listed below. At the end of the list, we also remind you of the additional, potential distraction for readers if writers do not cite and reference information in a conventional manner.

SILENT DISTRACTIONS

1. SPELLING

Academic *readers* often make severe judgments about writers' abilities based on the correctness of their spelling. It is common for readers to assume that an inordinate number of misspellings indicates laziness or irresponsibility in the writer. The assumption that writers just don't care is especially strong when they misspell common words (for example, "a lot" instead of "a lot;" "there" when it should be "their" or "they're"; "it's" when it should be "its") or make common errors, ones that readers have seen so many times that they become pet peeves or annoyances. *Writers* can correct spelling errors using a spell checker on the computer or a good dictionary. In fact, because spell checkers can't identify homonyms (a spell checker will find that "threw" is spelled correctly even if you really mean to use "through") or misplaced words ("She it the one who threw it."), it is important to have a dictionary on hand too.

Some people who have good visual memories are adept at spelling. Others, including many famous writers, need to look up words before letting a piece of writing stand on its own. If spelling is not particularly easy for you, you will need to take time to look up longer or uncommon words in a dictionary.

2. TYPOS

Like spelling errors, typos may be used by *readers* to make a quick determination of your skill and the commitment you have to your writing. *Writers* can locate some typos using a spell checker; others will get by since they may be correctly spelled words, but not the words you intended. One useful strategy for "seeing" typos is to read your essay from the end, moving word by word backwards through the text. This process can help highlight the typos for you. Final versions of essays need to be proofread for typing mistakes. If you notice a mistake just as you are turning in a final version of a paper, it is always better to correct it than to have a perfectly neat paper.

3. CAPITALIZATION

Capitalization has virtually no effect on the *reader's* understanding of a text but a misplaced capital, or a missing one, sends a distress signal to an academic reader that may take his or her attention away from your essay. Because capitalization errors are often the result of a typing mistake, it is important for *writers* to check that words that need capitals, like names of people or places and first words of sentences, are capitalized and that words that don't need capitals are not capitalized. Reading the essay backwards word by word is often a useful strategy for finding missing capitalizations too.

4. FORMATTING

Like spelling, typos, and capitalization, formatting has no effect on meaning. However, academic *readers* expect paragraph indentations and will be disturbed if your whole essay appears in one paragraph. It is a matter of *writer's* choice where to break paragraphs. Two page and single sentence paragraphs are unusual but are not incorrect. The general wisdom about paragraphing is that when you move on, in some way or degree, to a new topic, it is time for a new paragraph. Reread any chapter of this text (or any other academic text) to get a sense of paragraphing.

Other usual formatting issues are that most academic papers are double spaced, typed, have standard one-inch margins, use average size type, and are presented on standard weight, white, $8\frac{1}{2} \times 11$ inch paper. Academic papers are expected to look alike.

5. POSSESSIVES

We have listed possessives under silent distractions because the proofreading concern we want to highlight regarding possessives is the apostrophe ('). Whether or not we hear, in speech, the "s" signifying the possessive in "the boy's bike" or the boys' bikes, in college writing, *readers* expect the apostrophe to appear, standing for "belongs to." While checking for possessives, the *writer* should look for missing instances as well as for any apostrophes that appear in the text unnecessarily. Apostrophes are only used in forming contractions (like can't or wouldn't) and for possessives. No apostrophe should appear where a plural is intended except if it is a plural possessive.

6. SENTENCE BOUNDARIES

When we speak it is often not possible and it is certainly not necessary to identify where one sentence ends and the next begins. Like the first four distractions, sentence boundaries are of concern only to *readers*, not to listeners. Sentence boundaries seem to matter a great deal to academic readers even though, like the other silent distractions, they usually have no effect on one's ability to understand a text. In editing one's own essay, the *writer* should know that there are only two possible inconsistencies in the category of sentence boundaries: 1) fragments, in which you write part of a sentence but punctuate it as if it is a complete sentence and 2) fused or run-on sentences, in which you write two sentences together but punctuate as if you have written one sentence. Under certain circumstances–for emphasis–fragments are acceptable, though usually student writing is expected to be free of fragments; fused and run-on sentences are not acceptable in college writing, although long, correctly punctuated sentences are sometimes valued as part of a particularly "academic" style.

We know of no fully reliable rule for what makes a complete sentence in English. The general formula is that one needs a subject and a predicate, the person or thing the sentence is about and a description of that subject's action or state of being. "He stands" is a complete sentence, but "standing, idly by the streetlight, the sirens blaring, the horns honking" is not a complete sentence because there is no subject; you're left to say, "Who is standing, idly . . . ?" "The quiet, long-haired boy in the front of the line," is also an incomplete sentence because there is no predicate. You're left to say, "What about 'the quiet, long-haired boy . . !?" Our favorite test for complete sentences is to imagine that the sentence is all someone said when he walked into the room; would the sentence make some kind of complete sense or would you ask the kind of questions the fragments in the example above provoke?

It is difficult to notice fragments because they are usually made complete by attaching them to the previous or preceding sentence. So, when you are writing, you make that connection in your mind. Run-on or fused sentences are a little more difficult to detect, and it is our experience that they occur in student writing less frequently than fragments. If you have two complete sentences you can either divide them up with a period (.) or you can join them together with a semicolon (;) or with a comma and a conjunction such as "and," "or," and "but." You can't join two sentences together with a comma (,). The best technique we know of for checking sentence boundaries is to read a paper, sentence by sentence, backward. If you start with the last sentence of the essay, then read the next to last, and so on, you will be able to focus on sentence completeness without being influenced by the meaning of the text.

AUDIBLE DISTRACTIONS

7. AGREEMENT

The meaning of a sentence is rarely affected by the convention of agreement but non-standard agreement is a particularly powerful distraction for academic *readers*. Agreement means that there is consistency within a sentence. The main parts of the sentence are either both plural or both singular. The form of the verb depends on whether the sentence contains a singular or plural subject. In the same way, singular or plural pronouns match singular or plural antecedents. To meet the expectations of academic readers you will need to check for both subject/verb agreement and pronoun/antecedent agreement.

Using a handbook is often a useful way for *writers* to check for agreement. In general, you will need to review each sentence first to see that the form of the verb matches that of the subject: In the sentence, "Each student has a notebook," the singular subject "student" matches the verb form "has." In the sentence, "Students take tests in chemistry," the plural subject "students" matches the verb form "take." Second, you will need to see that in a sentence the antecedent, which is the word a pronoun refers to, is plural if the pronoun is plural, and singular if the pronoun is singular. In the sentence, "Musicians must practice if they want to become accomplished performers," the plural pronoun, "they" matches the plural antecedents, "musicians" and "performers." In the sentence, "A musician must practice if he or she wants to become an accomplished performer," the singular pronouns "he or she" match the singular antecedents "musician" and "performer." Again, agreement is a convention of standard, college writing that you can give attention to at the point in working on your draft, when you are making the presentation of your essay conform to the expectations of academic readers.

8. TENSE

The academic *reader* who encounters a surprising, non-standard tense shift in a college essay will, as with the other audible distractions, still be able to understand what is being said. He or she may pause to reflect on the writer's language history or background, surmising that this is a speaker of other languages besides English or other dialects besides the standard one. Even if the writer's background or history is the subject of the essay, the academic reader will expect the writer's knowledge of other languages and dialects to remain invisible in the finished text. (We believe that, at this time, the academic world is biased in favor of the standard form, although this bias is undergoing debate and change.)

In **Editing and Proofreading,** the *writer* will want to focus, again, on the verbs in the sentences, perhaps using a handbook to help. Are the verbs in their standard form? Is the tense consistent within sentences or paragraphs and, when there is a tense change, does it make sense in the context of the rest of the paragraph or essay?

9. WORD CHOICE

The final audible distraction is word choice or diction. Academic *readers* find acceptable a wide range of language and diction. But they expect words to be used in conventional ways. As a *writer,* you may want to review your draft for the accuracy and appropriateness of the words, something that is not always easy to distinguish. We advise you to choose words from your own vocabulary, which is enormous, rather than use a thesaurus to find unfamiliar words that you may not be able to use conventionally. We also encourage you to ask others if you are unsure of the choice you have made; be sure to ask for their explanation, not just their decision. Word choice options include not only replacing words that are used incorrectly, but finding the most precise words to express your ideas and reach your audience.

ADDITIONAL DISTRACTIONS
10. CITING AND REFERENCING INFORMATION

In writing this essay, you have integrated information you gathered from conversations and observations. As with all college writing, to be honest and to establish the authority of your information, it is necessary that you cite your information and that you do so using the conventions of direct and indirect quotations and of referencing. To refresh your memory about the details of these conventions, we have once again included some examples. As you read the examples below, be sure to notice the use of quotation marks and the placement of punctuation. If you are unsure about this, refer to your handbook.

You can include what someone said by using a direct quotation, an exact replication of what was originally said. The person who stated the words can be identified at the beginning, end, or middle of the quote. For example, inserting the speaker's identity into the middle of the quote, you might write:

> "The first time I used my pager," explained my friend Nancy, "I had no idea what some of the codes meant or how to find out their meaning."

And, if appropriate, the source of the reference—where or when it was initially spoken—is also included:

> Speaking at a school town meeting, Mr. Jones argued, "If our children are to become better readers and writers, we need to be willing to pay for smaller class size and better teachers" (October 1997).

You can also convey what someone said less exactly using an indirect quote or paraphrases; these are instances in which the writer rephrases, in a his or her own words and in a structure appropriate to the essay he or she is writing, the words of someone else. As in a direct quote, however, the source of the information is included. This can be incorporated into the body of the essay. For instance, an essay might include an indirect quote to Mr. Jones' comment about schools:

> Improving children's reading and writing skills is not something that can be done without expense to taxpayers. Mr. Jones, the local school principal, has argued to parents at the October school board meeting that the single best way to improve reading scores and help children write better is to reduce the number of students in each class. This, of course, would mean that more teachers would have to be hired and paid for their work.

✻ *A Final Rewrite*

Rewrite your essay one last time, carefully including all the editorial and proofing changes. You may find that some editorial changes lead you to further revision, as well.

Writing Log Entry 14

On Writing Essay 4

Write a page about what it was like to have written a second essay using information gathered from observations and conversation. What were the most freely flowing parts of the writing for you? Where did you get bogged down? How was this experience different or not from the writing of Essay 3?

❋ *Professional Demonstration Essays*
SOME QUESTIONS FOR CONSIDERATION

The following essays demonstrate several ways that writers have used information they gathered from talking with others and from general observations. The purpose of each essay is different—to make arguments, offer personal analysis, reveal and explain patterns. But what these essays share is that each one relies on stories, conversations, and observations that the writer has collected over time and from a variety of individuals. While several of the essays also include the writers' own personal experiences, these are not their primary sources of support for what they are saying.

As you explore the ideas you have already written about and brainstorm some new ones, you might refer to these essays to see the range of options available to you when you write from gathered information and to examine how writers integrate this information into their essays, using it to illustrate and support the purpose for which they are writing.

Use the following questions to help you study each demonstration essay in more detail:

1. In a sentence or two, how would you summarize the explicit purpose of each essay? Imagine you were to ask the writer what the essay was about and then ask, "So what?" How might he or she answer?

2. How do the writers make their points explicit? What are the sentences or parts of the essay that make these points available to the reader?

3. How do the writers use observations and conversations to support or illustrate the purpose of their essays? How is this information integrated into the text and used as a source of authority?

IN LOOKS, A SENSE OF RACIAL UNITY*

Lena Williams

Young Americans seem to be looking more alike these days. And that's not all. Young people of different ethnic backgrounds are acting and sounding a lot alike, too.

White males are wearing dreadlocks, fade haircuts and African medallions; black men and women are going blond and sporting Metallica T-shirts. There are black Valley girls and white home girls.

Large lips are the latest Hollywood look, so some white women are fattening theirs up with silicon injections. Meanwhile some black women are painstakingly making up their lips to achieve a thinner, more typically Caucasian lip line.

Michael Bolton, a white pop musician with a soul-inflected, blues-based vocal style, has beaten out black challengers for New York Music Awards' prestigious soul music title. And the hip street vernacular of black youths has become so mainstream that even Madison Avenue executives are using it in television commercials.

"I call it the darkening of white America," said Dr. Charles W. Thomas, a professor of urban studies and planning at the University of California at San Diego who is writing a book on the black-white crossover phenomenon. "What we are seeing is white people being totally engulfed in black life style and behavioral patterns. It started with the music. Now you see it in fashion, religion and expression."

At the same time, Dr. Thomas and other experts in black culture noted that more blacks are adopting white styles and social patterns than at any time since the early 1960's. They say many blacks may not realize that in imitating whites, who in many ways are imitating black culture, they in essence are reclaiming their own culture.

Dr. Thomas said, "We are seeing the black middle class doing what E. Franklin Frazier, the black sociologist, accused them of doing in the 1950's: 'poor imitation of whites' without understanding that they are reclaiming what is already theirs."

Alana Valencia, a 15-year-old black high school student who lives in Washington, is critical of the trend. "We call them the 'Wannabees,'" she said. "The black kids who 'wanna be' white and the white kids who 'wanna be' black."

The trend, which started in the mid-1980's, is predominant among young people, which has led to speculation that it is a fad. Some, however, believe the phenomenon is an expansion of a cultural exchange that dates to the Harlem Renaissance of the 1920's and 30's, when whites flocked to Harlem nightclubs and dance halls, regarding black life as exotic.

But the degree to which blacks and whites have immersed themselves into each others' culture and life styles, at a time when many cities seem to be more racially divided and reports of race-based hate crimes are on the rise, has even some of the experts scratching their heads.

"I've been puzzled by this," said Todd Gitlin, a professor of sociology at the University of California at Berkeley. "It's kind of like, one color fits all, I don't quite get it, although it's not unprecedented. Whites, no matter what their racial feelings, have tried to look darker for some time. This new phenomenon is in that tradition."

Dr. Alvin Poussaint, associate professor of psychiatry at Harvard University, said black styles have crossed over but that there is more going on than meets the eye. "The stigma has been removed from features that were Negroid and thus considered inferior, like thick lips," he said. "We're seeing a freeing up of style, just like there was a freeing up of sexuality in the 1970's."

The trend is not exclusively American. Around the world, a universal standard of beauty is emerging, projecting a multi-racial mix. Indeed, it's difficult to tell the race or nationality of models on some magazine covers.

"They're like a little bit of this and a little bit of that," said Audrey Smaltz, founder of Audrey Smaltz and the Ground Crew, a fashion support services concern in New York City. "They're these beautiful caramel-colored children who can be accepted by blacks, whites, browns and yellows."

A growing number of black celebrities are flaunting new looks and attitudes. There's Michael Jackson, who despite denials, appears lighter in complexion and thinner in nose and mouth; the new golden locks of Shari Belafonte, the actress daughter of Harry Belafonte; the occasionally green or blue eyes of Oprah Winfrey, courtesy of contact lenses.

Meanwhile, the managers of the white pop-music group New Kids on the Block acknowledge it is a clone of the black group New Edition.

Vernetta Lynch, a 20-year-old Washington college student who is black, said she once dyed her dark brown hair blond, but "just to see how it looked, not because I was trying to be white."

"It is unbelievable," she added. "The white girls are all wearing these imitation gold door-knocker earrings, have these short, sassy haircuts and talking like, 'yo, home girl,' and the black girls are acting like, 'wow, golly gee,' in their little Sperry docksiders. We're all mixed up."

Although some blacks view the imitation of their life style as a form of flattery, others say it is cultural theft.

"I think some blacks may feel a little vindication that the things that were rejected in the past, whites are trying to adopt," said Dr. Poussaint, who is black. "It is in a sense flattering. What bothers blacks most, though, is that they aren't given attribution for their contributions, and there is a feeling that it will be usurped by whites and blacks won't get any economic gain from their own styles or music."

Erik Simon, a 28-year-old white Californian who has a mop of two-toned dreadlocks that are mostly peroxide-yellow, said of his looks: "Some people are offended; usually older black women don't like it. But others think it's neat.

"I've never had anyone say, 'Why can't you just be white?' but you can tell just in the way they say things or look at you that they disapprove."

Mr. Simon said he started growing his locks about a year ago by not washing his hair for six months and vigorously rubbing his head every morning to snarl the strands. He said he decided to wear his hair in the Rastafarian style to shock people, more than anything else.

"It's not like we're stealing it from them," said Mr. Simon, who works in a Long Beach pet store. "It's the new punk. In the other direction, you can see black guys shaving their heads, which is a ripoff of the English punk-rock style, too. There always is that sort of trading between radical blacks and whites."

Jonathan Roberson, 32, a black New York hair stylist who recently dyed his hair blond, has noticed that a growing number of his black clientele are lightening their hair.

"I think blacks have come to a point where they are making more of a crossover than whites," Mr. Roberson said, adding that whites have always mimicked black hairstyles, like the Afro in the 1960's. "We used to be hung up on four walls of staying in this black identity. If you didn't, you didn't get the support of your brother. Now we're becoming more individual."

A survey being conducted on how 12- to 15-year-old black girls in Oakland define beauty has found that many have contradictory images of themselves.

"So far, I've found that many of these girls have strong identities as young black ladies, and yet they held on to these choices that seem to have more of a white standard of beauty," said Maxine Snow, a graduate student in sociology at University of California at Berkeley who is doing the research for her doctoral thesis. "For instance, they seem to borrow white standards of beauty in terms of long hair or blond hair and light skin. Yet, in terms of adopting styles, most of them say they didn't want to act or look white."

Ms. Snow said that the girls come from different socio-economic groups, but that many lived in homes where positive black identity was stressed.

The practice of adopting "white" standards of beauty was highlighted by an essay, "The Bluest Eye," in the January 1988 issue of Essence magazine. The author, Elsie B. Washington, a senior editor at the magazine, denounced the growing tendency of black celebrities, trendsetters and "just plain folks" to "alter their natural-born God-given dark eyes," by wearing tinted contact lenses.

"Green and blue contact lenses are a groping to identify with all that has been presented–erroneously and slanderously, I contend–as better than us," Ms. Washington wrote. "In my mind, I'm connecting this blue-eyes-green-eyes trend with the current anti-black mood around the country. I'm connecting it with another trend that glorifies and promotes mixed-race (read light-skinned) models and screen heroines, even in films that decry the maltreatment of black by whites."

But there is another view: that perhaps some of the preconceived notions, stereotypes and perceptions that blacks and whites have of each other are gradually changing.

"Everybody puts a little into their own special blend," said Orlando Taylor, a 15-year-old black sophomore at Aviation High School in Long Island City, Queens. "No one takes offense if there is a particular style that is black or white. Whether someone who isn't black or white is wearing it doesn't really matter."

VIDEO GAMES: BOYS VERSUS GIRLS*

J. C. Herz

Shortly after videogames became icons, one thing became glaringly obvious: This was a Guy Thing, programmed by and for males. When girls got near an arcade game, they were probably watching their boyfriends or brothers compete. Much to the chagrin of videogame manufacturers, half of the teenage population was conspicuously nonplussed. In an effort to attract girls, game companies tried a variety of stunts, the most successful being Namco's videogame character in drag: Ms. Pac-Man. In 1981, Ms. Pac-Man was the Gloria Steinem of videogames. She could do everything her male counterpart could do, backward, forward, sideways, and wearing a jaunty pink bow. She used the hear-me-roar feminist honorific. And she attracted legions of young women who fantasized about going on a rampage and consuming everything in sight. *Ms. Pac-Man* was an enormously successful game, because it was an oasis for the teenage girls in any arcade. There were a few others: *Centipede, Nibbler, Q*Bert, Burger Time,* and *Frogger.* These games invariably diverged from the standard shoot-and-slay premise and had better-than-average sound effects and usually featured some whimsical, cuddly character. Most of them were just as difficult as the panoply of side-scrolling shooters. But they were less homicide oriented.

Frogger, for instance, was hugely popular with girls. If you saw a cluster of teenyboppers in a video arcade in the mid-eighties, odds are they were standing in front of a *Frogger* machine. Consider: It is impossible to be aggressive in *Frogger.* The object of this game is to dodge traffic and avoid falling off logs so that you can reach your little frog nest safe and sound. It's a curiously nonconfrontational game. There are no villains to make you feel important and stoke your ego by challenging you to single combat. You're not considered a threat. You're not even acknowledged. Motor vehicles don't veer to run you down. Waves don't sweep up to wash you overboard. None of the obstacles in *Frogger* have anything, personally, against you. They just happen to be deadly. And you just happen to be in the stupid position of dashing through highway traffic and crossing

---

a river with no idea how to swim. You can't kill anything. You can only die. It's like crossing a minefield (*Mine Sweeper,* not coincidentally, was also a hit with girls). This is a game of don't-hurt-anything-but-just-don't-screw-up, just like *Pitfall.* Just like *Tetris,* which is more popular with women than any other game and notoriously addictive among female professionals.

Tetris is a very simple game–an animated puzzle that forces you to rotate and connect geometric shapes at a continually accelerating rate. Essentially, *Tetris* is about coping. It's about imposing order on the chaos. It's about detritus raining down on your head, trash falling into messy piles and piling up until it finally suffocates you. This is a scenario to which many modern women can relate. The challenge is to divide your attention somehow, so that all the runaway fragments fall into neat stacks and *the mess goes away.* The psychological payoff for the player is a state of rapturous relief. "Yes!" she thinks. "Yes! The Mess is vanishing! I can make the Mess disappear!" It's not about blowing things up. It's about cleaning things up. *Tetris* speaks volumes about the difference between women and men vis à vis videogames.

Barbara Lanza, a Byron Preiss game designer and gender-theorist-at-large, has a few ideas about *Tetris*'s popularity with women. In conversation, she is overwhelmingly voluble, staggeringly candid, and cheerfully bossy–a combination of Dr. Ruth Westheimer and Lucy from Charles Schulz's *Peanuts* comic strip. Her videogame gender theories basically boil down to: Boy Games Are From Mars, Girl Games Are From Venus.

"All desires to be politically correct to the contrary," she says, "boys and girls really aren't the same, especially when they're little. They may become more similar as they grow older, but when they're young, they're really not like each other. They're looking for different things. Girls are looking for experiences, and boys are looking for bragging rights. And also, boys are looking for something that they can learn to do that mostly takes perseverance. A guy will say, 'Look what I did–it took me three hours, but I got to level fifteen. Isn't that great?' A girl will look at that and say, 'Let me get this straight: you spent three hours, *three whole hours,* pushing a button so that you could get a phosphorescent glow on the screen. Run that by me again? And you say this is cool?'"

Lanza refers to *Ms. Pac-Man* as a paragon of distaff game design. "What in the world did *Ms. Pac-Man* do that other games of the time didn't do?" she asks. "First of all, the fact that it was called *Ms. Pac-Man* was extremely important. Rule Number One: If you're selling to girls, make it very clear that that's who you're selling to. They're highly socialized. They need permission. One of the cool things about *Ms. Pac-Man* was that it told you right off the bat: This is a female game.

"Now, aside from the fact that it was labeled for girls, *Ms. Pac-Man* has a very interesting game strategy. Notice that in *Ms. Pac-Man* nothing is shooting at you. This is extremely important: the fact that you are not a target. That allows you to cruise around and think about what you want to do. You get to sit back and plan more strategy, because you're not dodging things, because you're not being shot at. Being able to go forward, backward, left, right was extremely important. See, in a normal, typical side-scrolling game, you have to go from left to right. You can retreat if you want to, but it's not going to advance you in the game. It's really not part of the basic strategy. Retreating for a female is like breathing. We're used to the idea that you can win by giving ground. We get into a situation we think is too tight, we back off, we turn around, we find another way to attack it. You can go around it. You can avoid it. You can retreat. You don't have to go straight forward full speed ahead all the time. But too often, in traditional computer games, that's all you're allowed to do. You've got to do it their way. *Ms. Pac-Man* works because you can retreat. You can sneak up on your opponents. We're very big on sneaking up.

"These are the truly big selling points of *Ms. Pac-Man:* the fact that you could retreat, the fact that you could sneak up on your opponent, the fact that nothing was shooting at you but you could go and get *it*. Being chased is not the same as being shot at. Being chased can be exciting. Being shot at can be damned annoying." It's not that women are averse to violence per se. When properly presented, it can be quite appealing–witness the current female vogue for handguns, kickboxing, and *Virtua Cop.* But punching the fire button 380 times a minute is not a twelve-year-old girl's idea of fun.

The problem is, videogame designers, being mostly male, can't seem to figure out what girls want in a videogame.[1] Even if, at some point, a topflight videogame company in Japan or Silicon Valley decided to woo would-be female gamers, it's doubtful that a bunch of guys who've spent their lives clutching a joystick could design something that resonates in the mind of a fourteen-year-old girl. And it's a dubious assumption that they would even try–this is not the kind of swaggering, high-status project that traditionally attracts hot-shot designers. Like, oh yeah, what are

---

[1] This is an industry where "Females and Adults" is a categorical descriptor, used in the kind of automatic way that "women and children" is used aboard sinking ships or to describe wartime casualties.

you working on? "*Doom 5*. What are you working on?" Cough, mumble. *Sassy: The Game.*

Catering to boys is much more fun. Videogame companies are very good at it, and it makes them rich. And they don't want to mess with a winning formula. At this point, to paraphrase Christian Slater in *True Romance*, the industry's approach toward females is motivated by two things: fear and desire. There's a lot of money to be made if you can sell games to girls. On the other hand, there's a fear of developing games for girls. Because if you make a game that looks like it's too friendly to girls, the boys will ditch it in one hot minute, because boys don't want to play girl games. Stereotypes congeal at a tender age.

According to Justine Cassell, a cognitive psychologist at MIT's Media Lab, kids of both sexes make sweeping generalizations about gender just as soon as they can pronounce the world "cootie." "By age three," she says, "children are sex-typing games. Little girls will say, 'Oh no, that's a boy toy.' At three they start to do that with household objects like brooms and hammers. Those gender stereotypes are pretty fixed, and we know that you can get gender stereotyping for objects, professions, and traits— they can do all that by age five. We know that those girls who want to be girl-girls are going to stay away from aggressive activities because they would be betraying their gender alignment."

This begs the question, what type of game would actually appeal to girls without making them traitors to the prepubescent idea of femininity? The consensus (among people who don't make videogames) is that story-telling is a key element in what girls do for kicks. "Girls are very interested in narrative play," says Cassell. "There are patternists and dramatists. Patternists are people who enjoy numbers for their own sake, or putting puzzle pieces together. And dramatists are people who enjoy telling stories. Technology toys can also be divided into pattern toys and drama toys. And girls like drama toys. They like telling stories. Girls will tell stories about anything. I remember doing a biology assignment when I was in fifth grade about hydrogen and oxygen falling in love and setting up house together. And that's a very common girl approach to science."

The irony is that all this story-oriented play requires more sophisticated engineering than the most brilliant twitch response games. It's much easier to create a spatial dimension than a social dimension. Computers were designed with spatial logic in mind. They were not designed to deal with interpersonal interaction and storytelling. Making a game based on social logic presents some incredibly thorny code problems and may not be possible with today's technology, which is mostly good at making pretty pictures spin around in complicated ways. For boys, this is wonderfully satisfying. Girls are quickly bored by it and demand break-throughs in artificial intelligence.

This does not imply that girl games are necessarily gentle or friendly. Girl games can be just as ruthless–in some ways, more ruthless–as a round of *Mortal Kombat.* But there aren't as many open gunshot wounds and gushing bodily fluids. It's much more abstract. It's more subtle. It involves volleys of deftly inflicted psychic trauma. Science fiction writer Orson Scott Card said it best: "For those of you who think that girls are immune, remember that playing with dolls is another manifestation of power fantasies: all those lovely little people, always doing *exactly* what you want."[2]

In this spirit, Mattel has recently decided that what girls want in an interactive entertainment product is–you guessed it–Barbie! For $44.99, the *Barbie Fashion Designer* CD-ROM lets girls six and up mix and match Barbie's wardrobe and then force her to model these kicky vacation outfits and wedding gowns ad nauseam in virtual reality. You are the art director. You are the fashion police. You are the pint-sized image consultant who sends Barbie's 3E polygon avatar vamping down the perfect plane of a cartoon catwalk, hips swaying, her newly composed fashion statement swinging in the viscous Silicon Graphics atmosphere. She does a little swivel at the end of the runway, tips her chin, and smiles the quintessential Barbie smile–a flawless cheesecake come-on designed to spark girlish yearning for these fabulous computer-generated clothes. But not to worry, they can be yours! You *can* conflate fantasy and reality. Because *Barbie Fashion Designer* lets you print these ensembles on special ink-jet-compatible sheets of white fabric, cut them out, and tape them onto the real live plastic Barbie dolls you already own (the average girl apparently owns eight). This is what girls are supposed to want from Pentium PCs circa 1997.

But then, it's only fair that girls should get to see Barbie dolls on computer monitors, because boys have been seeing them for years. Until very recently, videogame heroines have been ornamental and completely incapable of any action–"window dressing," in industry parlance. They were scrumptious, partly because they were used as some kind of Cracker Jack prize–if you made it to the end of the game, the kidnapped princess appeared as a reward. But they were also scrumptious because they were part of a superhero universe where all the men have lantern jaws and broad shoulders and all the women are busty and nippy

---

[2] Orson Scott Card, "Power Fantasies, Moral Responsibility, and Game Design," *Compute,* May 1989, 10.

waisted. Videogames are like comic books that way. They drive visual ideas of femininity and masculinity to opposite poles of hyperreality.

That's just the nature of the beast–the beast being videogame designers rather than the medium itself. "It's an unspoken thing" says Brenda Garno, who designs role-playing adventures for Sir-Tech Software and is one of the few female veterans of the industry. "If a guy says, listen, there's two characters in this scene, Mary and Bob. Do me a 3D rendering of them. Mary, ten times out of ten, is going to have a big chest, tiny waist, and blond long hair or brown long hair. It's just accepted, because there aren't women in the industry right now. I don't think necessarily the male role in games has been that defined. Well I did, in a way, with this *Druid* guy. I actually sent a fax to our artists saying, 'I want him to look this way: Well-defined chest. Well-defined arms. Stomach blocks. Great ass. I'm definitely guilty of reverse sexism there, no question. This guy is exactly what I would like to look at when I get up every morning.'"

She sighs. "Maybe we need more female designers. We need people to start saying, listen, we're sick of being window dressing. Can you tone down the chest? Can you tone down the hips on that lady? Can you present us as just a little bit real?"

Female videogame characters may not be getting any more real, but they are becoming increasingly dangerous and, in some cases, damn scary. With the rise of fighting games as the preeminent videogame genre, female characters have become players. They are not window dressing. They are lethal. And in games that take their cue from Marvel comics, they are flamboyantly lethal, in a distinctively female way. If videogames are a bastion of death-mongering hypermasculinity, these are the digital Valkyries. *FX Fighter,* for instance, has two female gladiators, one of whom, stylishly decked out in a vinyl v-kini, thigh-high boots, and opera-length gloves, delivers a crushing knee-to-groin attack. The other, a hellion with Mandarin talons, has a list of martial arts combinations such as Claw Charge, Swipe Claw, and Face Rake. *Mortal Kombat 3* has comic-book she-demons in abundance, including a white-haired harpy who shrieks her opponents into stunned helplessness and has the choice of two Fatality Moves: "Screamer of the Week," which leaves her foe wind-blown and skinless, and "Hair Spin." The latter involves a whiplike action of her silver 'do, which cocoons a hapless opponent, then retracts, spinning him into an explosion of limbs and blood. And lest *Mortal Kombat 3* fall short on racial diversity, the roster also features an eight-foot black female bodybuilder from Hell (literally) who bleeds green and wears heavy metal cuffs on all four arms. Alternating Fatality Moves, she'll either punch your head off with a strong uppercut or literally skin you alive.

Both of these pumped-up, anabolic gorgons have a very obvious adult sexuality that's incredibly intimidating, especially to adolescent boys. I mean, what could be more frightening to a thirteen-year-old than a fire-breathing monster with triple-D breasts?

In videogames that draw from Japanese cartoons, the women are more proportionate and less threatening. That wide eyed Japanese cuteness makes them more approachable. They'll still pummel you in combat. They'll still humiliate you. But they're sort of girlish about it. In *Street Fighter 2,* there's a Mary Lou Rettonesque character named Chun Li who wears miniature Princess Leia hair buns. And when she wins a fight, she jumps up and squeals. Another Sega game, *Fighting Vipers,* is a veritable United Colors of Benetton ad: a Zapatista butch goddess in combat pants and dog tag earrings, a black martial artist/inline skater whose retractable razors give the phrase "roller blades" new meaning, an Asian schoolgirl whose lace petticoat, white angel wings, puff sleeves, and pigtails belie her fearsome force, and Picky, a skateboarding gamine who proves that this slacker stunt vehicle can also be used as an effective weapon.[3]

Not surprisingly, this latest crop of winsome female videogame ninjas have become pinups for the discerning readers of *Electronic Gaming Monthly.* And every year, they become more important to an arcade game's success. The unveiling (so to speak) of a new chick gladiator is a major event–they are to videogames what future model dream cars are to automotive trade shows. Guys are crazy about them. And why not? A martial arts superbabe is the girl next door who'll also trounce you with a heart-melting smile. Case in point: Sarah Bryant, the reigning queen of 3D polygon fighting game characters. She's a Jeet Kune Do expert built like an Olympic swimmer.[4] She's not delicate or curvy. She's not even particularly thin. This woman has powerful shoulders and strong legs, and she's tall–usually taller than her male opponents. All in all, she's considerably more realistic than Pamela Anderson.

And there she is in the pages of *Next Generation* magazine, lounging, poolside, seen from below against blue sky, as if some virtual cameraman had crawled up to her deck chair on his belly, as well he should. She's a monumental babe. And so casual! A few stray polygon hairs flying away

---

[3] Not to miss a cross-marketing opportunity, Sega has also designated Picky as a shill for the Pepsi Corporation. The Pepsi logo is texture-mapped onto her skateboard, and a Pepsi billboard and truck are in the background of all her fights. Score one for product placement.

[4] And a rather modestly attired one at that—blue head-to-toe halter bodysuit, black boots, black gloves. You can see her arms, basically. This woman is dressed for business, not for show.

from her blond ponytail (not too neat, nice touch), sunglasses on top of head, a tropical drink in red-fingernailed hand, eyes closed, soaking up the sun, confidently buff. There's even a vital stats sheet, à la *Playboy,* but quelle différence: "Heights: 5′11″. Bust: You wish . . . Waist: you in 30 seconds. Weight: You'll know when I body *slam* you! Ambitions: To kick everyone's butt and achieve world peace." All of this on a seventeen-by-twenty-one pullout poster under the headline "Sarah Bryant–She'll break your heart, then kick your butt." This is a wonderful message for the adolescent boys of North America. And they lap it up.

In the videogame industry, what teenage boys want, teenage boys get. And if they want pixillated distaff superheroes, boom, hundreds of millions of dollars are spent to flood raster monitors with female mercenaries. At the Electronics Entertainment Expo (E3), the numero uno videogame showcase in North America, 1996 was the Year of the Woman.[5] The EEOC couldn't have laid down a more messianic affirmative action policy. In Namco's new fighting game, *Soul Edge,* half of the characters are female, and so very multicultural–the Viking warrior princess with flying blond braids and the deadly Thunder Strike, the ninja assassin armed with windmill kicks and shooting stars, and an Asian highland nomad with combination moves like "Sparrow's Rush," "Spinning Sparrow," and "Mountain Crusher." In the space of an hour, dozens of guys line up to play this game, and every single one of them plays a chick fighter.

At the Capcom pavilion, a herd of fifty-five die-hard male game fans cheer as Chun Li fights a mirror image of herself on a twelve-foot screen overhead. The players controlling these dueling cupcakes are both guys, Capcom employees at the controls of a *Street Fighter 2 Alpha* cabinet. Initially, their enthusiasm seems to be fueled by the same impulse that makes men tune in to *Foxy Boxing* and the female segment of *American Gladiators,* that kind of let's-see-the-girls-get-all-greased-up-and-sweaty leer-o-rama. But no. When one Chun Li hits the mat and disappears, her doppelgänger squares off against an outsized martial arts ogre and wins, and the audience goes absolutely nuts. These are

---

[5]The notable exception to E3's femme fever is a GT Interactive title, *Gender Wars,* a combat strategy game set in the future, when men and women have decided that they can't even bother living together anymore and are instead engaged in commando warfare. At the beginning of the game, you get to choose your gender (this is, after all, the nineties) and conduct a guerrilla campaign against the opposite sex. So if you choose female, for instance, you have to select your squad leaders and troops and then accomplish missions like planting a listening device in the male central computer, killing off the military leader, blowing up the ammo supply, and stealing sperm samples from the enemy compound (why men would leave sperm samples hanging around the barracks is anybody's guess).

straight, white, middle-aged men screaming at the top of their lungs, "You go, girl!" And after the demo ends, they all line up at the machine so that they can play Chun Li, too.

At the Viacom booth, the trophy game is *Aeonflux,* starring MTV's favorite jackbooted female assassin kicking, diving, ducking, and pistol-whipping her way through a combat strategy game for the PC and Sony Playstation. A short distance away, Acclaim is showcasing a mystery adventure game, *D.* In this game, you play a young woman whose physician father has gone on a murderous rampage in Los Angeles National Hospital, and you have to wend your way through a labyrinth of blacked-out medical wards to track him down. (Spoiler: It turns out doctor dad is a vampire who at one point tries to convert you, and you have to decide in the end whether to kill or join him. Try *that* for psychodrama.)

But for aesthetic violence, these titles pale in comparison to the gothic fantasy world that is *Meat Puppets.* Part H. R. Giger, part Frank Herbert, part *Terminator 2,* the demo for this game begins with white letters on a pitch-black screen: "One girl. One gun. One game."

"Once upon a time . . .

"Someone gave an angry young woman . . .

"A beautiful, beautiful gun . . .

"(The gun was friend) . . .

"So Lotos Abstraction, as she was known, went out to play."

And then we see the hero of this game, this female Terminator character—sharp and angular and vaguely metallic—go ballistic. She sneaks up behind an effete enemy officer, puts a chain gun to his head, and pulls the trigger. She kicks over a large glass vat containing a hyperencephalic alien, which flops helplessly as its amniotic bath traces rivulets through shattered glass. At which point, she kicks down hard on its grotesque exposed brain, releasing a torrent of black goo.

It's tempting to think that, at last, someone understands.

But alas, these games aren't designed for girls. These are the same brilliant boy games in drag, and 95 percent of the people playing them are guys. While girls are busy playing *Barbie Fashion Designer,* guys are jostling to play female kickboxing champs and action adventure heroines. They're playing these empowered women, kicking ass and taking names while their sisters concentrate on making computerized mannequins look glamorous. When it comes to videogames, *teenage boys* are the ones with positive female role models. It's painful to say this, but boys' games have the only female characters worth playing.

They *always* get the cool stuff first.

ᴄᵉᴸᵃᴸᵒ

FROM WOMEN'S WORK AND CHICANO FAMILIES: CANNERY WORKERS OF THE SANTA CLARA VALLEY*

Patricia Zavella

Women had contrasting views about the Affirmative Action Program, but generally they supported the principle of equal opportunity for women. Cristina noted, "It was about time. We should be equal with men in everything." Lupe believed that "it's really good. Women are going into mechanics, forklift driver, regardless of their race. Everybody in the U.S. should have that right." Vicki agreed with the notion but had questions about whether women could handle men's work: "I'm all for it if you're capable of doing it." Vicki's job injury, incurred while she trained for a man's job, no doubt led to her caution. A woman entering a man's job created a stir. Lupe recalled the first time a woman went to work on the seamer machine: "Everybody was flabbergasted. They said, 'What's the world coming to?' 'This is terrible, a woman doing a man's job!' I was shocked." Workers referred to the program derisively as "women's lib."

There were many reasons why the changes ordered by the Affirmative Action Program would be slow in coming. Most women indicated that they were not adequately informed of the proposed changes and had to rely on rumors. As a floorlady, Luz had not had much direct experience with the program. She shrugged: "Things haven't changed that much. I don't think there's too much to it." Gloria, who worked in the lab, also saw few changes. Connie was dissatisfied with the training program because it focused on job bidding: "The affirmative-action training program is a farce." She explained her dissatisfaction:

> The first day we toured canneries. I had them come to my plant and took them all over, even in the basement where the women work and there are all the rats. The head of the training program told me, "You'll do anything to make a point." I told her, "You're right." Then they showed us slides of different jobs, which were right out of the Appendix A book [of the union contract]. [She rolled her eyes.] Next they were going to show

*Zavella, Patricia. Reprinted from Patricia Zavella: *Women's Work and Chicano Families: Cannery Workers of the Santa Clara Valley*, pages 120–126. Copyright © 1987 by Cornell University. Used by permission of the publisher, Cornell University Press.

us a videotape of how we look when we put in a bid for a job to management. I told them to forget it. I didn't give a shit how I looked when I put
in a bid. What really mattered was if I was qualified, if I had the seniority for the job. I refused to participate.

By contrast, Lupe had a positive experience in her plant: "She [the personnel officer] explained it real good, with everything in Spanish and English. She told us about the different positions that would be opened, how
you were hired, what wages and health benefits, everything. I was
pleased; they had never done it before." Lupe hoped that she would qualify for a promotion in the near future and believed that the Affirmative
Action Program was "the greatest thing that ever happened to the cannery." Luz had problems with the training program also: "They don't
allow a person to learn the job unless they want that particular person."

Some women did not support the notion of women taking men's jobs.
Estela, for example, said: "I don't go for that. Those jobs should be for
men; they have a family. I don't like to work hard anyway. I wouldn't take
a man's job because they're harder. It's good for widows and divorcees,
but if we have our husbands, why bother?" Lupe concurred, believing
women are physically weaker: "I myself wouldn't want to work that
hard. We can't handle it; our bodies can't handle it." Yet she observed
women successfully performing men's jobs: "Women drive semis, work
on axles." She had a look of amazement. "Some of them are pretty and
are not built that big." Celia felt guilty because she had taken a man's
greaser job. "Sometimes I feel bad because I've taken a man's job for the
last five years. And I figure we women with hard hats, we took men's
jobs." Celia also did not like to see men in women's jobs: "It's unusual for
men to work on the line. But when they do, they have to wear a hair net,
the women's aprons, gloves, like a woman. It makes me feel kind of
funny. To me, they must feel kind of, you know . . ." She couldn't bring
herself to conclude her statement, that men in aprons are emasculated.
She stammered a bit longer and then pronounced that at least she would
not take a warehouse job, "because those are men's jobs."

Vicki believed that conflict among workers was precipitated by the Affirmative Action Program: "Yes, there is competition because of women's
lib." Celia did not like the program: "There should be something different." She hoped that "women's lib" would remain confined to the job:
"Women should get paid if they work a man's job, but I don't believe in all
the other stuff. I like to have my door opened and other things."

Connie, on the other hand, did not support the view that women and
men should be confined to certain jobs: "We have families, too, that have

to live. And I don't feel like I'm hurting any man by supporting my own family."

The men also apparently believed that women should remain in women's jobs. This can be seen in the harassment women received when they got promoted. Women clearly had difficulties in using plant seniority as a vehicle for moving up the job ladder.

Men were sometimes temporarily assigned to women's jobs, but women had to fight through a series of steps to gain men's jobs. First they had to put in bids, since a man's job almost always means a promotion. Workers did not wear badges with their seniority numbers on them; the only way women could ascertain another worker's seniority was through gossip networks or a visit to the personnel office. Thus to bump someone took initiative and nerve. Women were discouraged not only by supervisors but through fear of the possible repercussions by their coworkers.

Once they succeeded in getting new jobs, women were often subject to devastating harassment. Supervisors insured that women received inadequate training. Vicki, for example, almost burned her face with acid while working with a cleanup crew because she was not advised of the dangers: "They don't teach you; they're in a hurry, and they don't go for women up there." Women would fail their job trials or receive job-related injuries and get discouraged. Familiar with this scenario, the bold Connie anticipated her treatment when she was promoted to shipping clerk. She told her supervisor and union representative alike: "I want it to go on the record that I have been told already that I'm going to be disqualified. But the only way you are going to disqualify me is to run over with that boxcar. I am going to make it." She described her training period:

> I learned to stack cases, which weigh up to a hundred pounds, and put up bars to the box cars, which weigh about twenty-five to thirty pounds, and you must lift them over your head. I wasn't taught to drive a forklift until I'd been there about six months. It would have made my job a lot easier, since I have to go up and down the dock, which is about two-and-a-half blocks long. But the boys there weren't allowed to teach me. They were told "definitely not; teach her to hand stock and put up bars." I used to come home so tired I'd just flop out on that bed, and I was out until the next day. I was *completely* exhausted!

Supervisors would add tasks to jobs and even assigned one woman work that formerly had been split between two men's jobs. For example, four-foot-nine-inch Maricela Hernández had to climb a ten-foot ladder to check temperature gauges, a task never assigned to the prior male worker. Lisa observed about her mother's experiences: "They used to hassle her!

They turned her meter back; she knew because she wrote the numbers down before she left. It was like a ritual: Every year they'd try and take her job away; she'd call in the union." Lupe observed: "The foremen were really upset because they had to train this one girl. They felt men should have the job because of the prestige; that's mostly what it was."

Patronizing comments by supervisors were commonplace. During her interview for an oiler-greaser job, one woman was told, "We don't want you using your sex appeal to get the men to do your work." Connie observed: "Most company people are male Anglos, and for some asinine reason they don't like working with women. They just don't want to give you the chance to advance."

Women's new male coworkers were also a source of irritation or outright harassment. On a new job, women were alternately ignored and taunted. They were admonished for depriving a man's family of its support, accused of being "man chasers," or called "uppity" or "loud-mouthed bitches." Men made fun of women's awkwardness in a new job with comments such as "leave it to a woman to do that" or teased them with statements such as "you wanted a man's job, now do it." Connie's coworkers were explicit: "They said, 'You're going to learn the hard way. Then it's up to you to learn the easy way.'" Luz, who worked temporarily in a higher-bracket job, said, "I know I sound paranoid, but those men who are fair are moved; they were very biased as to who you are. Men assume women can't do it with no testing." Cristina was upset: "They tell us vulgar things; all of this is very bad. It's discrimination, and sometimes even your own race is the worst." Celia had what seems to be a unique experience. She found her coworkers to be "real nice, very helpful. If I needed anything they helped and didn't make me feel like I took a man's job; they made me feel at ease." The fact that her husband, a Portuguese-American, was a foreman in another department in the same plant may have contributed to the cooperation she found from male coworkers.

Even subordinates discouraged the entry of women into better-paying jobs by refusing to respect their authority as supervisors. Connie supervised three crews of workers as part of her job. One of the new male workers refused to follow her directions on how to load the box-cars properly. This was during a rush period and created a lot of tension until she finally confronted him, demanding to know why he refused to work for her. According to Connie, he had responded: "It's just that I'm not used to a woman telling me what to do, much less yell at me. That made me mad." Connie observed: "I get my biggest problems from Chicano men. Any time I get a new worker out there, if he's Mexican or if he's Chicano, he's the one that gives me a hassle." I asked,

"Why is that?" Because Chicano men, Mexican men, have always dominated their women, and they don't want a woman to tell them what to do," she replied. She found it easiest to work with black men: "They have more respect for women." The fact that Chicanas were often placed in men's jobs in which they competed with Chicanos probably made these women more sensitive to slurs from them.

Furthermore, Chicanas may have responded differently to Chicano men because of their prior experiences with them. Connie described her own response to being in a man's role:

> It's just like in your home. Women are much more liberated now; we dare to answer back, but still a lot of times you feel guilty. There's times when I feel guilty, when I have to tell a man "you must do this because I'm telling you to do it." I revert back to when I was a child, and you didn't dare tell Daddy that. And you grew up, and you didn't tell your husband that either. It's just another male you're talking to, but it's the whole mystique of being a man: "You're so big and you're so strong." Women are supposed to be intimidated by men.

Apparently, male intimidation carried more force when the men were Chicano, because Chicano men conjured up images in Chicanas' minds that were more personal.

Women's complaints did not change things. Vicki noted, "Personnel could care less." Hence besides experiencing the difficulties of learning new jobs, women often felt humiliated and frustrated. Liz said: "I'm surprised I didn't get an ulcer. It was too much: I felt discriminated against as a Chicana and as a woman." Lisa observed, "My mom was a nervous wreck." Connie stated: "Every time a woman goes into a 'man's' job, she's harassed to the point that some women say 'you can have it.'"

The frequency of such harassment is subject to debate. A U.S. Department of Labor study claims that only one-quarter of the women they interviewed received such treatment. But every one of the women I interviewed who was working at a "man's" job had received patronizing treatment in one form or another and knew of other women who had also. Almost all of the women I interviewed had heard of such incidents. The consequent "spillover" effect of such intimidation went far beyond the individuals who faced it directly.

Women witnessed management practices that flouted the new system of promotions. Job openings were not posted; a foreman would inform friends of coming job openings so that they could apply first and so on. Connie worried because the incumbency rule was being used again. Luz believed that she could get promoted faster if "they ran the whole place fair; if jobs were openly and honestly available." Most women who were Spanish speakers believed that they needed more education and a command of English to move up. Lisa instead recalled the significance of work-based networks: "I'd have to be related to somebody important, to have the right friends and more contacts." Women clearly understood the stakes involved if they tried to move out of the "women's" departments.

VOCATIONALISM AND THE CURRICULUM*

Michael Moffatt

On paper, the curriculum of a large liberal-arts-based college such as Rutgers is a pluralistic universe of knowledge, a cornucopia of possible learning for the intellectually adventuresome student. Rutgers College students could study with about 950 faculty members in the wider university in the mid-1980s, organized into fifty-two different departments and programs whose majors were accepted by the college. All this choice might not be altogether a good thing, educational authorities sometimes worried. What guided the students through it? What general or unifying principles were they likely to discover in their college educations?

THE HIERARCHY OF THE MAJORS

For most of the students, however, the curriculum was organized in a very simple way. There were useful subjects, subjects that presumably led to good careers, and there were useless ones. Some of the useless subjects were "interesting," the students conceded. You might study one or two of them on the side in college, or if you could not stand any of the useful majors, you might actually major in something more eccentric:

Dorm Resident (Hasbrouck Fourth lounge, September 1984):   What did you say your name was again?

Anthropologist: Mike.

Student: Someone told me you're in anthropology?

Anthropologist: Yup.

Student: That seems like kind of a strange thing to be majoring in. I mean, what will you ever *do* with anthropology?

Anthropologist: I'm not majoring in it. I *am* an anthropologist. And what I'm doing with it right now is studying *you.*

Student: Oh, *you're* the guy . . . I've got to stop sitting around out here without my glasses on.

Oddballs aside, however, your bread-and-butter choice, your main field of study, ought to be something "practical," most of the students agreed.

Thus, in one recent year, almost three-quarters of the upperclassmen at Rutgers College were majoring in just ten departments while the remaining forty-two departments and programs divided up the other 28 percent of the undergraduates among themselves, in much smaller numbers. As most undergraduates understood them, eight of the ten top majors were sensible vocational choices. Economics presumably led to business, psychology to psychotherapy or to counseling, political science to law school, biological sciences to medical school, communication to work in the media, and mathematics to the sciences or to teaching. Accounting and computer science require no explanation. Only English and history were apparently pure liberal arts choices. But many of the students majoring in English had in fact double majors, and their other choice was usually a more useful one. Moreover, it was widely believed, the ability to write well made a difference in the business and professional world after college.

These top ten majors and all the rest then fell into a gradient of status in general student opinion, one that was based on three criteria. First, how good was the occupation to which a given subject presumably led? Second, and closely related, how difficult was that subject at Rutgers? And third, much less important, how much social good did the occupation or profession in question accomplish? By all three measures, biological sciences was number one. What real world profession, after all, was more prestigious than doctor? Doctors also made a lot of money and, conveniently, helped people. Premed was a very difficult major as well, the students agreed, known for its early "weeding courses," for its difficult prerequisites such as organic chemistry, believed by the students to be expressly designed to weed out underqualified undergraduates. Some of the other hard sciences were almost equally tough in undergraduate opinion, though they were taken far less often, perhaps because their target occupations were not as well known. And then came two very popular, respected choices: engineering and computer science.

Majors in the social and behavioral sciences ranked below most of those in the hard sciences. These subjects were definitely easier, the students believed, but they did still point you toward known professions or semiprofessions. And they were often about relevant, human things as well: psychology and psychotherapy, sociology and social work, and so on. Economics had a special position in the social sciences. Like the rest of them, it was considered to be only moderately difficult. This meant that many students could handle it, however; Bio-sci was simply too tough for the average undergraduate. And, though the students did not see business as a socially beneficial occupation, they did see it as one of the surer routes to personal benefit, to a middle-class or an upper-middle-class income. Economics was thus the most popular single choice by a factor of three over the next favorite major at Rutgers in the 1980s, and it had the same popularity nationwide in the 1980s.

Finally, bringing up the rear, behind the hard sciences and the bigger and the better-connected of the social and behavioral sciences, came the poor old humanities. The students often equated the humanities with all of the liberal arts; and every one of them, the students usually agreed, was a "gut" major that prepared you for nothing at all in life. Sometimes capable, hardworking students did choose to major in these subjects out of pure interest in them. But to do so, they had to swim upstream against student opinion; they had to be forever excusing themselves to their friends for their peculiar choice. "He's a throat personality in a gut major," an acquaintance of one such misplaced student joked about him in 1978.

What made most students think that some majors were more difficult than others? First of all, like many of their elders, the students firmly believed that mathematical and scientific knowledge was intrinsically harder to attain, more cumulative, and more precise than the knowledge typical of the social sciences and the humanities. You could not fake a knowledge of mathematics, they believed, whereas reading and writing, the cognitive skills that counted most outside the sciences, were much more "subjective." Reading as most students thought of it was actually entirely unproblematic; who, after all, could not read by the time they got to college? Writing, on the other hand, could be difficult. Writing was obviously not a talent everyone possessed. There was some difference of opinion among the students as to whether it could be learned or not. But if you could write, then you could "bullshit" your way through almost any course in the humanities or the social sciences, the students believed. For who could say why one paper received an A and another a B?

> Most engineers [believe] that their discipline is far more demanding in terms of time, brainpower, and competition than any others, except Pharmacy or the other sciences. . . . Non-engineering majors . . . have the easiest life in college. To study their material requires only reading whereas engineering requires reading, comprehension, and problem-solving. . . . However, I do respect [nonengineers] for the amount of papers they must write.
>
> *—Senior male, engineering major*

Nonscience majors sometimes tried to argue back against these collective put-downs of their chosen fields, but they also often accepted them as well:

> Sociology, sometimes known as the "articulation of the obvious," is an example of a discipline lacking esteem. People . . . more readily accept mathematical science because [it] represents concrete knowledge. Whereas Human Communication, Philosophy, Anthropology, and Sociology, some of the many liberal arts, are based more on abstract thinking and abstract principles.
>
> *—Sociology major, undergraduate paper*

> The most serious and intellectual of all students seem to be those in engineering and pre-medicine. . . . Unfortunately psychology majors are not seen as very intellectual or challenged academically. When a person is a psychologist, it is respectable, but before they get there they are seen as having a gut major and an easy course load. . . . For some it is a major to take when you don't know what else to major in.
>
> *—Junior male, psychology major*

The students had another, even more convincing reason for ranking the majors according to difficulty, however: their own correct sense that the various academic departments and programs in the college gave widely differing grades for widely differing amounts of required work. And the difficulty of a given subject did tend to correlate with its perceived vocational desirability, for a very simple reason. Administratively, the college and the larger university had been set up to operate as an academic marketplace. Under guidelines from the state of New Jersey, the resources the academic deans gave to the various departments—faculty positions, secretaries, budgets—were partially "enrollment driven." The more students your department taught, the more resources you could demand and the larger and more influential your department could potentially become within the university. The fewer, the smaller you were likely to shrink.

Therefore, professors in student-poor departments were often encouraged by their chairmen to "up their enrollments" by making their classes more attractive. Better teaching was one way to do so. Easier grading was another obvious technique. Faculty members in the student-rich departments, on the other hand, often felt overburdened. The deans never increased their resources fast enough, they complained, and therefore they had too many distracting undergraduates around: How would they ever get their research done? They could thus afford to be much

TABLE 1	Departments and programs, easiest to toughest grading (Faculty of Arts and Sciences departments and programs at Rutgers College). Capital letters represent those in the ten most popular majors.

1. American Studies
2. Italian
3. German
4. Hebraic Studies
5. Spanish and Portuguese
6. Chinese, Comparative Literature, and Slavic Languages and Literature
7. Women's Studies
8. Linguistics
9. Puerto Rican Studies
10. Labor Studies
11. African Studies
12. Classics and Archaeology
13. POLITICAL SCIENCE
14. French
15. Biochemistry
16. Anthropology

17. Religion
18. Sociology
19. Philosophy
20. ENGLISH
21. Geology
22. HISTORY
23. Art History
24. Statistics
25. PSYCHOLOGY
26. Physics and Astronomy
27. BIOLOGICAL SCIENCES
28. COMPUTER SCIENCE
29. Medieval Studies
30. ECONOMICS
31. Chemistry
32. Interdisciplinary Studies
33. MATHEMATICS

tougher in their grading. They could afford to "maintain standards." They could afford to "resist grade inflation." They could even institute weeding courses!

The degree to which this economy of supply and demand actually determined grading and the perceived difficulty of different majors was indicated by a list that the dean's office of the Faculty of Arts and Sciences, the biggest faculty unit serving Rutgers College, quietly circulated to all its departments once a year, probably in an effort to shame its easier departments into shaping up. In these lists, the departments and programs were ranked according to the percentage of A's, B pluses, and B's that each one had given across all its undergraduate courses during the previous year. The 1986 list (Table 1) had the easiest departments at the top, the most difficult at the bottom. The range was striking, as were the distributions. The department at the top was over two times easier than the department at the bottom. It had given 72 percent A's, B pluses, and B's, while the department at the bottom had given 30 percent. Also note the degree to which the humanities really were easiest according to this evidence, the social sciences somewhat harder, and the hard sciences hardest. Finally, note the generally direct correlation between the majors in highest demand and some of the tougher subjects (in capitals) in Table 1.

Most students did not know about the existence of this list, but they did have a working sense of what it reported. At the easier end of the scale, for instance:

> I've made the dangerous discovery that I can do a various amount and even quality of work and maintain good grades. Thus it has become a matter of how little work I can get away with and keep my [B average] or better. The nature of my major (English) aids in maintaining my lax study habits. Since exams are totally subjective and paper topics are chosen by the students, one doesn't need to read all of the books and attend all of the lectures. This year I have become amazed at just how little work is necessary.

> *—Junior female*

PART THREE

INTERACTING WITH
ACADEMIC TEXTS

Sources for Essay 5: Written Texts

15

LEARNING THE CONVENTIONS, MAKING YOUR POINTS, AND CREATING YOUR WRITTEN SELF

✱ *What's Left to Learn About College Writing?*

As a college writer, one of your challenges has been to identify and develop a perspective you can offer on any particular topic to make your voice heard and your words understood by the reader. You have been learning to situate yourself in relation to the academic community you are entering, as you would in any new language setting. You have also been considering ways in which what you write about and how you write are influenced by your own understanding of the writing process, your past writing experiences and expectations, and the cultural traditions and communication conventions that shift from one setting to the next. What remains at this point is to examine how one comes to know the conventions of speaking and writing, in particular, of college writing, and how these conventions can affect writers' growing understanding of what they want to say as well as the way they present themselves to their readers.

Writing Log Entry 1

Surveying What You've Learned About Language And Writing And How You Have Learned It

Before reading further, take a few moments to write your impression of what you have come to understand about language and writing during the past several weeks. How have you come to this

(continued)

Writing Log Entry 1

(Continued)

understanding? What have you done or read or talked about that has brought you to where you are now?

✤ *Learning the Conventions as a Speaker*

As we discussed in Part Two, establishing the confidence and authority to speak within one's family, within communities one enters or joins, or even within the world of wider communication depends largely on learning the cultural and personal traditions that affect these language communities–issues such as authority hierarchies, gender roles, sibling positions, and so forth. In the course of learning these traditions, one also learns how they shape language conventions–what is appropriate to say, when it is appropriate to say it, and to whom. But how does such learning occur? Family members don't sit you down and have you take notes from their lecture; the clubs you join don't hand out a list of "acceptable language traditions."

You learn many of these traditions, and the conventions that derive from them, without even trying to, without knowing you are doing so. As a member of a family, you are immediately integrated into its traditions, learning to speak in the context of that particular family and in relation to the conventions that have grown from its history. You learn that if you use certain words in certain situations you can expect certain results. Similarly, outside the family, without necessarily thinking about it, you watch people interact with one another. You listen to the words they use, their tone, the subjects they discuss, and then you try out comparable language in your own conversations.

Individual experiences and the lessons of trial and error teach us other conventions. When the way you speak achieves positive results, you may respond by trying to repeat the behavior or something about it. For instance, once you have a job interview and are hired as a result, you may try to recall some of what you said or how you said it the next time you interview for a job. If your nomination speech to the school results in your election, odds are good that you will review that nomination speech the next time you are running for an office. Similarly, negative results can often lead you to change your language behaviors. After your mother cautions, "Don't use those words in this house!" you may try to respect her wishes. Having been unable to convince your boss to let you have the day off one week, you try a new approach the next time you ask.

Many of the conventions of spoken language, then, are learned in a relatively passive manner—by continued exposure to them or by positive and negative rewards that either reinforce behaviors or cause you to change them.

But as you move further away from the context of family, friends, and familiar situations, into more distant circles of communication, conventions can become more complex and difficult to learn, and you may need to give active attention to learning what is appropriate and effective. Consider the following contrast. At home, you may want to convince a younger sister to do some chores for you. Your success in getting what you want depends, in part, on how well you express yourself to her—how well you know and use the conventions of brother/sister or sister/sister talk. Do you threaten her or use reason? Do you mention incidents from the past or stick only to the present? Most likely, the passive lessons of trial and error, of past observations and experience, will provide the answers to such questions.

Now, imagine that you are new to a job; you are in the employees' lounge, trying to convince a fellow employee to take some of your scheduled hours so you can go camping. Again, your success depends in part on your understanding and use of appropriate conventions. Though you may have had the automatic or entitled authority of an older sibling at home, what authority do you claim at work? What are the traditions about who can ask for time off—only older employees? only those with several months experience? only the boss's nephew? You may be able to gather some of these conventions through observing other employees and gaining experience. But the more unusual conventions may not be apparent until a seasoned employee takes you aside and explains them to you.

The difficulty of learning conventions through trial and error becomes even more pronounced in increasingly distant communication situations. Imagine you are at a bank, trying to convince someone that the balance the bank has on record doesn't include one large deposit you made. What traditions surround this conversation? To whom is it appropriate to speak—the teller? the manager? Should you demand a change in your record or politely question the bank's accuracy? Again, you may be able to learn about this unique language situation through trial and error, but it could be to your immediate financial advantage to ask someone in advance—perhaps a friend who had a similar problem or who is in banking or business.

Learning what the conventions are does not mean learning what is right or wrong, but what is most usual in a specific language situation, what is *conventional* and expected. In this scenario, it may be that the bank manager handles inquiries like yours. It would not be *wrong* to ask a teller, but doing so would be less likely to get you the result you are seeking, because it would not be the expected language behavior for that setting.

So far, our discussion of conventions has addressed two aspects of communication at once: *rhetorical conventions* and *usage conventions.* The broader rhetorical conventions concern what is usually expected or appropriate to talk about in different settings, to different listeners. The sentence-level, usage conventions concern how it is appropriate to speak, what words and phrasing are acceptable. Again, the more familiar the situation, the less you think about either rhetorical or usage conventions. With close friends, you usually feel free to talk about anything in any way you choose. In other situations, especially when you are new to a communication context, both rhetorical conventions and usage conventions may require your conscious attention.

Writing Log Entry 2

Identifying and Learning Community Conventions

Select one of the communities or organizations to which you belong. First, identify some of its speech conventions—the kinds of language or topics you expect to hear; the individuals you expect to be included in the conversation. Next, describe how you and other members of the community learned these conventions—whom did you watch or speak to or what did you read in order to come to know about and understand them?

❋ Learning the Conventions as a Writer

Writers, too, must understand the traditions of the particular language situation and the resulting rhetorical and usage conventions. In some cases, the differences between spoken and written language conventions are minimal, making the transition quite simple. Writing a letter to your parents is, generally, no more agonizing than speaking to them. But sometimes the conventions of writing can feel alien—particularly in those cases where writing is the only accepted means of communication. At the same time, learning these conventions may be more difficult in writing than it is in speaking.

The ways you learn traditions and conventions for speaking–gathering information from what you see and experience, from observation, and from trial and error–are available for learning written conventions, but they are not always so helpful. First, speech is constantly present in our lives in a way that writing is not. There are simply fewer examples to follow in writing. And second, since there are fewer opportunities to gain experience in writing, the most common approach for learning speech conventions–trial and error–may not be practical for writers. Finally, because each communication situation is different, the rhetorical conventions for writing may be harder to identify. While you can read a printed text and possibly become familiar with written usage, the larger issues of what is appropriate and expected may be less easy to figure out. The extensive experience you have as a speaker is a useful starting place in your development as a writer; also, thinking about the different demands of writing and speaking can give you a sense of the unique features of writing.

Consider some writing situations that might occur in everyday life: a letter to the IRS explaining your deductions; instructions for a friend who will be taking care of your pets while you are on vacation; or a description of a car accident for the purposes of collecting insurance. In our daily lives, we don't have sample "letters to the IRS" available to study or model "instructions for pet sitters" on hand. And even if we did, the models would not cover exactly what we need to say–though they might give us a sense of the tone and phrasing that is acceptable. In these instances, you might first apply what you know about the conventions of spoken language and, from there, use the lessons of trial and error. You may, for instance, adopt a formal, deferential voice with the IRS, trying to create a respectful, honest image of yourself; for the pet sitter, you may be much more informal and friendly, keeping in mind the numerous chores you want completed. These general conventions should work for either speech or writing. But at some point, the basic differences between the two modes of communication necessitate some differences in your approach.

The most obvious and yet, significant, difference between spoken and written language is that in the first, both the speaker and listener are present. In a conversation, we have an entire set of physical cues, gestures, and other information that is not part of written discourse. The availability of these cues means that spoken language does not always need to be as specific as written language–the speaker's hand movements, eye contact, and so on can provide a great deal of non-verbal information. The listener's response can let the speaker know what is clear or unclear so that the speaker can add details as needed. In addition, the presence of a responding listener and a much more open-ended time frame means that it is acceptable for spoken language to be more repetitive and less focused than written language.

Because of this essential difference between speech and writing–the presence of the audience–the conventions of one are not always applicable to the other. Telling the pet sitter in person about your dog–with the dog right there!–you don't necessarily have to remember every detail because the sitter will ask questions. In a letter, lack of detail is problematic: including no information about the temperament of your dog, may result in injury to the pet sitter; forgetting to mention that the dog has just recovered from hip surgery may result in improper care for the dog.

In our other hypothetical situation, the amount of information you provide is also critical. If you are sitting in an office, telling the claims adjuster about your car accident, he can stop you when he has heard enough detail on one point, asking you for information on another. However, in a letter to the insurance company, repeating the story of the car accident several times with slightly different emotional levels, you may inadvertently discredit yourself as a reliable witness.

The fact that speech provides much more immediate response allows us to learn its conventions more easily than we might with writing. In speaking, you receive reaction to each phrase, each word. You can even adjust your conventions along the way–changing "Tom" to "Mr. Kent" when you see Mr. Kent raising his eyebrows disapprovingly; you can shorten the points you're making when you see that Mr. Kent is looking at his watch. It's true that you can learn some of the conventions of written language in a similar, trial and error way. But the response to writing is most often neither so immediate nor specific as it is in speech. If, for instance, the insurance adjuster turns down your claim, it is unlikely that he or she will point out the specific features of your letter that made your argument unconvincing.

Writing Log Entry 3

Receiving the Response You Need from a Reader

Reread the three examples of writing we cite above: a letter to the IRS, instructions for a pet sitter, and a description of a car accident for the insurance company. Using one or more of these to

(continued)

Writing Log Entry 3

(Continued)

make specific points of comparison, write about an instance when you had to write for a particularly difficult situation, one in which the reader's understanding or agreement with what you said was most important. Were you successful? What conventions did you use? Were they like or unlike those in our examples?

❋ *Making Your Points*

Another challenge facing speakers and writers is how to hang on to the spark of what they want to communicate in the midst of these conventions and expectations. That spark–what interested, amused, concerned, or irritated them–was what initially motivated them to talk or to write. Yet sometimes, in the course of making adjustments for conventions, individuals can inadvertently decrease the energy of what they want to say or even lose track of it altogether.

We have claimed several times that writing and speaking are most effective when they grow from something you care about, are interested in, want to convey, or want to make happen. This personal connection is more often apparent in spoken than written language. That is, you most often speak because you want to, because you have something to say. Granted, there are times when you feel forced to answer questions or present information. But the majority of the time, and certainly when you were first learning to talk, the words came from your urge to say something. In familiar situations, when the conventions are well-known to you, you are able to focus all of your attention on what it is you want to say. Sometimes, as you move outside circles of familiarity (or in familiar but stressful situations) the complex sets of conventions you encounter can make it more difficult to hang on to your reason for speaking.

Imagine having to tell the bank that there is an error in your balance. You may know, according to convention, that you should talk directly to the manager, using a respectful, inquiring tone, selecting words that are somewhat formal ("I believe there has been an error" rather than "You are wrong"). But in the course of keeping these conventions in mind as you speak, what you want to say may be obscured or even lost. Your attention to being polite may muffle the urgency of your concern about your balance; in being deferential to the bank's authority, your own skill with accounting may not clearly come through. This conflict may sometimes explain why speakers find themselves speaking inappropriately in stressful settings–we know what the conventions are, but we are afraid of losing track of our purpose, so we rush ahead–shouting at the bank manager that he is a fool for making such a mistake. At least we've said what we are thinking, though we have probably lost our chance to be listened to by the bank manager. It's all too easy to leave a situation, only to realize that you never got what you wanted in the first place.

Making Your Points in Writing

As with speech, the further you move away from familiar circles of communication, the more difficult it can be to hang on to what you want to say as you write. Attaching a note to the TV: "Don't turn off the VCR–I'm taping!" you have made your point quite clear. Writing a letter to the president of a cable company to recommend against adding another home shopping network may be more complicated. In your attempt to follow convention, to sound polite and formal, the seriousness of your request may get lost.

Focusing on that obvious difference between speech and writing–the presence of both the speaker and listener–consider how much greater the risk is for writers to become so focused on the conventions that their reason for writing becomes not just overshadowed but completely lost. The physical distance between writers and their audiences can give the conventions inappropriate advantage. Since they are not face-to-face with an audience, writers may find themselves adopting an awkward, unnatural use of language in which conventions and their effects become exaggerated. The spoken version of an introductory convention, "Thank you for seeing me," may, in writing, become "I am grateful for the opportunity which you have given me to convey my concern." While the second version is not incorrect, it does risk undermining the purpose of the letter–to be heard as a serious customer with a valid complaint, not as a groveling customer who is grateful for a meeting.

Writing Log Entry 4

Finding Conventions in What You Read

In writing *Shoptalk*, we had to make sure that our intention to help students improve their understanding of college writing and

(continued)

Writing Log Entry 4

(Continued)

their own writing skills not be overwhelmed by the writing conventions expected in a college textbook, and, in fact, that these conventions allow us to accomplish this intention.

Reread the last two sections of *Shoptalk*, "Making your points" and "Making your points in writing," underlining any phrases, words, or sentence structures that seem to you to be particularly representative of the conventions of a college writing textbook. Looking over what you have underlined, select three or four that you find most representative; in your **Writing Log**, describe how each one works in relation to the book's intention.

✳ *Creating Your Self with Language*

Whenever you use language, the words you have selected and the way you put them together provide listeners or readers with an image of who you are. Earlier, we referred to this self when we talked about the stance that the writer takes in relation to the reader and the subject of the writing. You can create a formal, distant, general self with phrases like: "One can contemplate one's future and life in the next millennium," or an informal, personal, chatty one, "I've got to think about what I'll do after I graduate." This construction of the self, called "ethos," is the image of the writer that is created for your listener or reader by the words you put together. Whether you are aware of it or not, the language you use creates an ethos, a spoken or written self for your audience. Effective speakers take advantage of this aspect of language, creating an ethos that projects the kind of person they really are or the one they want to appear to be. The more confident and experienced one becomes as a speaker, the less one has to dwell on this aspect of communication. You know how to speak in familiar situations, and as the range of what is familiar to you expands, you are able to focus on your purpose in speaking, creating an effective spoken self in the process. Unfamiliar situations, however, may require that you give more conscious attention to the image you are projecting.

A speaker's physical presence as well as his or her actual voice qualities also contribute to the creation of this image, affecting the word choices speakers make. For example, imagine the contrast between asking your friend for a loan and asking the bank for a loan. Though you will want to convince both parties that you will repay the money, the way you present yourself to each will be different. Your voice is already familiar to your friend and is closely tied to the physical image of you that your friend has gained over time. The spoken self you create in your request for a loan either will be consistent with this image (a reliable, conscientious person) or, if it is more to your advantage, will attempt to replace your familiar image (an unpredictable con artist) with one that is more reassuring for your friend (someone who has seen the error of his ways and wants to make good). In contrast, the bank manager has never met you and may have never seen you or heard your voice. Consequently, you are creating a spoken self for the bank manager without any past history to rely on or play against.

The risk is even greater, if, in conversation, you know the conventions and hang on to your purpose, but your spoken self creates unexpected or unwanted consequences. For instance, you may want to get the day off, correct your bank statement, or avoid doing chores, but will you do so at the cost of your future reputation? You get someone to cover for you at your job, but your fellow workers conclude that you shirk responsibility and can't be relied on. Your sister does your chores, but she tells your parents you are a bully. The bank alters the bank balance, but the tellers are rude to you every time you come in after this event. Clearly, learning how to speak with authority is more than just learning how to get what you want. Part of getting what you want includes getting people to see you the way you want them to.

✿ Creating a Written Self

Your spoken self is closely tied to your physical presence and voice. To some listeners, your words may "sound" differently if you are wearing jeans and a t-shirt than they will if you wear a business suit. In addition, the presence of the listener will affect the spoken self you choose to create. The image you project will be, in part, a response to the person with whom you are speaking. You may decide to present yourself differently as you plan your speech about why you don't deserve a parking ticket depending on whether the judge is a scowling, impatient senior member of the bar or a young, attractive, new magistrate.

As these examples suggest, both listeners and speakers may let their impressions or biases influence the communication taking place. As in any other judgments made from superficial data, these judgments may be a distortion. The scowling magistrate may actually be the more open-minded judge; the speaker dressed in jeans may be the more formidable. In focusing on appearances, we may miscalculate how we should be presenting ourselves. We may find ourselves speaking overly formally to the older judge and too casually to the younger.

In writing, these difficulties are magnified since our audience is only imagined. With no immediate presence of a reader, writers may, initially, rely too much on the dictates of convention to create their written self. For example, the conventions of business letter writing may require formality, but the purpose of your letter, to convince the cable company not to add another home shopping network, may be severely weakened if these conventions aren't somehow adjusted. In order to keep the written self consistent with the points one wants to make, the work of writing includes creating an appropriate image of the reader. When you are writing to a stranger or a near stranger, adjusting your writing to this imagined audience may be especially challenging. Writing to the president of a company, you may be so intimidated by the image you have created of this person, an image that may be far more intimidating than would be the actual physical presence of the cable company president, that your writing becomes defensive even though you have not been directly challenged. You may have invented an unfriendly, narrow-minded man who cares more about making money than about your TV viewing pleasure and write: "Dear Sir: You must think I am an air-headed female who can't think for herself and who loves to shop so much that she would be thrilled by having another shopping channel ..." Creating, instead, the image of a president who knows that competition among cable companies is fierce, who wants to keep his customers, you may adjust your written self to one that is more agreeable: "Dear Sir: Given that the local cable network with which you compete recently replaced one of its shopping networks with another sports channel, your decision to add the House Beautiful Shopping channel is likely to lose you some valued customers." Writing provides us with an interesting opportunity to examine the images we hold of our audience and to create a sense of audience that serves us best as communicators.

Writing Log Entry 5

Identifying Your Written Self

Return to *Writing Log 3* in Chapter 2, where you wrote a letter to the person who coordinates the writing courses at your school about your fears and expectations toward college writing. Exchange logs with someone in your class, reading one another's letters. Analyze the written self that is created in the letter. What kind of ethos does the writer seem to create? What seems to be the writer's image of his or her audience? Point to particular words or sentences in the letter that create these images.

16

LEARNING CONVENTIONS, MAKING YOUR POINTS, AND CREATING YOUR WRITTEN SELF *AS A COLLEGE WRITER*

❧ *The Nature of College Writing*

Writing texts, including this one, create an illusion about the way we learn to write and become better writers. The illusion is that once you have read this book, completed its assignments, and written all of the essays, you will be done becoming a college writer; you will have finished the book, the course, and will have learned all you need to know about writing. We certainly believe that when you have finished this text and its assignments, you will be a better, more self-confident writer. But you won't be "done" becoming a writer. For, as we have suggested throughout *Shoptalk,* you will always have new choices to make as a writer; new situations to write in; new ideas to communicate; new audiences to write for. As a college writer, you will find yourself in new contexts, writing for the demands of different disciplines with varying conventions and expectations.

Of course, if there were no consistencies in college writing experiences, college writing texts wouldn't be possible. As we have identified throughout the book, there are some conventions that remain relatively constant for all college writing. Academic readers have certain expectations about the explicitness with which you need to express points, about the need for analysis, about the sources of information available to you when you write, and about the use of standard English. Necessarily, the expectations of academic readers influence the choices that college writers make as they learn appropriate conventions, how to make and hang on to the point of a college essay, and how to create a compelling ethos or image of themselves for the reader.

❧ *Learning the Conventions of College Writing*

The conventions of college writing may seem to be a mysterious code known only to instructors, not to be broken by students. Yet these conventions can be learned in the same way we learn those for all language: by trial and error, observation, and direct instruction. And like writers new to other writing situations, new college writers may find themselves relying on the least efficient method: trial and error. Trial and error is particularly ineffective as a means of learning college writing conventions because the feedback students receive to their writing in the form of general comments or grades does not usually provide enough of the kind of information writers need in order to improve their writing. Some of you may have experienced the frustration of trying to figure out how to keep the quality of your writing the same or how to improve it when the only prior information you have from an instructor is a broad category label such as "A" or "C."

Since each academic discipline is a unique area of focus with its own significant questions and ways of examining its subject, college writing conventions are especially complex. Consequently, a process of close and careful observation in a course or within a department, rather than trial and error, can be an effective means to learning the conventions and expectations for any particular discipline.

To appreciate the complexity of college writing conventions, consider, for example, that although several departments on campus may have courses available on the topic of man-made disasters, the conventions for examining and writing about the topic vary dramatically among the departments. In the English Department, you might read a novel like *Golden Days* and write a feminist analysis of the main character; in the Political Science Department, you might outline and examine the political events leading up to Hiroshima and Nagasaki, writing an argument for or against U.S. action; in Environmental Studies, you might visit the decontaminated site of a nuclear waste dump, interviewing local residents about the effects on their neighborhood; and in the Journalism Department, you might recollect and analyze your own memory of situations involving nuclear disarmament or waste, writing a profile piece of your retrospective account. So while the starting point–man-made disaster–is the same, in each course, the object and perspective of study, the kind of information that is collected and valued (personal experience, observation and interviews, written texts), and the focus of the writing in each discipline are quite different.

By carefully observing the content and materials of a course or a department, you can begin to determine what the appropriate conventions are. Here are some questions that might guide your observations.

1. What kinds of information are most frequently cited in the readings for the course?

2. What kinds of sources does the instructor most often introduce in lecture and discussion?

3. Looking closely at the assignments, what kinds of questions seem to recur—those about history? personal experience? other people? things you have read?

4. Looking at the course syllabus, what does the instructor seem to value and how will your performance in the course be measured?

5. Looking at the required texts, what is the tone of voice that is used by the authors—what is the ethos that is created? How is it created?

6. If sample essays have been distributed, how are the writers making and supporting their points? What is the ethos that is projected?

7. Reading carefully any comments the instructor has made on your writing, what conventions does he or she seem to be valuing most?

Because writing is by nature so time-consuming, most students wish for a formula that would make writing quicker and easier, a generic program into which the writer can plug ideas, push the "print" button, and come up with a perfect essay every time. As we will discuss later, for some very particular writing occasions, you can follow a formatting formula. But for nearly all other college writing assignments, you will need to figure out what matters in this course, to this particular academic reader, and why.

To address these complex questions, college writers can combine the kinds of observations we have described with the third way of learning conventions—direct instruction from or discussion with a teacher. It is worth making an appointment to talk with someone who teaches in a department you are taking courses in or planning to take courses in. Find out from the instructor about the written conventions of the discipline. Let the instructor know that you are collecting this information for a college writing class or for future writing assignments you will complete in the course. You want to understand what writing in this discipline "looks like," how its essays or reports are structured, what manner of citation is used, what kinds of research material are expected and accepted, and where the most convincing materials are likely to be published.

What you are learning from this form of field research–the process of observation and direct gathering of information–are the ways the professionals in a particular discipline think; what questions they find significant; what sources of information and methods of analysis they most value. The general college writing conventions we listed at the start of this chapter will hold for all disciplines; the unique disciplinary conventions need to be acquired as you move through those courses.

✤ *Writing with a Formula*

It would be dishonest of us to claim that there are absolutely no formulas for college writing. When there is a formula of sorts, there is, also, a reason the formula exists, one that has to do with the general purpose of the piece of writing.

First, consider some examples of disciplines for which formula-type writing is more expected than others. In business memos or scientific lab reports there are often quite rigid formats that writers are expected to follow. In these instances, the point of the writing is to convey information as quickly and directly as possible. Keep in mind, though, that these are *formats* within which information is to be presented. Even in "formula" writing, writers still have the job of coming up with ideas, conveying their message, appropriately addressing the audience, and so on.

A second, and most familiar example of college writing that has a formula, is the timed-writing exam. Students receive a question and are asked to write on the spot for a given time-period. Writers of timed exams are not expected to develop ideas and find meanings to the extent that they are expected to do so in untimed writing. Exams are an occasion to present quickly what you already know on a given question. Unless another pattern for the formula is given, you can usually rely on the following:

1. A brief introduction that restates the question or provides some background;

2. A brief statement of one or two highly explicit points you wish to make;

3. Several paragraphs or pages of specific explanation of these points using supporting examples;

4. Some brief concluding statements that reflect on the question and the information you have provided.

Readers of a timed essay do not usually expect to learn something new, as would the reader of an untimed essay. They expect to be able to see quickly if you have learned certain concepts or principles or remembered certain information.

This same formula is also expected in timed-essay exams that are not connected to specific course material, such as writing placement or exit exams. You may be given some reading material or a question to respond to. Again, readers of these exams are not looking for your unique perspective or your creative process in the way they might be were you writing an untimed essay. The formula provided above will be useful to you on these occasions as well.

Writing Log Entry 6

Figuring Out What "Counts"

Any writing assignment includes, in addition to the essay you write, other related "written texts": the assignment itself and the instructor's comments and corrections. Review these related written texts for an essay you wrote for this or another class you are currently taking. Analyze them to determine what seems to matter to that instructor for that particular assignment. Be sure to identify what you found in the related texts that led you to your conclusions.

�֎ *Making Your Point*

As you continue to grow and develop as a college writer, you may find that the very conventions and expectations that you are working so hard to understand and employ seem to frustrate, even prevent your attempts to make a particular point in your essays. Student writers can become so focused on the "formula," on figuring out what the teacher wants, that they lose sight of what they, themselves want. Remember that one of the most identifying conventions of college writing is that it makes its meaning explicit. This can only occur if writers know what that meaning is– what they have the urge to argue, explain, describe, propose–and, equally important, why they want to do so.

Remember that language, both spoken and written, most often emerges from the language user's urge to say something to an audience. But because college writing is initiated by someone else–an instructor– students are faced with a difficult dilemma: If college writing is initiated by someone else, how can you find within that your own "urge" to write. And then, how, in the midst of the conventions, can you hang on to it?

Your personal and cultural perspectives offer an important connection to all the writing you will do in college. In *Shoptalk*, one of our goals has been for you to try out writing strategies that develop and engage these perspectives and that give you a way to find that urge for writing within the writing prompt initiated by the instructor. To write effectively in college, you need to ask yourself, what do I have to say and how can I say it in such a way that I will be listened to?

Writing Log Entry 7

Finding the Reason to Write in the Words of the Text

Look again at the piece of writing you examined in the last **Writing Log.** Identify your reason for writing that essay, and how it, your own "urge" to write, fit with the reason for writing that was implied in the instructor's assignment. How might you have made this connection stronger? List particular areas of the essay in which you most explicitly accomplished your own purposes and the purposes of the assignment.

❧ *Creating a Written Self*

As a college writer, you have choices about the image of yourself you will cast for the reader of your text, the written self your words will create. But like the choices you have regarding conventions and making a point, choices about ethos in college writing come with their own peculiar challenges.

The majority of college essays are written at the request of an instructor who will be the primary–though not necessarily the only–reader or audience. In relation to the student writer, this audience has more education, has studied the subject of the essay more extensively–indeed, is most often a specialist in the particular discipline–and holds the power of evaluation and grading. Faced with such an audience, one option that occurs to many students is to try to meet the instructor head on, attempting to create an image that will impress the reader with its intelligence. However, while seeking to develop an impressive, intelligent voice or self-image, students can mistake convention for language. That is, they seem to act on an assumption that college writing is defined simply by its language, the inclusion of big, formal vocabulary and complicated sentences. What gets overlooked in this approach is the reason that particular vocabulary and syntax are used and their relationship to the conventions and expectations of the discipline.

For example, trying to sound "academic" when writing about a novel, a student might write, "Everything about the characters is discerned as the story progresses." Writing about the same idea, a more experienced college writer might instead write, "The narrator maintains an omniscient perspective throughout the novel." Both writers are making an observation about the amount of information that is shared in the story. The second writer knows, and chooses to use, some of the specialized language characteristic of literary writing. Using words like "narrator," "omniscient," and "novel," the writer can be identified as someone familiar with the conventionally accepted language of literature. Rather than selecting familiar vocabulary and syntax or using specialized language that is appropriate to the discipline, the first writer used "thesaurus speak," substituting "discerned" for "know" and created an unnatural sentence construction with no active subject (no one is doing the discerning). In an attempt to create an academic, impressive voice, students can inadvertently mark themselves as being unfamiliar with the discipline by using unfamiliar, uncomfortable language. In fact, the most experienced college writers might not try to rely on individual words pulled from a thesaurus or a literary glossary at all. Instead, these writers would know that what matters most to the reader of the literary college essay is a concrete observation followed by support drawn from the text itself: "In *The Great Gatsby,* Nick speaks as if he knows everything about every other character."

Think back to our earlier example of the operating room. What would happen if someone who is not a medical person and has only a patient's knowledge of health care tried to use medical terminology in the same way the doctors were? Rather than giving that person the voice of a knowledgeable physician or someone on par with the doctors, this person would be marked as an outsider who is pretending badly. The same thing can happen in college writing if one tries to create a voice for the purpose of impressing a reader by using words or sentence structures that are unfamiliar.

It's as if you are all dressed for school and decide, at the last minute, that your jacket isn't nice enough, but it's the only one you have. In desperation, you run to the closet and grab your father's lovely suede jacket that is several sizes too large for you. When your friends see you they notice the jacket alright, but what they notice is that it doesn't fit.

There is little chance that you can sound like one of your instructors or that you can successfully create an image similar to the professor's. But through the kind of close observation and instruction we have described, you can develop a sense of the special (not necessarily big) vocabulary that your instructor uses and that appears in the texts you read in class. You can also come to understand what kind of information "counts" in that course and how it is expected to be presented. Finally, you can take advantage of the perspective you have by way of your own personal and cultural experiences, letting these provide you with an avenue into whatever you are writing.

In this way, the image you create of yourself, the voice you use, will be at once your own, appropriate to what you want to say, and appropriate to the conventions of the discipline, consistent with your relationship to those conventions.

You will provide readers with the image of a writer worth listening to, a writer who brings a certain authority to the text and who presents himself or herself in a manner respectful of the conventions of the conversation he or she is entering.

Writing Log Entry 8

Creating a Written Self

Analyze the essay you examined in the last two reflective writings to determine what voice you have created in this essay. Be sure to identify words or language structures that allowed you to create this voice. Identify, too, any places where the voice changes or is inconsistent and explain how this happens.

❧ *Writing from Texts*

We hope that as you leave this writing course, you do so with an understanding of the kinds of choices facing you in future college writing. One final feature that distinguishes college writing from much other writing and adds to its level of difficulty is that it often requires the writer to interact with written texts, the last of the three sources of information we will discuss. While writers outside the university may draw on what they have read to inform their writing, inside the university it is *essential* for writers to know what has been said, in print, about their subjects. And the more "academic" a piece of writing is, the more heavily referenced it will be. A doctoral dissertation, for example, usually includes a full chapter or two entirely devoted to what has been said so far on the subject under investigation, quoting from these texts, and establishing the groundwork for the original material the dissertation will explore. If that same study were to be rewritten for a non-academic audience, it would likely make much less extensive reference to the background material and would document its sources less prominently in the text.

As a college writer, you will not be held to the demands of the professional academic, but you will often be expected to make use of material from written texts as a major source for your own writing. Frequently, college writing assignments are preceded by reading assignments. Students are asked to write in connection or response to something they have read. In a sense, a writing assignment in response to reading, means that students are being invited–or expected–to enter the ongoing conversations of other writers. Notice that in the majority of **Writing Log** entries you have completed so far in Part Three, you were asked to do just that–to write in response to, and with direct reference to, other written texts.

However, in the next chapter of the book, though your **Writing Log** entries will continue to be based on written texts, we will invite you to enter a particular conversation and to write from certain written texts that we have supplied. We will also provide you with some strategies for using writing as a means of finding your way into this particular conversation and into your own starting place for creating an essay.

17

PLACING YOURSELF IN A CONVERSATION IN COMPOSITION

❧ *Writing from Written Texts*

In the first two parts of the book, you practiced writing college essays using two sources of information available to all writers: personal experience and field research gathered from observations and conversations. Now we will ask you to write from a third source of information, the one that may be most common in college writing: written texts. Such texts include academic and general-audience books, essays and articles from professional journals, newspaper and magazine articles, even reference materials like encyclopedias or government documents.

An additional source of written texts is the World Wide Web, where writers have access to a seemingly endless supply of texts that have been entered into the Web by individuals and organizations from all over the world. Some of these texts replicate those we can find in the library (articles, newspapers, conference papers, journals, and so forth); others have been created specifically for electronic rather than print distribution (Web pages, on-line databases, on-line journals).

Like any information available to writers, written texts are not all of equal value nor can they be cited with equal authority. To some degree, words that appear in print or across the lines of an electronic-computerized network give the illusion of being important. However, because anyone who has access to the technology and knows how to make use of it can create a Web page or an electronic database, and because many of the tens of thousands of books and articles published each year are done so with little or no evaluation of their quality or reliability, writers must determine which written texts will provide their essays with the best, most credible means of support. In the academic world, this determination is based, among other things, on the authority and reputation of the authors and the means by which the texts were made public. Generally speaking, texts that have been written by individuals who are known to have a particular expertise in an area and/or texts that have been published through organizations that screen and evaluate for quality and truth-value (publishers, editorial boards, review boards, and so forth), provide the most valuable and convincing data for college writers. Electronic texts, particularly, need to be evaluated in these terms. Professional and scholarly organizations make use of the Web; academic texts are distributed there. But a vast amount of what is on the Web is self-published or published by groups or organizations with no credibility in the academic world. So, while the Web provides a powerful, even indispensable resource for college writers, the material published there needs to be evaluated carefully for its value and credibility.

❧ *Entering the Conversation*

In this chapter, we provide you with the written texts that will serve as your source of information for your final essay. We selected essays from the professional literature of one academic discipline, Composition. The essays we have included are connected to the discussions that have appeared throughout this book in that they address issues about college writing and learning to write, for the focus of the discipline of Composition is the subject of writing.

The writers of these essays are professors whose field of specialization is Composition and their intended audience for their work is primarily other professionals in the field. Although professional academics write for students as an audience when they write textbooks, most of their other writing is for other academics who specialize in the same or a related area. The literature of a discipline may be thought of as a conversation among those who are part of that discipline. However, in a preliminary way, you have already begun to enter the conversation of the discipline of Composition, since you have been investigating the subject of writing throughout your work in *Shoptalk*.

The articles you will read and write from for Essay 5 were first published in three of the many professional journals that members of this discipline read: *Language Arts, Writing Lab Newsletter,* and *College Composition and Communication*. The authors submitted their essays to the journal editors who, in turn, passed them on to reviewers who evaluated the essays and judged them to be appropriate and ready for publication.

In some cases the reviewers and editors may have asked for the authors to make revisions and additions before the essays were published.

In selecting these particular texts we were not looking for essays that focused on one specific topic; we were interested in giving you what we felt were interesting examples of different writing by authorities in the field that touched on a range of issues. You may find that the issues addressed in the four essays overlap, and that they overlap with some of the subjects of your own or your classmates' writing. You will see that in addition to written texts, these essays include other sources of information to make their points. Personal experience, observation and conversation, as well as written texts inform the research and scholarship of Composition.

As you read, your job is first to hear what the authors have to say, to make sure you understand their points and the way their arguments unfold, to ask questions about those points that you don't follow or implications that are unclear.

Then, your next goal will be to join the conversation, in some way, yourself. You may find that the essays trigger questions you wish to pursue in your own writing; or that you wish to examine some point that recurs in the essays; or that you wish to focus on some conflict with or support for ideas the essays raise for you. As in the other assignments, you will choose your own topic and purpose for writing, and your purpose and focus will develop as you work on the preliminary writing activities.

When a writer's primary source of information is written texts, probably the biggest challenge is to find one's own purpose for writing. Like all college writing, an essay using texts as its primary source needs to provide not simply a summary of what you have read. A college essay must make some kind of original contribution to the ongoing conversation.

When you work on this assignment, it would be helpful to think back to the ways in which you met the requirements for analysis and explicitness in previous assignments. In the first two essays, once you focused in on a particular experience or group of experiences, you had to locate some focus and direction, some pattern; you had to make sense of what you were noticing about the experiences. Similarly, in the second two assignments, when your source was information gathered from what others said and what you observed, you could not simply record your observations; you needed to reflect on them and to find your own perspective on your material. These analytical skills and the ability to find different perspectives that you have been developing in the previous four essays can be applied to this final writing assignment in which your information comes primarily from written texts.

As you read these essays, give careful attention to interacting with the words and ideas: responding, questioning, replying, and reacting while at the same time hearing and respecting the authors' words. Such interactive behaviors will, finally, help you establish your own authority and position from which to write. The response activities preceding and following the essays can help you not only to get a deeper understanding of what you have read, but to engage personally with the ideas raised for you by the texts. When you wrote essays in the first two sections of *Shoptalk*, you began by looking back to all the **Writing Log** entries you had done. However, because the **Writing Logs** in Chapters 15 and 16 served mainly as a way to reflect on the reading you were doing and as practice for the experience of writing from written texts, for Essay 5, you will only need to consider the **Writing Log** entries in this chapter, writing you will have generated in light of the essays that follow.

Writing Log Entry 9

Thoughts before You Read

As a starting point, take a minute to reflect on your first thoughts about these essays *before* you read them. Take a look at the titles and glance through each one. Write down your first impressions of what each essay seems to be about. What initial thoughts do you have on these topics?

✳ *Annotate, Underline, Scribble*

Ultimately, you are going to join this conversation yourself which means that you will need not only to read these essays but to interact with them. Before you begin to read essays, be sure to have a pen or pencil in hand so that you can mark up the pages as you read, not merely underlining all of the "important stuff," but, perhaps, developing a code for yourself that allows you to have a record of your reading: you might underline main ideas, bracket the examples, squiggle line those sections that confuse you. At the same time, use the margins of the text to write notes to yourself that record your reactions and thoughts for later ("That's surprising"; "Sounds like what we read in sociology"; "Find out about this . . ."). Take your time to read slowly through and annotate each essay.

༄༅

Minimalist Tutoring: Making the Students Do All the Work*

Jeff Brooks

A writing center worst case scenario: A student comes in with a draft of a paper. It is reasonably well-written and is on a subject in which you have both expertise and interest. You point out the mechanical errors and suggest a number of improvements that could be made in the paper's organization; the student agrees and makes the changes. You supply some factual information that will strengthen the paper; the student incorporates it. You work hard, enjoy yourself, and when the student leaves, the paper is much improved. A week later, the student returns to the writing center to see you: "I got an A! Thanks for all your help!"

This scenario is hard to avoid, because it makes everyone involved feel good: the student goes away happy with a good grade, admiring you; you feel intelligent, useful, helpful—everything a good teacher ought to be. Everything about it seems right. That this is bad points out the central difficulty we confront as tutors: we sit down with imperfect papers, but our job is to improve their writers.

When you "improve" a student's paper, you haven't been a tutor at all; you've been an editor. You may have been an exceedingly good editor, but you've been of little service to your student. I think most writing center tutors agree that we must not become editors for our students and that the goal of each tutoring session is learning, not a perfect paper. But faced with students who want us to "fix" their papers as well as our own desire to create "perfect" documents, we often find it easier and more satisfying to take charge, to muscle in on the student's paper, red pen in hand.

To avoid that trap, we need to make the student the primary agent in the writing center session. The student, not the tutor, should "own" the paper and take full responsibility for it. The tutor should take on a secondary role, serving mainly to keep the student focused on his own

---

*Brooks, Jeff. "Minimalist Tutoring: Making the Student Do All the Work." *Writing Lab Newsletter* 15.6 (1991): 1–4. All Rights and Title reserved unless permission is granted by Purdue University. Material will not be reproduced in any form without express written permission.

writing. A student who comes to the writing center and passively receives knowledge from a tutor will not be any closer to his own paper than he was when he walked in. He may leave with an improved paper, but he will not have learned much.

A writing teacher or tutor cannot and should not expect to make student papers "better"; that is neither our obligation, nor is it a realistic goal. The moment we consider it our duty to improve the paper, we automatically relegate ourselves to the role of editor.

If we can't fix papers, is there anything left for us to do? I would like to suggest that when we refuse to edit, we become more active than ever as educators. In the writing center, we have the luxury of time that the classroom teacher does not have. We can spend that time talking and listening, always focusing on the paper at hand. The primary value of the writing center tutor to the student is as a living human body who is willing to sit patiently and help the student spend time with her paper. This alone is more than most teachers can do, and will likely do as much to improve the paper as a hurried proofreader can. Second, we can talk to the student as an individual about the one paper before us. We can discuss strategies for effective writing and principles of structure, we can draw students' attention to features in their writing, and we can give them support and encouragement (writing papers, we shouldn't forget, is a daunting activity).

ASSUMPTIONS

All of this can be painfully difficult to do. Every instinct we have tells us that we must work for perfection; likewise, students pressure us in the same direction. I have found two assumptions useful in keeping myself from editing student papers:

1. The most common difficulty for student writers is paying attention to their writing. Because of this, student papers seldom reflect their writers' full capabilities. Writing papers is a dull and unrewarding activity for most students, so they do it in noisy surroundings, at the last minute, their minds turning constantly to more pressing concerns. It is little wonder that so much student writing seems haphazard, unfocused, and disorganized. A good many errors are made that the student could easily have avoided. If we can get students to reread a paper even once before handing it in, in most cases we have rendered an improvement. We ought to encourage students to treat their own writings as texts that deserve the same kind of close attention we usually reserve for literary texts.

Our message to students should be: "Your paper has value as a piece of writing. It is worth reading and thinking about like any other piece of writing."

2. While student writings are texts, they are unlike other texts in one important way: the process is far more important than the product. Most "real-world" writing has a goal beyond the page; anything that can be done to that writing to make it more effective ought to be done. Student writing, on the other hand, has no real goal beyond getting it on the page. In the real world when you need to have something important written "perfectly," you hire a professional writer; when a student hires a professional writer, it is a high crime called plagiarism.

This fairly obvious difference is something we often forget. We are so used to real-world writing, where perfection is paramount, that we forget that students write to learn, not to make perfect papers. Most writing teachers probably have a vision of a "perfect" freshman paper (it probably looks exactly like the pieces in the readers and wins a Bedford prize); we should probably resign ourselves to the fact that we will seldom see such a creature. Most students simply do no have the skill, experience, or talent to write the perfect paper.

BASIC MINIMALIST TUTORING

Given these assumptions, there are a number of concrete ways we can put theory into practice. Our body language will do more to signal our intentions (both to our students and to ourselves) than anything we say. These four steps should establish a tone that unmistakably shows that the paper belongs to the student and that the tutor is not an editor.

1. Sit beside the student, not across a desk—that is where job interviewers and other authorities sit. This first signal is important for showing the student that you are *not* the person "in charge" of the paper.

2. Try to get the student to be physically closer to her paper than you are. You should be, in a sense, an outsider, looking over her shoulder while she works on her paper.

3. If you are right-handed, sit on the student's right; this will make it more difficult for you to write on the paper. Better yet, don't let yourself have a pencil in your hand. By all means, if you must hold something, don't make it a red pen!

4. Have the student read the paper aloud to you, and suggest that he hold a pencil while doing so. Aside from saving your eyes in the case

of bad handwriting, this will accomplish three things. First, it will by-pass that awkward first few moments of the session when you are in complete control of the paper and the student is left out of the action while you read his paper. Second, this will actively involve the student in the paper, quite likely for the first time since he wrote it. I find that many students are able to find and correct usage errors, awkward wording, even logic problems without any prompting from me. Third, this will help establish the sometimes slippery principle that good writing should sound good.

I am convinced that if you follow these four steps, even if you do nothing else, you will have served the student better than you would if you "edited" his paper.

ADVANCED MINIMALIST TUTORING

Of course, there is quite a bit more you can do for the student in the time you have. You can use your keen intelligence and fine critical sense to help the student without directing the paper. As always, the main goal is to keep the student active and involved in the paper. I have three suggestions:

1. Concentrate on success in the paper, not failure. Make it a practice to find something nice to say about every paper, no matter how hard you have to search. This isn't easy to do; errors are what we usually focus on. But by pointing out to a student when he is doing something right, you reinforce behavior that may have started as a felicitous accident. This also demonstrates to the student that the paper is a "text" to be analyzed, with strengths as well as weaknesses. This is where the tutor can radically depart from the role of editor.

2. Get the student to talk. It's her paper; she is the expert on it. Ask questions—perhaps "leading" questions—as often as possible. When there are sentence-level problems, make the student find and (if possible) correct them. When something is unclear, don't say, "This is unclear"; rather, say, "What do you mean by this?" Instead of saying, "You don't have a thesis," ask the student, "Can you show me your thesis?" "What's your reason for putting Q before N?" is more effective than "N should have come before Q." It is much easier to point out mistakes than it is to point the student toward finding them, but your questions will do much more to establish the student as sole owner of the paper and you as merely an interested outsider.

3. If you have time during your session, give the student a discrete writing task, then go away for a few minutes and let him do it. For instance, having established that the paper has no thesis, tell the student to write the thesis while you step outside for a few minutes. The fact that you will return and see what he has accomplished (or not accomplished) will force him to work on the task you have given him probably with more concentration than he usually gives his writing. For most students, the only deadline pressure for their paper is the teacher's final due date. Any experienced writer knows that a deadline is the ultimate energizer. Creating that energy for a small part of the paper is almost the best favor you can do for a student.

DEFENSIVE MINIMALIST TUTORING

So far, I have been assuming that the student is cooperative or at least open to whatever methods you might use. This, of course, is not a very realistic assumption. There are many students who fight a non-editing tutor all the way. They know you know how to fix their paper, and that is what they came to have done. Some find ingenious ways of forcing you into the role of editor: some withdraw from the paper, leaving it in front of you; some refuse to write anything down until you tell them word for word what to write; others will keep asking you questions ("What should I do here? Is this part okay?"). Don't underestimate the abilities of these students; they will fatigue you into submission if they can.

To fight back, I would suggest we learn some techniques from the experts: the uncooperative students themselves.

1. Borrow student body language. When a student doesn't want to be involved in his paper, he will slump back in his chair, getting as far away from it as possible. If you find a student pushing you too hard into editing his paper, physically move away from it–slump back into your chair or scoot away. If a student is making a productive session impossible with his demands, yawn, look at the clock, rearrange your things. This language will speak clearly to the student: "You cannot make me edit your paper."

2. Be completely honest with the student who is giving you a hard time. If she says, "What should I do here?" you can say in a friendly, non-threatening way, "I can't tell you that–it's your grade, not mine," or, "I don't know–it's *your* paper." I have found this approach doesn't upset students as it might seem it would; they know what they are doing, and when you show that you know too, they accept that.

All of the suggestions I have made should be just a beginning of the ideas we can use to improve our value to our students. I hope that they lead to other ideas and tutoring techniques.

The less we do *to* the paper, the better. Our primary object in the writing center session is not the paper, but the student. Fixing flawed papers is easy; showing the students how to fix their own papers is complex and difficult. Ideally, the student should be the only active agent in improving the paper. The tutor's activity should focus on the student. If, at the end of the session, a paper is improved, it should be because the student did all the work.

GROWING WRITERS IN CLASSROOMS*

Glenda L. Bissex

I live on a hilltop in Vermont, three miles above a town of some 2,000 souls. Living with nature while being engaged in education has shaped my understanding of learning, and so I write about learning as growth.

Organisms, whether plants or animals, bean seeds or tadpoles, grow through orderly processes toward internally determined forms. Growth occurs through interactions between an organism and its environment. The organism provides its growth processes and its structure; the environment provides the nourishment to activate and sustain those processes, enabling the organism to grow to its potential form.

Manufacture is different from growth. A manufacturer takes inert raw materials and imposes upon them an externally determined form to fulfill the manufacturer's purposes. Children are not raw materials, teachers are not manufacturers, and schools are not factories, although some people talk and act as though they were. The industrial model of schools can be seen, for example, in a striving for the uniformity of mass production—homogeneous grouping, all children reading "at grade level"—and in an emphasis on the technology of teaching rather than educative relationships.

Studies of how children learn to speak have shown us some growth processes of language, processes children bring to their subsequent literacy learning. Without benefit of a programmed text, even very young children learn systematically, not randomly or by mere imitation. This is evident when children overgeneralize rules, as in regularizing past tenses ("They goed away") and plurals ("He has four foots"). Preschoolers' invented spellings, which are unconventional but consistent across children, are likewise rule-governed. For instance, nasals before consonants are unrepresented (DUP = *dump*) since that nasal is not articulated as a separate speech segment. Without instruction in sound-letter relationships, these young spellers abstract relationships from the letter names they know, leading them to many conventional consonant spellings but also to such inventions as H for "ch" (PKHR = *picture*).

Children learn to talk by interacting with an environment that provides rich information about language: they learn by speaking, being spoken to, asking questions and listening to speech. From models of older speakers they learn the values and functions of speech; they receive feedback, support, and encouragement. The first of three principles of language growth I will describe and relate to learning to write is that *children learn to talk by talking, in an environment that is full of talk.*

Some people believe that children all learn to speak because speech is somehow "natural" for us as humans while writing (and with it, of course, reading) is not "natural." But children who have grown up in isolation from human society–the wild boy of Aveyron in the last century and Genie most recently–have not grown up speaking. The capacity for speech may be innately human, but it develops only in a speech environment.

Although written language arose later than speech in the history of humankind and is not yet universal, it was preceded by drawing, another form of writing down meanings, of representing graphically what we know. Our use of an alphabetic writing system may lead us to forget that there have been in human cultures writing systems that did not represent speech sounds but were closer to drawing. Children in our culture remind us of this connection as they take one of their first steps toward literacy, differentiating writing from drawing.

I was taught much about the naturalness and forcefulness of the urge to write among children growing up in a literate society by my undergraduate Education students at Johnson State College. I asked them to write their autobiographies as writers, reaching as far back into childhood as they could. The earliness and vividness of their memories astonished me:

> I started writing as soon as I could hold a pencil. I can remember sitting up in my high-chair with the tray up, working on my homework, like my brothers and sisters. I would yell to mother, "Is PTO right?" And she would say, "Yes, I guess so." I would say, "Yes, PTO is right," and go on pretending to do my homework. The only word I thought I could spell right was PTO, which I later learned wasn't even a word.

> I can remember wanting to learn to write so badly! I would watch my brothers and sister as they scribbled nonsense on paper. They looked so official, so grown up. I would imitate their grandeur. I quite often played "restaurant" where I would "write" orders on paper and hand it in to the "chef."

> My writing career began at an early age. When I was a pre-schooler, I would study my older brother's school papers. The thing that intrigued

me most was the letter C, which the teacher used to indicate that the paper was correct. I worked on making my own C's. I practiced them in orange crayon all over the bathroom walls in our house.

I remember, before school years, doing a lot of scribbling, although this scribbling meant nothing to my family. I can recall being able to read the whole thing. As the family giggled and thought how "cute" it was, I would sit in my chair and read my scribbles.

Since I can remember, I wrote. I remember taking crayons and writing on the walls and my mother would yell at me because it was scribbling. But would it be funny if I wrote a word; she probably wouldn't have yelled at me then. I really remember wanting to express with my pencil, pen, or whatever, but I couldn't, no one understood!

When I became aware of letters I was amazed, and I learned to write words. I remember my teachers making me always write in pencil because I'd have to erase my errors. I always wished it could have been in pen so I could just keep writing without stopping.

Just as children learn to talk by talking in an environment that is full of talk, children learn to write by writing in an environment full of writing and writings. In the classrooms of Vermont Writing Program teachers, children of all ages are learning to write by writing every day in environments that are full of writing in progress as well as finished products. Teachers write, often at the same time as their students do. They share their writing problems or drafts with their students and may ask for their help as an audience, as critical listeners or readers. Through writing conferences, modeled and guided by their teachers, students become eager to share their writings with one another. They know they are writing to produce reading, not exercises for the teacher or "dummy runs." They come to understand, through the power of their own experience, that text conveys, above all, meanings.

Which brings me to a second principle of language development that also holds true for writing: *Children learn language among people who respond to their meanings before their forms.* We are eager to attach meanings to babies' first speech sounds. We do not immediately correct a beginning speaker's misarticulations; in fact we sometimes imitate them. We do not insist that beginning speakers talk in complete sentences, but may expand their one or two word sentences to check if we have understood their unverbalized meanings. How differently some beginning writers are treated in classrooms!

One youngster had his own "dictionary" in which the teacher recorded words he needed to have spelled for his writing. He had been writing at home for over a year and was already spelling a good many words conventionally, so I was surprised to find the word *dog*–one of the first words he'd learned–in his dictionary. When I asked him if he didn't know it already, he said, "Yes, but I didn't know how to make the *g*." While at home he had written at length and in a variety of forms, at school he wrote one sentence on the few lines beneath his picture the way the other kids did. As he must have seen it, writing at school meant writing correctly formed letters in correctly spelled words on the lines. Instead, he spent much of his time elaborating his drawings, for which there weren't expectations of correctness.

In contrast, beginning writers in Vera Milz's classroom (1980) write notes to their teacher, to each other and to penpals–all of whom respond to their messages. They write journals whose content their teacher responds to in writing at the end of each week. They write books that their classmates read. They know they are writing messages–meanings–and their skills grow through constant practice within a literate environment rich with information about print and through the genuine motivation of being understood.

Children learn language–written or spoken–among people who respond to meaning before form. That is the principle of writing conferences such as this one from a primary classroom in Vermont. Tiffany reads her story aloud to Amy. The story tells about mice chasing another mouse. Echoing a question her teacher asks in writing conferences, Amy leads off with, "Tiffany, where did you get the idea?"

Tiffany: I just thought about it. I got it from writing some stories on a piece of paper.

Amy: Why don't you tell what happened to the other mice?

Tiffany: That's a good idea.

Amy: 'Cause how would I know that? They ran after him. What did they do after that?

Tiffany: I guess they just ran back 'cause they knew he was too far away to catch him.

A little while later, she adds to her story: "The other mice were running back to have a drink."

In a high school classroom, Jeanne is finishing reading to Martha a draft of her piece about someone in a hospital:

. . . This was the toughest part of the visit because there wasn't much to say, and everything they did say was due to the fact that they forced their words out. Very soon the talk would die and her visitors would stare at the ceiling till someone suggested that they leave. A procession left the room, and just like everyone and everything else at the hospital, it too traveled slowly.

Now satisfied with their departure but joyed with the thought that they cared enough to visit her, she looked around her dull brown cell and wondered when she could get out, back into the real world.

Martha asks, "Are you talking about your own experience?"

The writer, Jeanne, answers: "Slightly my own experience, and then a couple of weeks ago my mom was in the hospital and a lot of my own feelings came out just walking down the hall to visit her. I didn't like it at all."

Martha: I kind of think you have two purposes: one being how different people change when they talk to people in the hospital, and then that it's a really scarey thing–that they want to get it over with fast. Well, I'm trying to decide which one is the purpose. Which one do you mean?

Jeanne: I don't know. Maybe a little bit of both. I was looking mostly at the personality changes 'cause when I went down you just sit there and you're really quiet. You try to say something and it's always, you know, "Well, how's it going?" and you really don't care. You're just down there to be nice and polite.

Martha: Do you mean to say–is your focus on the patient or on the visitor?

These writing conferences did not just "happen"; they were guided by teachers who put first things first and trained their students to do the same. Once Jeanne and Tiffany have revised their pieces in response to their readers' questions about content, they are ready for an editing conference where they will work on form–spelling, punctuation, and such.

Good writers have been found to focus first on meaning, while poor writers, conceiving of good writing as correct writing, focus from the start on correctness and neatness, on avoiding errors. Their premature corrections, according to Sondra Perl (1979), break the flow of their writing and thinking without making substantial improvement. Of course correctness is desirable, but placing it before meaning confuses the means with the ends of writing–like hitting the right notes but missing the music.

Good writers, seeing personal value in writing, write spontaneously outside of school and thus get additional practice. At home or at school they have models of writers and an interested audience that responds to the content of their writing. Poor writers, on the other hand, view writing as an externally imposed task. They do not see adults writing, and their teacher audience at school "corrects" their writing rather than responding to its message (Birnbaum 1980). Children can be taught to be poor writers or good writers. The role of the teacher is crucial, especially for children who have less opportunity to learn to write at home.

Finally, *language grows from being telegraphic and context-embedded toward being elaborated and explicit.* Children start speaking not single words but one- and then two-word sentences. "Car" may mean "I hear a car," "sweater chair," "my sweater is on that chair." Generally the most concrete and significant words are stated, while the rest of the meaning may reside in the context shared by the speaker and the listener; for example, they both hear the car. Soon after children begin using telegraphic sentences, more and more of the deleted elements appear on the surface—are stated rather than assumed.

We see the same process as children begin writing. In invented spellings, more and more of the omitted speech sounds become represented: from H to HS to HAOS for *house.* Text often develops in the same way, as seen in some writings by first graders in September:

> Jamie drew a monster (labeled MSTR) standing beside his cave (CAV). He chose the most important and concrete words to write; the deleted words emerged when he told his teacher his paper said "This monster lives in a cave."

> On the first day of school Jennifer drew a house and wrote H. The next week both her drawing and writing were elaborated: a house (HS) with a smoking chimney and a lawn in front on which stood two smiling figures, Mary (M) and ME. She told her teacher it said, "I am at my friend Mary's house."

> An eight-year-old with a learning problem who is also in this classroom shows the same pattern of development. The first day of school he drew a square green wagon with a large wheel (labeled WE) and dictated, "My wagon has wheels." The next week he drew a pelican (PLEN) in wavy water (WTR) with a dock (DC) at one edge of it: "I saw a pelican in Florida near the dock." Toward the end of September his sentence was fully represented in writing: THE FIS IS IN THE WTR.

Teachers who grow writers in their classrooms also regard pieces of writing as growing things to be nurtured rather than as objects to be repaired or fixed. These first grade writings were nurtured by a teacher who provided an hour every day for children to write on subjects they chose, who listened to each child read what she or he had written and then responded to it, who repeatedly encouraged children to figure out spellings for themselves, who typed their favorite writings into books for other children to read and for the authors to see their own words in conventional spellings, who collected each child's writings in a folder so the parents, the child and she, the teacher, could see the child's progress.

Once their sentences become explicit and elaborated in writing, children need help in making explicit their meanings on a larger scale, as happened dramatically through a third grade whole-class writing conference. Tanya chose to read to the class the first piece she had written in September. In order to minimize interruptions during writing, the teacher had told her students to put down the letters they knew in a word if they didn't know the spelling or couldn't figure it all out; thus "h,n," represents Hunger Mountain.

> I went on a hike to h,n, and I had a picnic the food was fruit and meat and I like it and it was fun my frend Jenny went with me. We came out.
> The end

Her classmates and teacher asked a lot of questions about what she'd written:

> Which Jenny?
> You should say where you camped out.
> It doesn't make sense "the food was."
> What was the weather like?
> What did you have to drink?
> Did you walk from your house to Hunger Mountain, or did you drive there?

The teacher then asked Tanya, "If you went back to work on it, what parts would you work on?" "I think I need to work on *all* of it," said Tanya. And she did. The next day she wrote her second draft, a much fuller version:

> I went on a hike up to hongger montain. I went by car. I had fun climming up hongger montain. When I got up on top I met my freind Jenny Adams. I ask what was she doing here. She said "That her father drove her" I was glad she was here. We had supper and after we went to bed in the morning we had breakfast and after that are parnets came and pit use up and took use home. I ask Jenny's Father and mother if she could stay other night her parnets said 'yes' I was glad that she could The end.

The writing problems of adult literacy students as well, Elsasser and John-Steiner (1977) observe, come from failures to transform compact inner speech into elaborated written language that is comprehensible to readers who do not share the writer's context.

Language–both spoken and written–develops from being telegraphic and context-embedded toward being elaborated and explicit. It is learned among people who attend to meaning before form. And it is learned in a language environment, not merely by imitation but by re-creation–by constructing and testing rules. That is, children learn language not just as little mimics but as little scientists. Each child needs to make sense for himself of how language works. That seems to be how language grows.

When we try to manufacture what must be grown, we are in trouble. The self-regulating systems of growing things, interacting with their environments, create the energy for growth. Manufacture requires new, external energy. When both teachers and learners are cut off from their natural energy sources, we have to "motivate" learners and combat teacher "burn out"–acknowledgements of our educational energy crisis.

When teaching is seen as control rather than nurturance, it is not surprising that students are seen as and become "irresponsible," for they are not being responded to; they are being "made into" something. They are raw materials for our educational technology–materials to be ground down to uniformity so they can be "efficiently" processed according to the designs of publishers, test makers, and curriculum committees.

As Robert White (1952, p. 363) has said

> the task of rearing and guiding children can best be represented by the metaphor of raising plants. This should be encouraging, because raising plants is one of mankind's most successful activities. Perhaps the success comes from the fact that the husbandman does not try to thrust impossible patterns on his plants. He respects their peculiarities, tries to provide suitable conditions, protects them from the more serious kinds of injury–but he lets the plants do the growing. He does not poke at the seed in order to make it sprout more quickly, nor does he seize the shoot when it breaks the ground and try to pull open the first leaves by hand. Neither does he trim the leaves of different kinds of plants in order to have them all look alike. The attitude of the husbandman is appropriate in dealing with children. It is the children who must do the growing.

Works Cited

Birnbaum, June. "Why Should I Write? Environmental Influences on Children's Views of Writing," *Theory into Practice* 19 (1980): 202–210.

Elsasser, Nan and John-Steiner, Vera, "An Interactionist Approach to Advancing Literacy." *Harvard Educational Review* 47 (1977): 355–369.

Milz, Vera E. "First Graders Can Write: Focus on Communication." *Theory into Practice* 19 (1980): 179–185.

Perl, Sondra. "The Composing Processes of Unskilled College Writers." *Research in the Teaching of English* 13 (1979): 317–336.

White, Robert W. *Lives in Progress.* New York: Dryden Press, 1952.

ᘓᕙᘔ

Doing His Own Thing: A Mexican-American Kindergartner Becomes Literate at Home and School[*]

Margaret M. Mulhern

"Did you bring books? How much did this cost? Where did you buy it? Do you have a library card?" This was one of the many strings of questions asked by kindergartner Rubén Gutierrez when I visited his home. Rubén, never at a loss for words, was described by his mother as *"muy preguntón"* (very inquisitive). At school, his teacher noted that Rubén had a knack for "doing his own thing," rather than following her directions. High on Rubén's agenda was learning to read and write, a task he approached with as much gusto as he ate jalapeño peppers, biting into them whole and raw, with great joy.

Looking back, it is not surprising that Rubén caught my attention during my first visit to his classroom in the early fall of his kindergarten year. Eventually, I selected him as one of three Mexican-American children whose Spanish literacy development I would document at home and school (Mulhern, forthcoming). Though most of the children in the classroom were eager learners, Rubén's energy was electrifying and contagious. I wanted to find out more about Rubén, especially his home life and the ways in which his home and school worlds would connect during his kindergarten year. To do so, I spent one day a week in Rubén's classroom in the fall and two or three days a week between January and June, alternately observing the three focal children. I also accompanied Rubén home from school weekly, interacting with him and his family members for three or four hours. His family welcomed me, a Euro-American woman who had learned Spanish as a second language, into their home during that year and I continued to visit them for the two years I remained in Chicago.

WHY RUBÉN?

Rubén, like most of his classmates, was the child of Mexican immigrants, many of whom themselves had not had extended opportunities for schooling. Almost all of the children in Rubén's Chicago neighborhood and school were of Mexican origin and, like Rubén, many were placed in Spanish bilingual classrooms. His classroom was crowded with 27 children identified as needing additional instructional support. Rubén was one of four children who had attended preschool and this probably contributed to his teacher's and my identification of him as a child with a high developmental knowledge of literacy as compared to his classmates. For instance, Rubén was able to write his first name and seemed comfortable with literacy activities, while many children struggled to copy one letter of their names.

My interest in studying Rubén and his classmates was driven by the lack of information on how children construct literacy as they move between their home and school worlds (Sulzby & Teale, 1991). I believed that, by attempting to look through the eyes of a child crossing the home-school border, a fuller understanding of the varied ways that children go about becoming literate could be revealed. Those ways are undoubtedly influenced by family perspectives on literacy learning (Goldenberg, 1989; Solsken, 1993) and teachers' approaches to literacy instruction (Dahl & Freppon, 1995). By looking through this broad lens, I hoped to gain insights into the ways in which home-school links and literacy instruction could be strengthened to better meet the needs of children.

My use of the term literacy refers to print literacy or written language, rather than the multiple literacies that are part of children's lives. Farr (1994) notes that the Mexicano families she worked with, who also lived in Rubén's neighborhood, viewed literacy (the ability to read and write) as a cultural tool connected to schooling. In clarifying my primary focus on children's acquisition of school literacy, I do not want to discount the importance of "funds of knowledge" (Moll & Greenberg, 1990), oral literacy activities (Vasquez, Pease-Alvarez & Shannon, 1994), and *consejos*, "spontaneous homilies designed to influence behaviors and attitudes," (Valdés, 1996, p. 125) that have been documented in Mexican-origin families.

In recent years, much attention has been placed on the need to involve parents (especially those from low-income backgrounds) in their children's early literacy learning. The burgeoning family literacy movement is one manifestation of the goal to increase parent involvement (Mandel, 1995). While such programs may be valuable for those families who choose to participate in them, I wanted to document the ways in which

Mexican-immigrant parents are already involved in their children's education. I believe that parent programs should not lessen the responsibility teachers have for learning more about home literacy practices and reaching out to parents who may be unfamiliar with instructional approaches in U.S. schools. If parent involvement programs are implemented at all (see Valdés [1996] for arguments against them), they need to take into account the sociocultural practices of families (Auerbach, 1995), including the ways in which written language is used in homes.

In this article, then, I share Rubén's experiences as a literacy learner who negotiated meaning as he crossed the home-school border. I have included additional information on Rubén's home background, for readers who may be less familiar with the home lives of Mexican-immigrant children. While what is true in Rubén's case cannot be generalized to apply to other children, it does provide insights into the potential for interconnectedness between a child's home and school learning experiences. His experiences can also inform teachers who wonder about home support for literacy learning and the role of the school in communicating with families like Rubén's. Finally, Rubén's talent at making links between a variety of literacy activities, both within the classroom and between home and school, suggests ways that teachers can foster similar linkages for other students.

RUBÉN AT SCHOOL

Rubén was a child who commanded attention in the classroom. Physically, he was always shooting up his arm or jumping up with excitement. Verbally, his constant initiations, rapid speech, and deep voice drowned out many of the children. Rubén's enthusiasm for learning to read and write was evident in his choice to continue his engagement with literacy during free play periods and in his persistent questioning about the texts that surrounded him. Even reminders from his teacher that he needed to listen did not sidetrack Rubén from his pursuit of literacy. The result of this interactive stance was that Rubén could easily "steal the show," as he vocally participated in whole group activities far in excess of any other child.

Setting His Own Agenda

Rubén was intently focused on learning, but what he had in mind to learn did not always match his teacher's agenda. This caused some tension for both Rubén and Mrs. Martinez (a ten-year veteran of kindergarten teaching), although, for the most part, Rubén was able to negotiate lessons to fit his interests. For instance, during a phonics lesson on 'B' syllables, Mrs. Martinez said, *"Eso es una ballena"* (That is a whale), and Rubén followed with, *"Si viene un niño, la ballena se come un niño"* (If a child comes, the whale eats a child). Rubén's comment momentarily turned the phonics lessons to one of his favorite topics—animals, what they eat, and how they live. Thus, one way Rubén remained engaged during skill instruction was to personally create a more meaningful context for the syllables presented.

Sometimes Rubén told his teacher he didn't want to complete the assignments as directed. For instance, when instructed to write an ending for a story, Rubén said, *"Maestra, ya no quiero escribir"* (Teacher, I don't want to write anymore). When she didn't answer, he tried again, *"Maestra, ya no quiero hacer nada"* (Teacher, I don't want to do anything anymore), and finally, *"Maestra, ya acabé"* (Teacher, I finished already). This tactic didn't work, however, and Rubén was told to continue writing. While other children appeared to have similar feelings on occasion, few were as vocal as Rubén in expressing their opinions.

Rubén's frequent assertions could, at times, get him into trouble and he had to stand apart from the group for a few minutes. Mrs. Martinez felt that Rubén liked to make jokes so the other kids would laugh. One day, as she explained that only mothers or fathers could come pick up report cards, Rubén suggested that the cat could also come. Another time, when Mrs. Martinez started to read a book saying, *"Vamos a ver quié es el autor"* (Let's see who the author is), Rubén interjected his best friend's name and, once again, he had to take a *time out*.

Rubén's tendency to want to follow his own agenda was apparent to Mrs. Martinez who often told him that he wasn't listening and told me that Rubén "does his own thing." It appeared to me that Rubén's desire to make his own choices resulted in his tendency to do as he pleased. He thought worksheets were "easy" and wanted to rush through them so he could read a book. If an activity was interrupted because the children had to leave the room, Rubén didn't want to stop working and he would stand at the table writing, even after the lights were out and all the children had left. Finally, he would run out the door and catch up. Rubén did test the teacher's limits at times, but, for the most part, he figured out how to negotiate doing his work as well as doing what he wanted.

ENGAGING IN LITERACY ACTIVITIES

In Rubén's classroom, literacy instruction was conducted almost exclusively in Spanish, thus allowing the children to acquire literacy in the language they knew best before making the transition to English instruction. The traditional approach included direct instruction of Spanish syllables (i.e., *ma, me, mi, mo, mu*) and the completion of worksheets. There were also regular opportunities for the children to explore written language through shared book experiences and independent reading, as well as writing stories, journal entries, and letters. Mrs. Martinez sometimes made connections between the syllables the children had been taught and the whole text activities; however, most of the phonics instruction was isolated from more meaningful contexts. The classroom was print rich; the walls were covered with posters and signs and there were over 300 books available for reading.

Overall, Rubén enjoyed the literacy activities available at school. He caught onto graphophonemic relationships easily and would name the beginning syllables of words he encountered throughout the day. If he had any questions about them, he was not hesitant to ask an adult for assistance, and he elicited information at his level this way. Rubén was very attuned to environmental print. For example, he asked me to read posters and bulletin boards when we walked down the hallways and he always knew whose birthday would be celebrated, by referring to the classroom bulletin board. Rubén eventually learned the letters of the alphabet and the associated pictures posted in the classroom, although these were not a focal point of instruction.

Rubén had a great affection for books. During shared book reading, he sat in the front of the group, often getting up on his knees to see the book better. He had so many comments and questions (15 or 20 per book was not unusual) that Mrs. Martinez had to ask him to hold his questions until the end. Even with this warning, Rubén interrupted frequently, commenting on content (*¿Verdad que el tigre es el amigo del león?*–Isn't the tiger a friend of the lion?) and graphophonemic relationships (*Búho empieza con la 'bu'–Búho* [Owl] begins with *'bu'*). Rubén read both alone and with others. He did this during independent reading as well as many other times, but always after requesting permission from the teacher. Claiming that he could read, Rubén reconstructed the meaning of books from memory and picture cues.

Rubén was eager to obtain books to read at home. He often spoke of getting a library card, as Mrs. Martinez had suggested, and one day he asked me to give him a dollar for the card. He asked the school librarian when he would be able to check books out, and he often ran over to peruse the piles of books at the beginning and end of library class. Short texts in basal workbooks did not hold Rubén's interest however. When he left one of these selections on the table one day, I reminded him that the teacher had asked the children to take them home and read them to their parents. He grimaced at the idea and told me to take it, instead.

Rubén's desire to engage in writing activities wavered, depending on his mood and his confidence in his ability to write. Assignments which involved writing to a known audience (e.g., a card to a classmate's mother who recently had a baby and, on another occasion, a mother's day card) were exciting. Being able to choose his own topic also seemed to foster Rubén's interest in writing. Rubén was the first child in the room who noticeably started to think about encoding his message using his graphophonemic knowledge. In January, while writing about a zoo visit, he isolated and recorded Z for *"zoológico"* (zoo). Then he said, *"Yo miré focas"* (I saw seals), and wrote the letter *O* for *"foca."* (In Spanish, invented spelling often consists of vowels rather than initial and final consonants.) Rubén often used me as a sounding board, wanting me to verify his letter or syllable choices and read his invented spelling. Yet there were times that spelling seemed to be too much work for Rubén and he wrote children's names and lines across the page "to finish quickly." Mrs. Martinez commented to me that Rubén didn't want to make a "mistake" and therefore became very hesitant in his writing. This hesitancy may also have stemmed from the phonics lessons where the children were expected to write initial syllables correctly.

Rubén often chose to go to the writing table during free time. He sometimes succeeded in calling his friends over to write and draw with him, but they didn't seem to have his staying power. Near Valentine's Day, though, four children joined him after he started writing notes to his friends and putting them in a postal area set up for the holiday. Most often, Rubén drew favorite objects, sometimes connecting the pictured items with an oral "story." He also labeled his drawings, especially those portraying Ninja Turtle characters. As he wrote, Rubén told me that he would show his work to his mother because she would compliment him. Rubén also used the free-play period to listen to books on cassettes, read books, and complete leftover worksheets. At the end of the school year, Mrs. Martinez commented about Rubén, "When we have free play he won't play, he wants to just do writing."

RUBÉN AT HOME

Rubén walked home from school with his mother until close to the end of the year when he began to walk alone or with me on the Thursdays I visited. Rubén's street was like many in the neighborhood. It was filled with three- or four-story older houses that were divided into several apartments. While the conditions of the housing varied, the buildings were old and problems with plumbing and roach infestations were common. The steps to the homes came right to the sidewalk and there were few gardens or lawns and very few trees. When Rubén and his classmates got excited about seeing a squirrel at the zoo, it struck me that they didn't see them in their neighborhood very often. The sidewalks had many gaping holes that were slowly being repaired by the city; meanwhile, old tires or pieces of wood covered the holes to prevent accidents.

A few blocks from Rubén's home was the central commercial area of the neighborhood. Local businesses catered to the community–there were photo studios for special occasions, *tortillerías, panaderías* (Mexican bakeries), and stores selling clothing, music, and other merchandise from Mexico. The high concentration of *Mexicanos* made the neighborhood a comfortable entry point for immigrants who often already had an established social network of family members and neighbors from their home towns in Mexico. However, gang activity was a great concern within the community.

The Gutierrez's apartment made up the entire second floor of one of the houses. The front door opened into a large living/dining room, warmed by a large space heater. Rubén and his sisters, four-year-old Erica and two-year-old Lucia, and I watched TV, read books, or played in this room. Several photographs of the children hung over the couch and their artwork adorned the door. When he could not work at his construction job because of foul weather, Rubén's father played cards with friends and relatives in this room. Three bedrooms, a kitchen, and a bathroom made up the rest of the apartment.

Rubén's parents were 24 years old and had emigrated eight years before from the Mexican state of Durango where they had lived on *ranchos.* Their home was busy with people coming and going, so it took me a while before I sorted out who lived there. Señor Gutierrez's brother, his wife, and Señora Gutierrez's brother also lived in the apartment. Having at least five adults in his home, it became clearer to me why Rubén felt so at ease with adults in the classroom.

On a typical school day, Rubén played outside, watched television, and did literacy related activities until he went to bed. Rubén watched cartoons or the public television channel his teacher had recommended. He enjoyed the programs about animals, and asked me to interpret the English narration for him. Rubén's chores were to take out the trash and put away his toys. On the weekend the family mostly stayed at home, but Rubén liked to go to the park or play outdoors when the weather was favorable.

On warm days, the streets were full of activity—everyone was relieved to be outdoors after the cold winter. On the sidewalk in front of Rubén's house, the neighbors sold corn on the cob and cucumbers from a small stand. On the hottest and muggiest days of summer, the fire hydrant was opened and cold water flooded the street as the children cooled themselves off. Sometimes Rubén's grandfather came by with his popsicle cart and treated the children. Ball games, hopscotch, and piggyback rides were the children's favorite outdoor activities. Rubén was asked to watch his youngest sister if she went outside with him. He had to be very mindful, since she was as active as he was—Rubén had to track her down once when she climbed in the window of the neighbor's house. Rubén, too, could get into dangerous situations—on the way to the store, one day, he picked up a discarded hypodermic needle he saw under a car. His mother explained to him why it wasn't safe to pick it up.

Rubén's activities within his home and neighborhood provided rich contexts for learning outside of school. He interacted with the many adults in his extended family, as well as with family friends and neighbors. Rubén had responsibilities within the family and integrated play and literacy learning into his daily activities. In the next section, I provide some background information regarding Rubén's family members' perspectives on literacy learning, in order to further contexualize his home literacy experiences.

SITUATING RUBÉN'S HOME LITERACY INTERACTIONS

Of the family members, Señora Gutierrez and her sister-in-law, Amanda, had the highest levels of formal education and read and wrote most frequently. They were also enrolled in school, Amanda in the eighth grade, and Señora Gutierrez in ESL classes at a community center. Señora Gutierrez took care of many of the literacy needs in the home—reading school notices, communicating with her family in Mexico, and filling out forms related to her husband's employment. The majority of observed and reported literacy events in the home were related to education (e.g., doing homework, playing school, reading children's books, and reading school notices) and daily living routines (e.g., shopping, writing letters, reading mail, paying bills, and taking down phone messages). Rubén's mother was the most involved in his literacy interactions, answering his questions and checking his school papers. She informed the teacher when Rubén had the chickenpox and asked for homework to bring home to him.

Señora Gutierrez, herself, had enjoyed school in Mexico, finishing the six years of primary school. She remembers her brother helping her write the alphabet. She was taught through a syllabic approach using a school textbook, and noted that literacy was being taught to her children in a similar way. One difference she noticed between U.S. and Mexican schools was that the schools in Mexico were harder, with more homework. She gave the example that, if one misspelled a word, it had to be practiced five times. Señora Gutierrez continued to write new words several times when she was studying English.

Asked about literacy and the availability of books in her parents' home in Mexico, Señora Gutierrez recalled her school books. There was no library in the town, and her family did not have money to buy books. When I spoke of my mother reading to me, she explained, *"Es que no había este costumbre allá, pero la gente que tenía dinero iba al pueblo y compraba libros para sus niños y la gente que no tenía ni sabía que habían libros"* (It's that there wasn't this custom there, but the people who had money went to the town and bought books for their children and people who didn't have money didn't even know that there were books). Lack of resources also prevented her from pursuing her education after primary school. At the age of 16 she came to the United States with her older brother so she could help support her family in Mexico.

Rubén's father did not like school, as a child, and after four years, he decided to leave to work with his father. When I asked Señora Gutierrez what her husband read, she told me *"Él no lea, no le gusta"* (He doesn't read, he doesn't like it). If Rubén asked his father a question about written language, he would refer him to his mother. But, according to Señora Gutierrez, her husband thought highly of Rubén's great interest in learning. *"Pues, dice que está bien porque a él no le gustaba. Dice ¡qué bueno! que a él le gusta porque ahora que está grande dice que hace falta saber. O sea como no salió de sexto dice que a él le gustaría haber salido"* (Well, he says that it's good because he didn't like it [school]. He says it's good that he [Rubén] likes it because now that he's older he realizes that it's important to have knowledge. As he didn't finish sixth grade, he would have liked to have finished).

Señora Gutierrez did not particularly like living in Chicago, but she planned to stay for her children's schooling. She felt that the most important value she could teach her children was *"la educación,"* which included both the importance of behaving well with others and studying. Her hope was that her children would "come out ahead" in life.

ENGAGING IN HOME LITERACY ACTIVITIES

No less talkative at home than at school, Rubén used the dinner hour to tell his mother about various school events–things he did there (that he had read five books to me, or that he had played Red Riding Hood in a dramatic reenactment), something interesting he had learned, or other children's behavior. Señora Gutierrez felt that Rubén knew a lot because he asked so many questions, often about literacy. If she was too busy to answer his questions, he found someone else to ask. Rubén used any available print at home to learn about written language–he asked his mother to read him school notices, frequently referred to the calendar, dictated letters to his mother to send to his grandmother in Mexico, and he often played school.

Rubén's interest in literacy was evident during all of my home visits. On the days I visited, Rubén engaged me in literacy interactions, and I learned from his mother the extent to which similar activities took place when I was not present. He initiated most of the activities we did together, pulling me away from the kitchen table, getting my bag of books and saying, *"Quiero hacer algo"* (I want to do something). Besides reading books, Rubén wanted to draw, write, and do "work." For instance, Rubén initiated a letter naming activity in which I was to put an 'X' on any letter he did not name correctly. Letter naming was not a common literacy activity at school, but Rubén made good hypotheses about letter names. For a letter name Rubén didn't know, he generated a hypothesis that, if he said the beginning sound of a word that started with that letter, it would be the correct letter name. This worked for some letters, like *B* (pronounced/be/in Spanish) for the word *bebe* (/bebe/). Yet, he called the *Q*/ke/ instead of the Spanish /ku/, because he associated the letter with the word *queso* (/keso/, cheese) which was pictured next to the *Q* at school. Similarly, he called the letter *G* /gwa/ instead of /he/ because he though of the pronunciation and spelling of his classmate's name, Guadalupe. This activity again indicated to me how aware Rubén was of the environmental print in the classroom and that he was applying the knowledge gained at school to his home activities.

When a classmate asked Rubén why I went to his home, he responded, *"para leer libros"* (to read books). Indeed, reading and talking about the books I brought were major activities during my visits. Rubén took advantage of my access to children's books since the books in his home were limited to a Bible, a set of medical encyclopedias, and books related to the family members' schooling. His first question when I walked in the door was, *"¿Trajiste libros?"* (Did you bring books?). He would sometimes run to the kitchen to show his mother a book and tell her that he wanted her to get him some. Despite frequent requests for books, Rubén was, at first, not very successful in obtaining them. His mother was concerned about him being responsible enough to care for books, and she worried he would leave them out where his little sister could get them. Moreover, Señora Gutierrez did not know where she could purchase books. Unfortunately, the two best Spanish language bookstores in Chicago were located at the other end of the city; the local bookstore had a small selection of children's books, most of which were highly priced and poor in quality. Yet, later in the year, she was able to borrow some books from the community center where she studied English, and Rubén brought them to school so Mrs. Martinez could read them to the class. Rubén listened to his mother read the books I lent or gave him and he engaged in pretend reading on his own. His mother was grateful for the bit of quiet time this activity allowed.

While reading seemed to be Rubén's preferred home literacy activity, he also liked to write. Labeling his drawings, writing names of family members, and occasionally writing a letter were most typical. When Rubén wrote at home, he solicited assistance with spelling from me and his mother. He wanted his mother to validate, by reading aloud, the emergent writing he did on his own at home. But she was often unable to read his invented spellings and modeled conventional spellings. According to Señora Gutierrez, one day when Rubén had brought a paper to her saying, *"Aquí dice tortuga"* (Here it says turtle), she told him, *"No, así no lo dice"* (No, like that it doesn't say it), then she wrote the word correctly for him. Her response reflected her experiences with learning to write in rural Mexico. In addition, although an emergent approach to writing was being used in Rubén's classroom, no explanations of this perspective were provided to parents, who continued to draw upon the literate practices they had been exposed to as children.

Rubén was not always pleased with his mother's view of his writing and responded to her comment that his writing didn't say anything by telling her that she "didn't know." He tried to better understand how written language worked, by asking his mother, *"¿Por qué tú haces muchas letras y dice algo?"* (How come you make a lot of letters it says something?). She explained that she had already learned how to write and he was still learning. Thus, there was some tension around writing at home, as there was at school–Rubén was unsure when his writing was legitimate and he wanted to spell correctly. Still, he held onto his desire to write and continued to take risks as a writer.

Rubén's family contributed to his literacy learning. His parents were pleased with his avid interest in learning and his mother responded to his many inquiries about written language. Señora Gutierrez talked with Rubén about school, made sure he completed his homework, participated in writing activities with him, read to him at his request, and made an effort to provide books for him.

LEARNING FROM RUBÉN: IMPLICATIONS FOR FOSTERING CONNECTIONS IN CHILDREN'S LITERACY EXPERIENCES

By spending time with Rubén, I learned more about his world and the role of literacy in his life. Rubén's orientation to literacy learning was similar at both home and school, and he managed to "compose a place" for himself (Dyson, 1993) as he moved between these two settings. This process involved the negotiation of some tensions that arose because of differences between how Rubén and others perceived literacy learning. Many of the strategies Rubén used in becoming literate were effective ones. He had a strong sense of himself as a reader/writer and he seemed to instinctively know what would help him to become literate–access to books, time to read and write, choice of books to read and topics for writing, and adult scaffolding. His inquisitiveness and straightforwardness allowed him to pursue literacy by "doing his own thing" and resulted in rapid acquisition of knowledge about written language.

The following points highlight the lessons I learned from Rubén about how teachers might foster literacy learning in and out of school.

Connect Skill Instruction to Meaningful Contexts

Rubén was a highly motivated child who realized that he could learn more about the world through books and that he could communicate with others through his writing. His teacher helped foster these understandings by providing opportunities for reading and writing. Planned activities that were the most authentic (i.e., reading trade books, writing to a known audience) seemed to engage Rubén the most. He showed disinterest in or resistance to writing on assigned topics that did not spark his interest and he disliked reading basal stories, preferring to keep the "word" connected to his "world" (Freire & Macedo, 1987).

Rubén was attuned to meaning and wholeness when he engaged with print. He found ways to add meaning to teacher-directed skill lessons, by associating the syllables to words that were meaningful to him or by commenting on words such as *ballena* (whale). Rubén was also adept at noticing beginning syllables of words in books and other print, picking up on his teacher's modeling during read alouds. His ability to listen for the initial consonant or syllable of any word he wanted to write was exemplary, especially since there was infrequent discussion or teacher modeling of ways to think about using the syllables the children were taught during skill lessons. Rubén's strategies indicate how important it is to connect skill learning to contexts that are meaningful to children. Teachers can observe the strategies children use to make sense of print and they can have children share their strategies with their peers (Mills, O'Keefe, & Stephens, 1992).

Connect Home and School Literacy Experiences

Rubén's case suggests ways in which the connections between home and school literacy experiences can be encouraged. Because these links were a central focus of my research and because I was present in the home and school settings, I had a greater role, in making the connections recommended here on an informal basis, than Rubén's teacher did. However, as a result of the study, she came to see the need to improve home-school relationships.

Ruben's love of books and his ongoing crusade to obtain them suggest the need to increase children's access to books. Señora Gutierrez was not familiar with the cultural practice of sharing books with children, but she enjoyed reading to her children those books I made available. It is critical to understand that the infrequency of reading to young children in some Mexican-origin families is neither an indication of neglect nor disinterest in children's educational success (Heath, 1986; Valdés, 1996). Rather, many parents had not been introduced to this practice in Mexico and are not familiar with ways to access books. Given the importance of book reading for young children and, as in Rubén's case, children's enjoyment of books, support for this activity could be provided by allowing children to borrow books from the school or classroom library. Currently, many schools do not allow kindergartners to take books from the library. Modeling of shared book reading could occur by inviting parents to visit the classroom, or by sending home a teacher-made videotape of lap reading.

In suggesting that books be sent home with children, I am not implying that parent-child book reading is the only or most critical use of the books, or that some parents are not already reading with their children. Parents may not read the books with their children for various reasons, including limitations on parents' time and literacy abilities (Purcell-Gates, 1996) or lack of knowledge of English, when only English books are sent home. Yet, children can benefit by engaging in pretend reading, or reading books with a sibling or neighbor, as Rubén did. An explanation of the value of pretend reading is warranted because parents or older siblings who have not seen young children engage with books may expect children to be able to read them if they are sent home by the school. While this was not true in Rubén's case, I have observed this reaction in other families.

Clearly, teachers must make efforts to inform parents about school literacy practices. Tension arose between Rubén and his mother over writing because Señor Gutierrez was not aware of the school practice of allowing children to write using invented spelling. While some tension in literacy learning is inevitable (Solsken, 1993), and may, in fact, be helpful in furthering children's understandings of written language, Rubén's case study points to the need to better inform parents. It was when I interviewed Señora Gutierrez about Rubén's home literacy activities that I learned of her perspective on his writing. Señora Gutierrez's conception of literacy learning, which required correct answers, made sense, given her own literacy background and the worksheets Rubén was bringing home. However, when I provided an explanation of the concept of emergent writing, Señora Gutierrez seemed to better understand how Rubén's spellings were indicative of his competence with written language. Having a particular perspective on literacy learning does not preclude parents from considering alternative perspectives. Changes in literacy approaches have necessitated educating all parents about the ways children are being taught. Non-mainstream parents, who do not directly question teachers about their methods, should not be left out of discussions of literacy instruction.

One caution to educators as they foster home-school connections is to avoid advocating only literacy activities valued by schools, in case culturally-specific literacy practices are replaced (Auerbach, 1995; Valdés, 1996). While this critique has been made of family literacy programs, it also applies to teachers' approaches to involving families in their children's schooling. Auerbach (1995) notes that ethical issues are raised whenever we intervene in families' lives, so "we need to proceed with caution and humility" (p. 649). It is critical to learn more about the ways in which families use literacy and how they perceive written language learning, simply because there is variability across families. Moreover, it is necessary to acknowledge home activities as potential learning experiences for children, which can be tapped into when planning school instruction (e.g., see Moll & Greenberg, 1990).

Learn about Students' Out-of-School Lives

Rubén's case study provides not only a description of his literacy learning experiences, but also a portrait of an active, inquisitive child from a loving family. Just as Rubén was able to share his school activities with his mother, his home experiences could be tapped into for literacy learning at school. Mrs. Martinez helped children make home-school connections when she provided space for children to discuss their home lives, when she allowed children to choose their own topics for writing, and when she shared with the class books children brought from home.

By doing so, she opened the door to learning more about the children she taught.

Too often in my work, I hear negative stereotypes about Mexican-immigrant families and their role in their children's education. In sharing a small piece of Rubén's world, I hope I have dispelled some of these stereotypes by offering an inside look at the whole child and how literacy fit into his world. Clearly, Rubén's family, like others I know, and those written about elsewhere (Carger, 1996; Delgado-Gaitan, 1990; Delgado-Gaitan & Trueba, 1991; Goldenberg, 1989; Moll & Greenberg, 1990; Valdés, 1996), are interested in their children's educational and social success. Educators working with children like Rubén will be best prepared to teach them if they make the effort to learn more about their lives and to understand their parents' perspectives on education. Such efforts open the door to increase communication between parents and teachers and smooth the transition for children as they learn at home and school.

References

Auerbach, E. (1995). Deconstructing the discourse of strengths in family literacy. *Journal of Reading Behavior, 27* (4), 643–661.

Carger, C. L. (1996). *Of borders and dreams: A Mexican-American experience of urban education.* New York: Teachers College Press.

Dahl, K. L., & Freppon, P. A. (1995). A comparison of inner-city children's interpretations of reading and writing instruction in the early grades in skills-based and whole language classrooms. *Reading Research Quarterly, 30,* 50–74.

Delgado-Gaitan, C. (1990). *Literacy for empowerment: The role of parents in children's education.* Philadelphia, PA: Falmer Press.

Delgado-Gaitan, C., & Trueba, H. (1991). *Crossing cultural borders: Education for immigrant families in America.* Philadelphia, PA: Falmer Press.

Dyson, A. H. (1993). *The sociocultural worlds of children learning to write.* New York: Teachers College Press.

Farr, M. (1994). *En los dos idiomas:* Literacy practices among Chicago Mexicanos. In B. J. Moss (Ed.), *Literacy across communities* (pp. 9–47). Cresskill, NJ: Hampton Press.

Freire, P., & Macedo, D. (1987). *Literacy: Reading the word and the world.* South Hadley, MA: Bergin & Garvey Publishers.

Goldenberg, C. (1989). Making success a more common occurrence for children at risk for failure: Lessons from Hispanic first-graders learning to read. In J. B. Allen & J. M. Mason (Eds.), *Risk makers, risk takers, risk breakers: Reducing the risks for young literacy learners* (pp. 38–78). Portsmouth, NH: Heinemann.

Heath, S. B. (1986). Sociocultural contexts of language development. In *Beyond language: Social & cultural factors in schooling language minority students* (pp. 143–186). Los Angeles, CA: Evaluation, Dissemination and Assessment Center.

Mandel, L. M. (Ed.) (1995). *Family literacy: Connections in schools and communities.* Newark, DE: International Reading Association.

Mills, H., O'Keefe, T., & Stephens, D. (1992). *Looking closely: Exploring the role of phonics in one whole language classroom.* Urbana, IL: National Council of Teachers of English.

Moll, L. C., & Greenberg, J. B. (1990). Creating zones of possibilities: Combining social contexts for instruction. In L. C. Moss (Ed.), *Vygotsky and education* (pp. 319–348). New York: Cambridge.

Mulhern, M. (forthcoming). *Esperanza, Rubén and Yesenia: The emergent literacy of three Mexican immigrant children.* Albany, NY: SUNY Press.

Purcell-Gates, V. (1996). *Other people's words: The cycle of low literacy.* Cambridge, MA: Harvard.

Solsken, J. W. (1993). *Literacy, gender, & work: In families and in school.* Norwood, NJ: Ablex.

Sulzby, E., & Teale, W. (1991). Emergent literacy. In R. Barr, M. L. Kamil, P. Mosenthal, & P. D. Pearson (Eds.) *Handbook of reading research. Volume II* (pp. 727–757). New York: Longman.

Valdés, G. (1996). *Con respeto: Bridging the distances between culturally diverse families and schools.* New York: Teachers College Press.

Vasquez, O. A., Pease-Alvarez, L., & Shannon, S. M. (1994). *Pushing boundaries: Language and culture in a Mexicano community.* New York: Cambridge.

༄ཟ྅ཟ

"So What Do We Do Now?" Necessary Directionality as the Writing Teacher's Response to Racist, Sexist, Homophobic Papers*

David Rothgery

Then he waited, marshaling his thoughts and brooding over his still untested powers. For though he was master of the world, he was not quite sure what to do next.

But he would think of something. (221)

So ends Arthur Clarke's classic *2001: A Space Odyssey,* and, as David Bowman contemplates with some dismay his seeming mastery of the universe, his unstated question is one the contemporary writing literature teacher might well appropriate for his or her own contemporary pedagogical dilemma: So what do I do now with my students? It is the question a high-school English teacher once asked me as she read some Derrida and Nietzsche as part of a required Contemporary Theory and Pedagogy class I was teaching. Her pedagogical quandary was not an isolated one. I answered her with another question: "What if a student in your freshman writing class submits to you a rough draft of a paper which you consider to be racist–very racist? Would you, or should you, with that paper–or perhaps one that asserts that it is the duty of Christians to ferret out every gay and 'beat some sense into him'–mark it as any other paper?"

She seemed to squirm in her seat. She had, in fact, once gotten a racist paper, and her response had been unequivocal: she did not allow the paper and "sat the student down and set him right." Whatever truth there is to Foucault's assertion that each "society has its régime of truth, its 'general politics' of truth–i.e., the types of discourse which it accepts and makes function as true" ("Truth" 131), and whatever personal power agendas are working subtly at the heart of any particular discourse, still, to that teacher that morning, there were some things you could be *certain* about. In the case of a racist paper, some seemingly

---

*Rothgery, David. "So What Do We Do Now?" From *College Composition and Communication* 1993. Copyright 1993 by the National Council of Teachers of English. Reprinted with permission.

universal principle far beyond "political correctness," beyond situational truths, was at issue.

Still, as she struggled through some of the assigned readings for the course, it was clear she was having some difficulty reconciling her own moral fervor with what Bakhtin, Derrida, and other theorists of the "anti-foundational" persuasion were arguing: that the human condition does not permit certainty regarding any "Transcendent Truths" as our moral underpinnings, but rather some "truth" in a far less fundamental sense, no matter what we may "feel."

Patricia Bizzell, in restating the dilemma, points to a resolution which works for her and which has implications for any classroom teacher:

> We have not yet taken the next, crucially important step in our rhetorical turn. We have not yet acknowledged that if no unimpeachable authority and transcendent truth exist, this does not mean that no *respectable* authority and no *usable* truth exist. (665 emphasis added)

She implies that teachers must proceed by these "usable" truths and center pedagogical discussions not so much on how one piece of discourse can be made less value-laden, but rather on how all discourse *is* value-laden and therefore political. Dale Bauer, sensitive to a too "authoritative rhetoric" in the classroom, one necessarily tied to a "political position" (391), directs students' attention to "how signs can be manipulated" (391) so as to ensure a "mastery that is not oppressive" (395). On the surface, just as foundationalism in its search for the objective principle is an appealing way to go, so too the kind of anti-foundationalism represented by Bizzell and Bauer—with its recognition that we really can't be certain that any principle is "objective" beyond our saying it is—is appealing in a post-Nietzschean world wherein we have become acutely aware of the linguistic fictional nature of our "non-fictional truths" (consider, e.g., the Margaret Mead version of Samoa). It's all part of the same game. We knock out the big "T" (Truth or Transcendent Truth) but remain, nevertheless, committed to a "respectable authority," a "reasonable truth," an analysis of how power agendas "manipulate signs," and, while showing how our deep-seated aversions to racism, sexism, and homophobia can be subjected to the same process, we, nevertheless, push forward with our convictions. Surely we can and will do this. We will continue to evaluate student papers as to mechanics/usage, style, organization, thesis, and by way of thesis development we will surely "do in" our dangerously myopic, intellectually backward students with appropriately low grades. Our "situational truth" is, if not transcendently valid, certainly more valid than the kind of truth such students promote.

Something about this approach, however, smacks too much of "having our cake and eating it too": there are no Transcendent Truths, but rather "usable truths", which we, as teachers, will make serve as our moral underpinnings. I am uncomfortable. And if I refuse to buy off entirely on the anti-foundationalist argument, I do not believe that makes me a victim of wishful thinking, of a refusal to accept in some way the reality of our essential rhetoricity. Admittedly, the fundamental "situatedness" of the human condition does not allow for the certainty of Transcendent Principles emblazoned across the sky, but neither does it allow for the certainty of there *not* being universals which suggest a direction.

Again and again I have heard professors admit (not in these terms of course, for it is not quite academic to make such admissions) that pedagogical *practice* and contemporary *theory* have to be inconsistent. That is, if it is true we must now discard forever notions of universal principles, it is also true we cannot live (and teach) as though no universal principles underlie anything. In the classroom we encourage a healthy conviction because it leads to the purposefulness which, in turn, increases the probabilities for more creative and powerful rhetoric. This inconsistency is to me, though, as indefensible as an auto manufacturer's claim that it "builds the strongest car possible" when in fact it does not.

On the one hand, the teacher who received the racist paper could have evaluated the rough draft by way of the usual criteria: thesis or essential argument, validity and relevance of supporting evidence, logic and hierarchy of ideas. What better approach than letting the student demonstrate for himself or herself the untenable nature of racist arguments? Such an approach surely works with the arguments, untenable or not, set forth in any paper from "American Management Styles: Finest in the World" to "Survival of Our Wetlands: More Priority, Please." After all, even with these papers we could argue that, in each case, something bordering on "fundamental" is at work: in the first paper, respect for the laborer perhaps; in the second, concern for our children's children. Still, teachers are not likely, with such papers, to react as our teacher did to the racist paper, which she regarded as a paper of an entirely different species. I suppose we could include in that extreme "different species" category (whether we ever receive them or not) papers which argue that we burn epileptics as devils, raze gay bars, lynch Blacks who dare to date White women, burn cats in satanic rites, or return women to their proper roles as child-rearers and sex toys.

My point in invoking these extreme examples is that, indeed, there is a *continuum,* a "more fundamental" at work, a sense of directionality. I take issue with those who believe we can buy into a universe of "situational ethics" or "usable" truths–that is, until we are willing to grant there is nothing to be gained in striving toward "fundamental" or "transcendent" principles which such papers violate in promoting cruel behavior towards humankind and the other creatures which populate the earth. Burning epileptics at the stake, abusing children, promoting by willful neglect the extinction of an animal species–such acts don't properly merit some gradation of ethical value relative to a particular culture or period of time.

Rarely do we come across extremely reprehensible papers–such as those which do openly promote cruel behavior. But our writing classes do become the setting for argument about capital punishment, euthanasia, abortion, women's rights. If we regard these discussions as having at most only "situational" weight–a "this time and place" payoff–then the dynamics of shared ideas is not allowed its proper role in the *necessary directionality* for the human condition and the condition of the planet we inhabit–that of alleviating suffering and cruelty, physical, mental, and spiritual–no matter which status the cosmic deities or demons accord such cruelty.

What is this "continuum," this "necessary directionality"? Consider the subject of racism. At one end of the continuum are non-racist papers arguing the merits of affirmative action, and at the other end are Skinhead-oriented papers arguing the supremacy of the White race. In between are many kinds of papers, such as one I once received which questioned why White students must be forced to mingle in small group discussions with Hispanics and Blacks. Surely, for most teachers, something *more* fundamental is at stake in the Skinhead paper, and something *less* fundamental is at stake in the paper on classroom grouping. But this "more"/"less" continuum is, for the teacher, a different vision of ethics than "usable truth," which by its very nature admits of no true sense of continuum. My point is "more fundamental" and "usable" cannot inhabit the same world. At what point, for example, does the seemingly fundamental truth about cruelty and insensitivity to those of different color become the "usable" truth of arrangement of students within classroom groups or the "reasonable" and "situational ethic" of "Does Affirmative Action Succeed in Its Goals?"?

I am certainly *not* arguing that a teacher could not legitimately deal with papers presenting reprehensible ideas by way of the usual criteria of structure, logic, grammar, and style. The question I pose is this: Has contemporary theory, with its insights into the "situatedness" of our existence and perspectives, left us any sense of a valid–indeed, a *necessary*, "we-can-no-longer-go-back-to-that"–directionality by way of shared ideas? Can we indeed go back to treating women as objects. African-Americans as possessions, homosexuals as freaks, epileptics as devils?

Stanley Fish argues, in *Doing What Comes Naturally,* that

> questions of fact, truth, correctness, validity, and clarity can neither be posed nor answered with reference to some extracontextual, ahistorical, nonsituational reality, or rule, or value; rather, anti-foundationalism asserts, all these matters are intelligible and debatable only within the precincts of the contexts or situations or paradigms or communities that give them their local and changeable shape. (344)

Fish speaks only of what he can be certain. He cannot be certain of Transcendent Truths. Nor can we. But does this mean we cannot be committed to moving toward truths which are *so comprehensive* that their force cannot be ignored?

Necessary Direction away from cruelty is just such a truth. The question is not so much whether or not we must assign to these "truths" the status of "undeniable absolutes," but whether we must assign to them some essence which is *so fundamental,* so clearly pointing to a necessary direction, that *we must insist that, pedagogically, an unqualified moral conviction must assert itself.* As long as "better" is given its proper "transcendent" due, a true moral purpose remains, and a true moral conviction in the classroom can continue. The confrontation of values, of situational ethics, that defines any composition classroom dynamics is not a naive affective or fictional game that we as teachers must continue to play to produce what Stanley Fish calls the "small . . . yield" of a "few worn and familiar bromides" (355); on the contrary, it is a confrontation founded in our sense of a *necessary* direction–one of less cruelty to ourselves and the rest of humankind.

This is not a starry-eyed meliorism or naive social evolutionism. Surely we do need in our classrooms the kind of discursive analysis the anti-foundationalists call for. A deconstructionist reading of *Mein Kampf* could not have been all bad. But Fish and Bizzell leave us too precarious an anchoring. Without that sense of a *necessary direction,* hate crimes such as the burning of crosses will necessarily be prosecuted only as vandalism, and the Andersonville and Auschwitz behavior will be defended by way of "following orders." We have moved *beyond* that. Indeed, humankind's condition seems to be defined in great measure by "situatedness." But what is functional and reasonable for one time and place must always push against other times and places–other situations on a greater scale. Racist and sexist behavior of any sort that promotes unnecessary cruelty must never be afforded the justification a too-unexamined moral pluralism may allow.

Otherwise, the kind of phenomena I experienced in my Writing Theory class in the spring of 1992 will be the norm. We were discussing Michel Foucault's *The Archaeology of Knowledge.* I had written on the board the sentence "Saddam Hussein is a Hitler." On the other hand, I recognized, as did the students, that the politically "correct" position on this (or on Hussein and the Gulf War in general) would vary greatly from campus to campus. Furthermore, Fish's comment that anti-foundationalism's super-self-consciousness is not a way out, that

> any claim in which the notion of situatedness is said to be a lever that allows us to get a purchase on situations is finally a claim to have *escaped situatedness,* and is therefore nothing more or less than a reinvention of foundationalism by the very form of thought that has supposedly reduced it to ruins (348–49 emphasis added),

still seemed valid here. Thus, the immediate reaction to the "Saddam Hussein is a Hitler" sentence in my class of relatively sophisticated rhetorical-theory students was in line with Foucault (and Fish): that we had to look at who said it and other dimensions of the "enunciative modalities," what "institutional sites" were being represented, and so on. The students suggested several such "sites" each with its own particular "political" baggage, its own appropriation of the statement, and I put them on the board:

Bush	Hussein	*NY Times* Editors	Soldier's Mother

"SADDAM HUSSEIN IS A HITLER."–REALITY?

W.W. II Veteran	Berkeley Anti-War Activist	Kurds

Our "situating" of a bit of discourse was, for a while, only an *academic* exercise–much as composition classes, I fear, tend to be for anti-foundationalist teachers. But when we finished congratulating ourselves on the incisiveness of our dissection, I put the chalk down and took a different approach. "But what if Hussein really *is* a kind of Hitler?" I asked. "What of the *very real possibility* that Hussein was *greatly* responsible for the unnecessary and perhaps cruel deaths of thousands of Kurds? What then? That is, what do we do now beyond analyzing the 'discursive formation' of that sentence?"

The students were literally unable to speak for almost a minute. It had not occurred to any of the students, all of them very bright, that *even in the classroom* there are questions that require more than being asked—that must be *answered.* I was not asking my students to take arms against Hussein but to sort out for themselves the truths regarding the possibility of a very real atrocity.

The classroom may be a laboratory, but it is a laboratory for the world we live in. Analysis and determination of power zones is of course essential, and too little of that has been done in our classrooms in the past. But when the *only* result for the classroom of anti-foundationalist and post-modernist insights is a discursive analysis which takes on the character of some linguistic Rubic's Cube, then we have plunged into the same idiocy that allowed learning theory to transform classrooms into robotical M and M dispenser systems.

As writers and teachers of writing, we must continue to grope in the recognition that our moral convictions do not translate as self-contained situational ethics alone, that they will continue to be measured along greater and greater scales—scales so large we must of necessity grant *some* of them a "highest order" status. "Better"—though it may and will be misappropriated and misapplied by the inexperienced, the uneducated, the cowardly, the wicked—must continue to be an operational term. We must continue to act, to "do," to "write" not only *as though* our writing is just one more version of Foucault's "discursive formations," emanating from this "institutional site" or that, but indeed *because* some of our convictions *are* better—because we can now discard *forever* some situational ethics.

What is the "new pedagogy" for our composition classrooms? Can it reside in "style," in anti-foundationalist situational truths which do not even consider the possibility of necessary directions (i.e., directions defined by *what can no longer be acceptable*)? That is indeed a "small yield," and the resulting classroom environment will produce too many students with a "small yield" attitude about not only their papers but the convictions which underlie them. Whatever naiveté there may be in the persistent groping in the dark for "first" principles to understand our universe, the real force of the greatest literature, or of that "one in a hundred" student composition, lies in that *groping* beyond the imprisonment of our situatedness. And a pedagogy that chooses to ignore the moral sweat, if you will, does a disservice of the profoundest order to the appreciation of good writing, of great writing. Yes, the groping between student and teacher may clash, but in the areas of racism, sexism, homophobia, the clash should be loud and morally meaningful in recognition that Necessary Directionality remains a valid concept.

Works Cited

Bauer, Dale. "The Other 'F' Word: The Feminist in the Classroom." *College English* 52 (Apr. 1990): 385–96.

Bizzell, Patricia. "Beyond Anti-Foundationalism to Rhetorical Authority: Problems Defining Cultural Literacy." *College English* 52 (Oct. 1990): 661–75.

Clarke, Arthur C. *2001: A Space Odyssey.* New York: Signet, 1968.

Fish, Stanley. *Doing What Comes Naturally: Change, Rhetoric, and the Practice of Theory in Literary and Legal Studies.* Durham: Duke UP, 1989.

Foucault, Michel. *The Archaeology of Knowledge.* Trans. A. M. Sheridan Smith. New York: Pantheon, 1972.

_____ . "Truth and Power." *Power/Knowledge: Selected Interviews and Other Writings, 1972–77.* Trans. Colin Gordon, Leo Marshall, John Mepham, and Kate Soper. Ed. Colin Gordon. New York: Pantheon, 1980. 109–33.

Writing Log 10

Asking Others about What You Have Read

Once you have completed your reading, make a list of three or four questions about each text. These should be real questions that you have about what the texts are saying or how they are saying it. Be very specific in writing your questions: cite the particular page, quote the actual paragraph, sentence, or sentences that were the source for your questions.

Working in groups with your classmates, try to answer each other's questions. Continue to be specific in your responses to one another, keeping the texts in front of you so you can identify what in the text suggests the responses you have.

Writing Log 11

Points of Personal Intersection

Rereading the notes and annotations you wrote while you read, list where you, Brooks, Bissex, Mulhern, and Rothgery come together in your thinking, and where you diverge. Are there experiences in your own life as a student or writer that support and/or conflict with what you read in the essays? Again, be specific about what passages you are referring to in the essays.

Writing Log 12

Points of Intersection with Writing in Your Class

Reviewing the four essays again, are there points of connection between the essays and any of the writing you or your classmates did so far in this course? With a small group of other students in the class, identify any writing the members of your group did that connects in some way to issues raised by any of the essays. Reread the writing from your group that is related in some way to the essays and reflect on what specific connections you find.

Writing Log 13

Writing after You Have Read

Select two or three sentences from each essay that feel to you to be representative of what is important or compelling or provocative in that essay. They may appear at different places in the essay or they may be side by side within a single paragraph. The idea is to locate sentences that seem to you to be interesting enough to hold the power of everything that the author is writing. Once you have made and written out your selections, explain your choices.

Writing Log 14

Extending the Conversation

Working with three other students, imagine and write the conversation/discussion that Brooks, Rothgery, Mulhern, and Bissex might have with one another if they were invited to your school to discuss, in a public forum, what is important to know about learning to write or another topic suggested by the essays. Each one of you should represent one of the four authors and should rely on the essays you have read to recreate and extend their arguments.

CHAPTER

18

DISCOVERING AND
CREATING YOUR DRAFT

Essay 5

Among the thoughts, points of view, arguments, and ideas that occurred to you as you read the four professional essays in the last chapter, select something that you would like to reflect on more extensively. Use the **Perspectives** and **Focusing** activities to analyze and interpret your thoughts about the readings and to find an explicit purpose you wish to convey to the reader. As you develop your essay, use the observations, narratives, or arguments of these four authors—or any other professional or student writing you have read this term—to support and develop your purpose. It is necessary to keep track of which texts provide you with ideas, which specific words might lend support to the points you wish to make, since an important convention of writing from written texts is that you cite this information appropriately with footnotes or internal references and a bibliography. (The professional essays cite their sources in this way, and you may refer to them as examples.)

WRITING ESSAY 5

In the course of your reading and writing about the essays so far, you may have already come across questions and observations that could become the focus for your essay. Using freewriting, focused freewriting, and rereading, you can reconsider what you have already written, looking for connections, surprising perspectives, important sets of belief or opinion, or other points from which your essay might be formed. As with any other essay, for an essay based on written texts to be meaningful for both the writer and the reader, it needs to grow from the writer's own perspective and desire to be heard.

DISCOVERING AND CREATING YOUR ESSAY

The following activities may help you to generate ideas and to focus your thinking for Essay 5. As before, we have included two different kinds of activities: **Taking on different perspectives** and **Focusing your direction.** Because your source of information for this essay is the written texts you have just read, the **Perspectives** and **Focusing** writings are somewhat different from what they have been in the first two parts of *Shoptalk.* We have adjusted them to help you find your own points of interest in relation to your reading of the professional essays. In order not to prejudice your thinking about these texts or inadvertently lead you away from a particular purpose for writing that you might otherwise find, we have not included demonstration selections from the writing of students who have already worked through this assignment. We are confident that by the time you reach the end of this chapter and have completed these activities, you will have generated a first, exploratory draft, begun to discover your own purpose for writing, and then will have written a second, more focused draft.

TAKING ON DIFFERENT PERSPECTIVES
PERSPECTIVES: *Questions and Connections*

Reread all the **Writing Log** entries you completed in Chapter 17. Jot down some notes about how they speak to each other. Make connections among the various entries. For example, you might consider the following kinds of questions: Are there certain concerns that come up more than once in your writing? Are there particular kinds of arguments that you find yourself being most in agreement with or most disturbed by? Do your own experiences support or conflict with any of the authors' points? Do you see any way that two or more of the authors might, given the chance, come together to make a single proposal or argument? Are there one or two **Writing Log** entries that seem especially intriguing to you and about which you may have more to say? There may be many other connections you see from your **Writing Logs** that are not referred to in these questions.

PERSPECTIVES: *Conflicting Points of View*

One way to find an observation or question you are interested in developing in your essay is to ask yourself what is missing from what you have already read. Thinking about the four essays and the viewpoints presented among the authors, what isn't accounted for? What points of view or arguments would you have expected to see represented that you didn't? What stories from real life are not considered?

PERSPECTIVES: *Metaphoric Thinking*

Reread all of the **Perspectives** writing you have done so far and identify a concept or an object that appears in or is suggested by the writing. Make several comparisons between the original concept or object and something else that, somehow, it reminds you of. Then, freewrite for a few minutes about how the comparisons work and what they show you about the concept or object that you might not have noticed before.

FOCUSING YOUR DIRECTION

FOCUSING: *Questions and Connections*

Looking back at the essays you read, which ones interest you most? Write half of a page about each essay, explaining how it fits with any ideas you have been exploring. Underline or bracket any words or phrases in the essays that represent the authors' points, engage you the most, frustrate, or confuse you.

FOCUSING: *More Connections*

Write three or four sentences about an observation or question that you see emerging for yourself. At this point, what can you say or what would you like to know more about?

FOCUSING: *Writing More*

Use the sentences that you wrote above as a focus from which to begin this freewriting. Push yourself to write two pages or more. The only parameters are those set by the sentences you have already written.

FOCUSING: *Rereading and Writing Again*

Reread the pages you have written; while doing so, underline sentences or sections of your writing that jump out at you in some way, ones that catch your eye and stay with you. Take three or four of these as your focus and freewrite further.

FOCUSING: *Rereading, Reseeing and Rewriting*

Together, all of the writing you have done so far in this chapter makes up the exploratory draft for Essay 5. Reread what you have written in these activities, paying particular attention to the focused freewriting at the end. Ask yourself what explicit purpose for writing emerges from this first draft. What is it that you are writing about and to what end?

With this tentative subject and purpose in mind, and with all the writing you have done so far at hand, write a second draft.

EVALUATING YOUR INFORMATION AND GATHERING MORE

At this point, in order to provide adequate and convincing support for your purpose, take time to evaluate the information you have included in your second draft and decide whether you need to collect any more persuasive references and illustrations.

Earlier, we pointed out that writers need to be concerned with the authority of the written texts they use for support. They must also consider whether they have used the most appropriate texts for the particular purpose of their writing.

At this point, review the words and ideas you have included from your sources. Ask yourself whether you have made clear what is your interpretation of this information. Will the reader understand why you cited the works you did? Have you used this material in a way that shows clear support for your own idea, that lends greater authority to the explicit point you are trying to make? Or, have you offered enough commentary on the works you cited, so that the reader will understand what you make of this information? Have you explained, adequately, the information you include from other texts, so that the reader will be sure to interpret it in the way you intended? Are there additional texts or portions of the texts you might cite that would add support to your essay?

The four essays you have read serve as professional demonstrations for this chapter. Look closely at these essays to see how their authors have cited other written texts. Do they include quotations or summaries? (These strategies are explained more fully in Chapter 20.) How fully do they explain the ideas or words that they draw from others texts? How do they use this kind of support as opposed to support from personal experience or field research?

19

RESPONSE AND COLLABORATION

By now you are familiar with ways of responding that can help you as you progress through the revising of Essay 5. Be sure to ask as many other individuals or groups of students in your class as you can to read and respond to your draft. At the end of this chapter, we have included some additional response strategies that address how you have used written texts as the source of information for this essay.

Though you may not get all of the responses that we have included here, and you may have the opportunity to seek responses from only one or two sources, the value of any individual response is enriched if you take the time to see how it might help you revise or rethink the draft and, later, to see what issues are raised by the way the individual responses agree or disagree with one another.

✻ *Four Ways of Responding*
LISTENING

The first kind of **Response** most writers need is simply to be heard, to know that someone is really listening and taking in what they have written. This form of **Response** is critical to all the other forms; it is the foundation for your ability to be a helpful responder.

LISTENING 1: RECEIVING

Listen carefully to the essay as it is read. Respond without words. Your job is to receive the writing, to take it in, to have any reactions you naturally have. That is, you might find yourself nodding in agreement or smiling or feeling sad but you will not, at this time, articulate your response in words. Simply say "thank you" to the writer for reading, or clap for the writing if you are in a larger group. The writer has had an attentive audience hear what she or he has to say.

LISTENING 2: ECHOING

Use the writer's own words as your **Response.** As you hear the piece of writing again or read it to yourself, jot down or underline words and phrases that stand out for you, that strike you in some way. Without using any other words, repeat the writer's words you have noted. By echoing back the writer's own words, you are letting the writer know what especially got through to you.

REPORTING

Next, the writer can benefit from knowing how different readers understand his or her writing. Your job in reporting is to report on your own reading of the text. You cannot know with certainty exactly what the writer intended, but you are an authority on your own reading. The following are strategies for reporting your reading to the writer.

REPORTING 1: MAIN POINTS

List for the writer what seem to you to be the main points he or she is making in the draft. What seem to be the main ideas that are included so far in what you have read?

REPORTING 2: FOCUS

What do you feel is the focus for the whole essay, so far? Is the writer's purpose or reason for writing explicit and clear? How does the essay accomplish this? You might come up with a title that, for you, represents the heart of what the draft seems to be saying.

REPORTING 3: SUMMARY

Give a summary of what you read. The summary gives more detail than the list of Main Points, but of course it doesn't include everything. You might summarize by writing down a few sentences that elaborate your understanding of each main point or by recording what you remember from the piece without looking at it.

REPORTING 4: STORY OF YOUR OWN READING

Tell the writer what you thought and what you felt as you read the piece of writing. The idea is to try to tell the story of what happened to you, in you, as you read. The story of your own reading is not a summary or an analysis, it is a narrative of what went through your mind and what feelings you had at specific points as you read or heard the draft.

ELABORATING

In the next kind of **Response,** you move beyond your immediate reaction to the text to make connections between your own experience and knowledge and what you have read. Elaborating helps you provide the writer with a broader understanding of his or her material since different readers will make different connections to and have different commentary on what the writer has said.

ELABORATING 1: CONNECTIONS

What does the writing connect to in your own experience? What have you read that corroborates what has been said? What can you add to the points the writer has made? What further examples can you think of? In what ways do you agree with the piece of writing? What parts of the writing do you particularly agree with or feel particularly connected to?

ELABORATING 2: CONTRADICTIONS

Is there anything in the piece of writing that contradicts your own experience or something you have read? What alternative perspectives can you offer on the points the writer has made? What is there in the piece of writing with which you disagree? Is there something that seems to you to be left out of the piece?

QUESTIONING

Finally, it is valuable to ask the questions you have about a work-in-progress. Don't hold back on any questions that come to you, for it will be useful to the writer to know what questions the piece, in its current version, raises for different readers.

Questioning 1: What I'd Like to Hear More About

Ask the writer about any aspect of the writing you would like to hear more about. The writer may choose to include some of this material or may choose not to add this information in subsequent versions of the piece depending on his or her purpose and the audience for whom the writing is intended.

Questioning 2: What I Don't Yet Understand

Ask the writer for clarification of any points, ideas, words, or phrases that you have questions about. Again, the writer may find that in the next draft she or he wants to make some changes as a result of the questions she or he was asked.

Questioning 3: The Writer Asks You Questions

At this point, the writer can ask for comment about any aspect of the draft she or he wants response to that doesn't seem to have been addressed. Again, the feedback is a non-judgmental form of response.

❧ *The Writer's Use of Information from Written Texts: Questions for Response*

Though the ways of responding that we have listed above could be applied to any draft, some **Response** that you ask from readers is specific to the kind of information that you have incorporated into your essay. That is, one of the lessons you are learning as you write college essays is how to use the kind of information available to you the most convincingly, effectively, and appropriately. The following are some questions responding readers might ask to help you think about how you have used information from written texts, the information source for this essay. Before answering these questions, responders should remind themselves of what they found to be the essay's explicit purpose or meaning. Keeping that purpose clearly in mind, answer these questions to give the reader your sense of how he or she used the information in this draft.

1. How does the writer use information from written texts to support or develop the purpose of the essay? To what extent are the specific references to written texts an integral part of the essay? That is, how do the references advance the explicit purpose or meaning of the essay and help to establish the authority of the writer? Are there other

references that might be added? Are the references that are included commented upon and explained in the essay?

2. What particular claims or observations does the writer make based on his or her interpretation or understanding of the texts that are cited? Tell the writer what makes these claims convincing for you. Tell the writer any claims that feel unconvincing to you. What would make these claims more convincing?

3. In what ways are references to written texts being made: quotations? paraphrases? summaries? In what ways do these seem to be effective choices or not? If whole passages are cited, how does the writer make use of these, and do they seem to be valuable, as they stand, to the essay?

4. How do the references to written texts fit into the content of the essay? Is there more you would like to know about how the writer is interpreting or understanding any particular citation or about its original source? (Note that an explanation appears in the next chapter about how to cite or reference written texts.)

✳ *A Reminder for the Writer as You Turn to Revision*

Once you have received a complete response to your draft, it's time for you to use this feedback to revise your essay. As you make your choices and plans for revising, consider all of the responses together, reflecting on each comment and question in light of the other responses you received, and in relation to your own reading of the draft and your intended purpose.

Chapter

20

EDITING, PROOFREADING, AND FINAL REFLECTIONS

✻ *Editing and Proofreading Strategies for Essay 5*

Use the descriptions below to remind you (as either a reader of your own draft or of someone else's) of the kinds of possible silent and audible distractions for readers. They are followed by additional distractions that can occur for readers when writers do not cite and reference written texts in expected ways.

SILENT DISTRACTIONS

1. SPELLING

Academic *readers* often make severe judgements about writers' abilities based on the correctness of their spelling. It is common for readers to assume that an inordinate number of misspellings indicates laziness or irresponsibility in the writer. The assumption that writers just don't care is especially strong when they misspell common words (for example, "alot" instead of "a lot"; "there" when it should be "their" or "they're"; "it's" when it should be "its") or make common errors, ones that readers have seen so many times that they become pet peeves or annoyances. *Writers* can correct spelling errors using a spell check on the computer or a good dictionary. In fact, because spell checkers can't identify homonyms (a spell checker will find that "threw" is spelled correctly even if you really mean to use "through") or misplaced words ("She it the one who threw it."), it is important to have a dictionary on hand too.

Some people who have good visual memories are adept at spelling. Others, including many famous writers, need to look up words before letting a piece of writing stand on its own. If spelling is not particularly easy for you, you will need to take time to look up longer or uncommon words in a dictionary.

2. TYPOS

Like spelling errors, typos may be used by *readers* to make a quick determination of your skill and the commitment you have to your writing. *Writers* can locate some typos using a spell check; others will get by since they may be correctly spelled words, but not the words you intended. One useful strategy for "seeing" typos is to read your essay from the end, moving word by word backwards through the text. This process can help highlight the typos for you. Final versions of essays need to be proofread for typing mistakes. If you notice a mistake just as you are turning in a final version of a paper, it is always better to correct it than to have a perfectly neat paper.

3. CAPITALIZATION

Capitalization has virtually no effect on the *reader's* understanding of a text but a misplaced capital, or a missing one, sends a distress signal to an academic reader that may take his or her attention away from your essay. Because capitalization errors are often the result of a typing mistake, it is important for *writers* to check that words that need capitals, like names of people or places and first words of sentences, are capitalized, and that words that don't need capitals are not capitalized. Reading the essay backwards word by word is often a useful strategy for finding missing capitalizations too.

4. FORMATTING

Like spelling, typos, and capitalization, formatting has no effect on meaning. However, academic *readers* expect paragraph indentations and will be disturbed if your whole essay appears in one paragraph. It is a matter of *writer's* choice where to break paragraphs. Two page and single sentence paragraphs are unusual but are not incorrect. The general wisdom about paragraphing is that when you move on, in some way or degree, to a new topic, it is time for a new paragraph. Reread any chapter of this text (or any other academic text) to get a sense of paragraphing.

Other usual formatting issues are that most academic papers are double spaced, typed, have standard one-inch margins, use average size type, and are presented on standard weight, white, 8½ × 11 inch paper. Academic papers are expected to look alike.

5. POSSESSIVES

We have listed possessives under silent distractions because the proofreading concern we want to highlight regarding possessives is the apostrophe ('). Whether or not we hear, in speech, the "s" signifying the possessive in "the boy's bike" or the boys' bikes, in college writing, *readers* expect the apostrophe to appear, standing for "belongs to." While checking for possessives, the *writer* should look for missing instances as well as for any apostrophes that appear in the text unnecessarily. Apostrophes are only used in forming contractions (like can't or wouldn't) and for possessives. No apostrophe should appear where a plural is intended except if it is a plural possessive.

6. SENTENCE BOUNDARIES

When we speak it is often not possible and it is certainly not necessary to identify where one sentence ends and the next begins. Like the first four distractions, sentence boundaries are of concern only to *readers,* not to listeners. Sentence boundaries seem to matter a great deal to academic readers even though, like the other silent distractions, they usually have no effect on one's ability to understand a text. In editing one's own essay, the *writer* should know that there are only two possible inconsistencies in the category of sentence boundaries: 1) fragments, in which you write part of a sentence but punctuate it as if it is a complete sentence and 2) fused or run-on sentences, in which you write two sentences together but punctuate as if you have written one sentence. Under certain circumstances–for emphasis–fragments are acceptable, though usually student writing is expected to be free of fragments; fused and run-on sentences are not acceptable in college writing, although long, correctly punctuated sentences are sometimes valued as part of a particularly "academic" style.

We know of no fully reliable rule for what makes a complete sentence in English. The general formula is that one needs a subject and a predicate, the person or thing the sentence is about and a description of that subject's action or state of being. "He stands" is a complete sentence, but "standing, idly by the streetlight, the sirens blaring, the horns honking" is not a complete sentence because there is no subject; you're left to say, "Who is standing, idly . . . ?" "The quiet, long-haired boy in the front of the line," is also an incomplete sentence because there is no predicate. You're left to say, "What about 'the quiet, long-haired boy . . . '?" Our favorite test for complete sentences is to imagine that the sentence is all someone said when he walked into the room; would the sentence make some kind of complete sense or would you ask the kind of questions the fragments in the example above provoke?

It is difficult to notice fragments because they are usually made complete by attaching them to the previous or preceding sentence. So, when you are writing, you make that connection in your mind. Run-on or fused sentences are a little more difficult to detect, and it is our experience that they occur in student writing less frequently than fragments. If you have two complete sentences you can either divide them up with a period (.); or you can join them together with a semicolon (;) or with a comma and a conjunction such as "and," "or," and "but." You can't join two sentences together with a comma (,). The best technique we know of for checking sentence boundaries is to read a paper, sentence by sentence, backward. If you start with the last sentence of the essay, then read the next to last, and so on, you will be able to focus on sentence completeness without being influenced by the meaning of the text.

AUDIBLE DISTRACTIONS

7. AGREEMENT

The meaning of a sentence is rarely affected by the convention of agreement but non-standard agreement is a particularly powerful distraction for academic *readers*. Agreement means that there is consistency within a sentence. The main parts of the sentence are either both plural or both singular. The form of the verb depends on whether the sentence contains a singular or plural subject. In the same way, singular or plural pronouns match singular or plural antecedents. To meet the expectations of academic readers you will need to check for both subject/verb agreement and pronoun/antecedent agreement.

Using a handbook is often a useful way for *writers* to check for agreement. In general, you will need to review each sentence first to see that the form of the verb matches that of the subject: In the sentence, "Each student has a notebook," the singular subject "student" matches the verb form "has." In the sentence, "Students take tests in chemistry," the plural subject "students" matches the verb form "take." Second, you will need to see that in a sentence the antecedent, which is the word a pronoun refers to, is plural if the pronoun is plural, and singular if the pronoun is singular. In the sentence, "Musicians must practice if they want to become accomplished performers," the plural pronoun, "they" matches the plural antecedents, "musicians" and "performers." In the sentence, "A musician must practice if he or she wants to become an accomplished performer," the singular pronouns "he or she" match the singular antecedents "musician" and "performer." Again, agreement is a convention of standard, college writing that you can give attention to at the point in working on your draft, when you are making the presentation of your essay conform to the expectations of academic readers.

8. TENSE

The academic *reader* who encounters a surprising, non-standard tense shift in a college essay will, as with the other audible distractions, still be able to understand what is being said. He or she may pause to reflect on the writer's language history or background, surmising that this is a speaker of other languages besides English or other dialects besides the standard one. Even if the writer's background or history is the subject of the essay, the academic reader will expect the writer's knowledge of other languages and dialects to remain invisible in the finished text. (We believe that, at this time, the academic world is biased in favor of the standard form, although this bias is undergoing debate and change.)

In **Editing and Proofreading,** the *writer* will want to focus, again, on the verbs in the sentences, perhaps using the handbook to help. Are the verbs in their standard form? Is the tense consistent within sentences or paragraphs and, when there is a tense change, does it make sense in the context of the rest of the paragraph or essay? We will say more about tense and agreement in the next section of the book.

9. WORD CHOICE

The final audible distraction is word choice or diction. Academic *readers* find acceptable a wide range of language and diction. But they expect words to be used in conventional ways. As a *writer*, you may want to review your draft for the accuracy and appropriateness of the words, something that is not always easy to distinguish. We advise you to choose words from your own vocabulary, which is enormous, rather than use a thesaurus to find unfamiliar words that you may not be able to use conventionally. We also encourage you to ask others if you are unsure of the choice you have made; be sure to ask for their explanation, not just their decision. Word choice options include not only replacing words that are used incorrectly, but finding the most precise words to express your ideas and reach your audience.

ADDITIONAL DISTRACTIONS

10. CITING INFORMATION FROM WRITTEN TEXTS

You wrote Essay 5 in response to written texts, and you used these texts to provide some of the evidence or support for the claims you made. So, in this essay, you will need to cite your sources of information according to the conventions of standard American college English. The main concern here is that you honestly and correctly identify words and ideas from other people's texts, whether these texts originally appeared in a journal, a book, a newspaper, or on the computer screen.

In American culture, ideas are treated like property, as if they were "owned" by the person who uttered or wrote them. Consequently, not identifying the "owner" is comparable to stealing someone else's property, an act that is called "plagiarism." When your sources are not cited in the conventional way, your instructor may assume that you don't understand the concept of plagiarism and simply ask you to rewrite your essay. However, sometimes, instructors will feel quite strongly that even though you do not know the formal conventions for citing written sources, you are still responsible for the citations you use. In this case, the penalty for plagiarism can be quite severe—ranging from a failing grade on an essay or in a course to suspension or expulsion from school.

But the process of identifying written sources and the formal conventions for making such citations are no more difficult than they were when you identified sources for other kinds of information. In the essays you have already completed, when your information sources were recollection and memory of personal experiences or observation and conversations, you identified the experiences or events and the people with whom you spoke, making clear which of the ideas in your essay originated in these sources. Similarly, now that you are writing from written texts, you need to indicate the individual authors whose words and ideas you have included. Citing this information presents you as an "honest" writer, but even more significantly, it adds great strength to your own writing. For you will be supplementing your own authority with the authority of another, published writer. Or, if you are refuting an author's words, you strengthen your claim by showing that the argument you are making is in response to an on-going, published conversation.

As we indicated earlier in this section, different disciplines value different kinds of information. And even among those that value the support of written texts, the particular kind of text may vary. For example, your essay may be supported most effectively by quotations from the primary text (the novel, play, poem, you're analyzing), secondary sources (articles or books about the primary text), or statistical evidence from your own research or from others'. Whatever the discipline calls for, there are some common conventions you should know for quoting or paraphrasing from written texts.

1. In a "direct quotation," writers use someone else's words or sentences as they originally appeared and insert them into their own writing. When you use a direct quotation, be sure to quote *exactly* from the original source, without changing any words or punctuation.

2. When you use part of a direct quotation, your own words need to introduce the quote appropriately and grammatically. Make the other's words "fit" into the structure of your sentence.

3. Check to be sure you have used both opening and closing quotation marks to indicate the complete quotation for the reader.

4. Whether you use direct quotations that repeat others' words or indirect quotations that paraphrase or summarize them, you must identify the original source either with a parenthetical notation that corresponds to a list of authors and texts on a Work Cited page or with a footnote that corresponds to a notation at the bottom of the page. Even electronic sources must be cited to include the author's name, the article or document title in quotation marks, the newsletter, journal, or conference title; the number of the pages or paragraphs; the medium of publication as *on-line;* the computer network name, and the access date.

Whether you use a parenthetical notation or a footnote number depends, in part, on the editorial style conventions of the discipline in which you are writing. Notice that the essays included in Chapter 17 include MLA style documentation, parenthetical citations with a works cited page at the end of the text. In addition to *The MLA Handbook,* several other guides exist to outline other academic styles: *American Psychological Association Publication Manual, Turabian Guide, The Chicago Style Publication Manual.* Your own handbook most likely includes descriptions of each. Find out which one your instructor expects you to use, and then follow its citation guidelines. Though the differences among them may appear slight, to the readers who expect them, they are, indeed, significant.

❧ *A Final Rewrite*

Rewrite your essay one last time including all the editorial and proofing changes. You may find that some editorial changes lead you to further revision, as well.

Final Writing Log Entry

On Writing Essay 5 and Completing Shoptalk

Write a page about what it was like to have written your final essay. What do you want your reader to learn from it?

As your final essay for the course, how does Essay 5 reflect your development as a writer this term? How does it demonstrate what you have learned through taking this course, reading this text, and completing so much writing? What are some of the most important ideas and concepts you take with you as you finish *Shoptalk* and proceed into the next phases of being a college writer?

INDEX

Academic papers, appearance of, 80, 101
Academic readers. *See also* Reader;
  Readers' responses
  expectations of, 243–244
  and misspellings in writing, 78
  usage distractions for, 78–84
Agreement, as audible distraction, 82,
  103, 180–181, 200, 312–313
*American Psychological Association
  Publication Manual,* 315
Analysis, 219
  Writing Log 4 and, 18
"Androgynous Man, The" (Perrin),
  107–109
Annotation, 256
"Anorexia: The Cheating Disorder"
  (Murphy), 56–63
Apostrophe ('), usage of, 80, 102
Appearance, of academic papers, 80, 101
Assumptions, Writing Log 4 and, 18
Audible distractions
  agreement as, 82, 103, 180–181, 200,
    312–313
  tense as, 82–83, 104, 181, 201, 313
  word choice as, 83, 104, 181–182, 201,
    313–314
Audience. *See also* Academic readers;
  Voice
  college instructor as, 248–249
  dealing with biases of, 240–241
  making points in writing and, 238
  in spoken language, 236
  Writing Log 3 and, 13–14
  in written language, 236
Authority
  in conversation, 126, 127–128
  establishing to speak in communities,
    133–134
  in familiar language situations,
    129–130
  in family structures, Writing Log 4
    and, 130
  speaking with, 240
  Writing Log 2 and, 127

Bissex, Glenda L., "Growing Writers in
  Classrooms," 263–271
"Black Writer and the Southern
  Experience, The" (Walker),
  116–120

Brooks, Jeff, "Minimalist Tutoring:
  Making the Students Do All the
  Work," 257–262

Capitalization, as silent distraction, 80,
  101, 178, 198, 310
Careers
  language conventions in, 134–135
  Writing Log 8 and, 135
Chicago Style Publication Manual, The,
  315
Citation
  of information from conversations
    and observations, 182–183,
    201–202
  of information from recollection and
    memory, 83–84, 104–105
  of information from written texts,
    314–316
Close-to-home languages, 129–131
Code language, 131
  Writing Log 5 and, 132
Code switching, 140–142
  and college writing, 144
Code words, 139
Collaboration
  response and, 65–76, 171–175,
    303–307
  in writing outside of school settings,
    68
"College Brings Alienation from Family,
  Friends" (Gonzales), 51–52
*College Composition and
  Communication,* 254
College instructor, as audience for
  writing, 248–249
College writing
  code switching and, 144
  courses outside of English
    Department or writing programs,
    26–27
  creating written self in, 248–250
  defined, 28–29
  formulas in, 246–247
  history of, 21–25
  learning the conventions, making
    points, and creating written self in,
    231–242, 243–251
  making points in, 247–248
  nature of, 243–244